A SHARPENED

Preparing An Arrow For Th

The account of God's preparation and use of the life of Ian Taylor
Missionary and Bible Teacher

IAN S. TAYLOR

A SHARPENED ARROW

A SHARPENED ARROW

Preparing An Arrow For The Archer's Use

TABLE OF CONTENTS

To my parents, Doris and Silas Taylor

With diligence and much patience they put into practice and lived the following verses, setting in motion the future direction of my life.

"Train a child in the way he should go,and when he is old he will not turn from it." Proverbs 22:6

"These commandments that I give you today are to be upon your hearts. Impress them on your children. Talk about them when you sit at home and when you walk along the road, when you lie down and when you get up."
Deuteronomy 6:6-7

ENDORSEMENTS

"A Sharpened Arrow" is the inspiring tale of God's grace, as told in this fast-moving account of Ian Taylor's personal experiences with his faithful God. From his earliest call to mission work, to his ongoing ministry of biblical teaching and leadership, Ian's story demonstrates the value and impact of a life devoted to serving others.

This is not really a book about Ian and his adventures, even though there are many to recount – from guerillas and alligators to the human tragedies of death and its grief's. Rather, the stories that unfold provide an inspiring reminder that God is in complete control of every detail of our lives, and he is working to sharpen every one of us for His glory one day at a time, one experience after another.

I have known Ian for a significant part of his journey, having worked together in various youth, camp and educational ministries for over 30 years. His authentic life of faith continually points me to God as my ultimate source of hope and strength.

Philip Boom, President Emmaus Bible College

Hold on to your seat as you ride a roller coaster of emotions throughout this action-packed true story about the life of Ian Taylor, missionary to Colombia. High seas and jungles, alligators and guerrillas, tragic death and new life, all of these and more will keep you spellbound to the end. Ultimately, you will be challenged and encouraged by this book, and blessed by the prevailing message that "God is in control!"

Jean C. Bassett, Author of *Wisdom's Children* and *William Says a Verse*

"A Sharpened Arrow" is the story of one man's journey whose passion from the very beginning was to serve the Lord. In a life fully surrendered to God this powerful journey shows some of what it takes to become *"an instrument for noble purposes, made holy, useful to the Master and prepared to do any good work"* (2 Tim. 2:21 NIV). But the journey is not easy! The author deliberately points the reader to God's faithfulness both in the midst of great joys and heart wrenching calamities. My prayer for you, the reader, is that you will be helped and encouraged in your journey with the Master for He keenly desires to equip you for every good work.

Philip C. Parsons, Christian Missions in Many Lands

ACKNOWLEDGEMENTS

I would like to thank, first of all, my wife Barbara. After hearing so many stories of God's work in my life she would say, "You should write a book!" When preaching, and using my life-stories, she noted that many were good illustrations of Bible lessons; and eventually she began to pressure me to start writing. I am also thankful that my father kept a date-order file with all the family newsletters that Ann and I wrote. These have been crucial in providing correct dates as well as some accounts I had forgotten.

As I began writing, Barb handled the first and many succeeding proof readings. Together we arranged the order and preparation of the book. Barb had heard my stories often, and was able to suggest accounts that needed to be clarified for better understanding. In several places you will see the local Colombian believers calling me "Hermano Juan." Ian is a difficult name for Spanish speaking people not having anything like that in their language. Ian has a Gaelic background and so popular in Scotland where my immigrant grandparents came from. Ian is Gaelic for John and so I adopted Juan (John) as my name in Colombia.

Finally, others would help with proof reading, as it neared completion. I am thankful to Jean Bassett for her painstaking reading; seeking to help make this book not only grammatically correct but also something easy to read. Thanks also to Diane Tencate, Jillian Hawke and Bethany Neumeyer for their literary skills as they applied their grammatical expertise to the manuscript. My daughter Diane, who lived through many of these experiences, was also a help in clarifying details and proper timelines for some events.

When writing about experiences in a foreign culture the writer can easily take for granted that the reader will fully understand a situation. The suggestions for better explanations, from these proofreaders, were needed. These helped to amplify some thoughts and were a tremendous help to me.

I am blessed in having family members who are also sympathetic to my feeble efforts; and I don't have sufficient words to express my deep gratitude to all who have had a part in this production. All of my family and many dear friends have encouraged me in this project and declare that they believe this book will be an encouragement to others. Above all, I am truly thankful to the Lord Jesus Christ who walked with me through all the experiences on these pages.

Ian Taylor

FORWARD

By
Dr. Franklin Jabini
Professor of Intercultural Studies, Emmaus Bible College

Ian Taylor is a veteran missionary. He has served the Lord for over 45 years in full-time Christian ministry. In this book, Ian shares the joys of serving the Lord and seeing God at work in planting churches, providing for the material, physical and spiritual needs of His people. Just like the angels in heaven, there is great joy in seeing people's lives changed to the glory of God. This book also reminds us, that ministry is not only about these mountaintop experiences. There are also valleys, where one has to deal with unfaithfulness and dishonesty among those who trusted Christ. The book also focuses on the personal life and circumstances of the worker. It shares the tears of pain and sorrow when one tragedy after the other hits a servant of the Lord in his own house. The unfair and unjust attack of the enemy on a foreign missionary is told to remind us of the broken world in which we are living. The book is not a hagiography, the story of a saint. It is an honest and open account of what Ian called an arrow in the service of the Archer.

Ian belongs to the generation that has influenced my understanding of the life and work of a missionary. Some of these men and women, whom I have prayed for, appreciated, and looked up to, are mentioned by name in this book. These workers are passionate about the Lord's work. They dedicate their all and use every possible means reaching out to the lost and teaching the saved. They are like centipedes, driven by "a holy stubbornness" that is misunderstood by some. This stubbornness equips them to find a way to do what is humanly impossible, often at the expense of their own comfort.

In this book, Ian is passing the baton to the next generation. Will someone hear the voice of the Lord of the harvest through these pages? The harvest is still plentiful, but the workers are few (Matthew 9:37). We are still living in a world in which 66.7 percent does not accept Jesus Christ as the Savior of the world. Moreover, even among the 33.3 percent who claim to be Christians, there is a majority who are not true believers. The task of missions remains one of the primary responsibilities of the church.

May this book find the young people that God is preparing somewhere to send out as workers into His harvest.

x

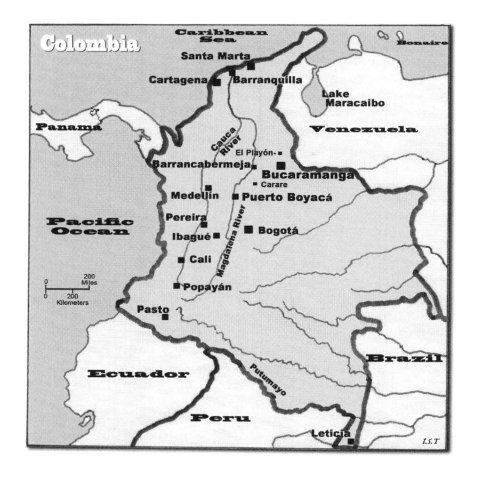

AUTHOR'S NOTE
A SHARPENED ARROW

Jeremiah 51:11 *"Sharpen the arrows, take up the shields! The LORD has stirred up the kings of the Medes, because his purpose is to destroy Babylon."*

God brought the Medes to judge and destroy Babylon. Blunt arrows would not pierce the hardened leather shields or the leather armor worn by the enemies. The warrior had to sharpen the arrows he would use. The sharpening process takes the rough edges off the metal arrowheads so that they will be effective in the battle.

In the same way, God must smooth the rough edges of pride, self-confidence, independence, or any impediment in the servant's life, so that he will be useful to his Master, and ready to face the challenges of any ministry. For this reason, the human arrows need to be sharpened by adversity or trials, which have the purpose of doing away with self-reliance. This allows the servant to come to the place of total confidence and trust in the Lord. Knowing that the Lord really is in control of all the circumstances that surround us, we will come to realize that God's plans and purposes are always the best. Sometimes the honing or filing process may include sickness, the death of a close family member, personal attacks by those opposing the faith, and even death threats.

When we realize that God is the Creator and Planner with purpose and objectives, and the servant is just a tool or an arrow to be used as He sees fit, we come to a place of complete confidence in Him. We learn that we can trust Him in any circumstance that may come upon us. The Archer sharpens the arrows in order to be ready. They will bear the marks of the sharpening tool; with the rust removed they will glisten and shine in the heat of battle. In this way the Lord prepares us and equips us for the ministry he has planned for our lives; and our submission to His will brings us into a close relationship with Him and a readiness for anything the enemy might throw our way.

In our own lives there is a spiritual battle going on. We are in no way capable of defeating the enemy of our souls in our own strength. But as Paul states, *"I can do everything through him who gives me strength."* (Philippians 4:13) When we allow Him to take us and use us as His instruments, then we can also say, *"We are more than conquerors through Him who loved us,"* (Romans 8:37).

An arrow must be sharpened after each use, so that it is ready at all times for the Master's use. Continual submission - a readiness and availability - makes the arrow dear to the Archer. Isaiah 49:2-3 *"He made my mouth like a sharpened sword, in the shadow of his hand he hid me; he made me into a polished arrow and concealed me in his quiver."*

In Gill's Exposition of the Entire Bible he writes,

"Make bright the arrows,... Which were covered with rust; scour them of it; anoint them with oil; make them neat, clean, and bright, that they may pierce the deeper; hence we read of a "polished shaft", or arrow, one made bright and pure, Isaiah 49:2; agreeably to this some render the word "sharpen the arrows." The word has the signification of "choosing"; but, as Gussetius observes, whether the direction be to choose the best arrows, or to scour clean and polish them, the end is the same; namely, to have such as are most fit for use."

A dull arrow with only a hint of purpose must be sharpened every day, so that it might fight the continuous battle between its spirit and the world. Arrows do not sharpen themselves; in order to be useful they must intentionally submit to the Master's plans and preparation. The marks of the sharpening will be seen and they will glisten in the sunlight showing the readiness of their polished blade.

Setting out as a young missionary, I had hopes and dreams of doing great things for God. I felt we, as a family, could meet any and every challenge that might come. Wasn't I doing what God wanted? Wasn't I in the center of His will and ready to work hard as I served Him? He had called me in a very definite way and prepared me for the mission field. I had felt almost invincible, until the most difficult trial I ever had to face took away all the youthful exuberance and feelings of personal spiritual strength. This was just the beginning of the honing process to sharpen a blunt, rusty and unprepared arrowhead that had no power of itself and could only be useful when the

Master Archer used it in the way He deemed best. He began the sharpening process that would make the arrow usable, not trusting in its own power, but confident in the hands of its Creator.

Struggles, dangers, strife, hardships, and trials would be the tools he would use to sharpen and prepare me for many tasks and situations. These would also bring me to the realization, that He is truly in control and His ways are so much better than my ways; I could trust Him in any and every situation. He is the One who would place the sharpened arrow on the bowstring, ready to fly at the moment of His choosing, into the dangers, troubles and strife of Spiritual warfare.

Isaiah 55:8-9 *"For my thoughts are not your thoughts, neither are your ways my ways," declares the LORD. As the heavens are higher than the earth, so are my ways higher than your ways and my thoughts than your thoughts."*

The purpose of writing these experiences is not to draw any attention to the "arrow," but to the Lord Jesus who is the One True Archer. He allowed every situation, showing Himself as a loving and purposeful God. He is able to use an ordinary person and has assured us that He will control the lives and actions of those who are ready to follow Him. When we are yoked together with Him we will find that in every circumstance, in spite of any trial or hardship, we will find His yoke easy and His burden light. (Matthew 11:29-30) As you read this account of how God not only sharpened me for service, but also protected me and my family so many times, I trust you will be encouraged to allow God to sharpen you for whatever service He may have for your life.

The pathway of obedience is truly the pathway of blessing.

Ian Taylor, 2016

PART ONE

PREPARATION

Proverbs 1:8,9 *"Listen, my son, to your father's instruction and do not forsake your mother's teaching. They will be a garland to grace your head and chain to adorn your neck."*

Preparing to serve God in any capacity begins long before He tells you to "go".

Part One relates to the many people who taught and influenced me in my journey of following God's call to missionary service. As scripture tells us, it is wise for us to listen to instruction and obey God's commands if we expect to be blessed by God and become a sharpened arrow used by Him.

1

HUMBLE ROOTS
AND GODLY INFLUENCES

Heritage

My father, Silas Taylor, grew up in Saratoga, Australia about 50 miles north of Sydney. After completing six years of school, his father made him quit so that he could milk the cows at 4 AM, again at 4 PM, and work in their market gardens during the day. After attending to the three or four cows, he then carried the heavy milk cans around to the homes in the Saratoga area dispensing the milk into the "billycans" and chatting with the customers as he went the rounds.

A group of believers from the Sydney churches regularly went to Saratoga for youth camps at a large boarding house called, "Buena Vista," looking out over the Brisbane waters. Gosford could be seen on a good day about four miles across the water. Some of the young people decided to start an outreach work. Through their endeavors my father accepted the Lord as his personal Savior. Eventually a small local church was established. My mother met Silas through this outreach work and, after they married, they became house parents for the camps at Saratoga.

My mother, Anna Doris Corson, (born on November 4, 1915) was the daughter of Scottish immigrants - William Thomas Corson and Janet Hay (MacIntyre) Corson. They arrived in Australia in the early 1900s. She was one of ten siblings having two older brothers William and John, and three older sisters, Sadie, and twins Bessie and Bertha. Her younger siblings were Ronald, David, Jenny, and Ken.

Mum's mother Janet, had been with the Plymouth Brethren church group in Scotland and when she arrived in Australia soon joined with a Brethren church at Gore Hill on the north side of Sydney Harbor. As a result, all ten children grew up attending the Gore Hill Assembly (as we called our church) and all made a profession of faith in their early years. William Thomas Corson, while not in any way against his wife and family attending any church, did not ever attend the Gore Hill Church with the rest of the family; in fact, he was a Free Mason, which he regarded as his "church". He was also a gymnast and soccer player and provided for his family with his own printing business. It seems that some of his influence came through to me, as I was also involved in several of these types of activities in my life.

As an older teen Anna Doris was one of the young people who went to Saratoga where she met Silas and eventually they married in 1936. Dad affectionately called Mum "Dot." They lived on the family homestead and "Sile", as Mum called him, continued working the cows and market gardens. But being a city girl, she did not really adapt to the country life or to her father-in-law, Laban Taylor, who acted more like an overlord than a loving parent. Norma, their firstborn was born in Gosford and shortly after, with Dot's encouragement, they moved to Sydney. Three years later I was born and by that time Sile and Dot had put a down payment on the home they were purchasing in Naremburn, a Sydney suburb. Three years after my birth, my sister Anne came along, completing the family. My parents continued to direct the camps at Saratoga for many years and one of my earliest memories is being at the guesthouse "Buena Vista" at one of these camps.

Having been born on April 11, 1940 I lived through World War II. I remember as a three- year-old running out to our backyard whenever I heard the war plane squadrons flying over our home on their way north to fight the Japanese. One memorable time was the night when sirens sounded and my Dad got my sister Norma and me out of bed and made a place for us to sleep in the hallway, just outside the bathroom. We could hear the loud explosions from the guns overlooking the entrance to Sydney Harbor. These were firing on submarines off the coast. Destroyers were also setting off depth charges as the Royal Australian Navy sought and destroyed miniature Japanese submarines inside the harbor. Although my parents did not have a lot of money, we were not poor either, and we always had enough to eat. I often received hand-me-down clothing, but my sisters and I were blissfully unaware of the hardships my parents faced. As a small child I did not really realize what the war meant to us, nor that it was a time when life was difficult for all families.

Our family was no different from others except that my parents had a strong faith in God and the knowledge that in all things He would make a way to provide for our needs. As a family we attended church regularly, there was never a question whether we might go to church or not. We went if the doors were open and participated in all events. Another one of my earliest memories is that of going to church sitting in a stroller and going past a children's park, just the other side of the Sydney Harbor Bridge, on the way to the Harrington Street meeting. I must have been two years old at the time. I remember watching the kids in the park and wanting to go and play with them. However, my parents taught me very early that it was more important to be in God's House (church) when there was a meeting, to worship and learn from the Bible about how to live for God.

The local church we eventually attended was about three miles away and, together with my two sisters Norma and Anne, we would walk there and home again for each of the meetings throughout the week. The usual schedule was the regular Sunday morning worship

Norma, Ian and Anne

service then Sunday afternoon a Sunday School with about 100 students for the usual classes. There was always a Gospel meeting Sunday nights. During the week there was the regular prayer meeting and Bible study night. On some special occasions we would have an Sunday School anniversary program where the children all took part in singing, reciting verses of a poem, and sometimes presenting a play. When I was about seven, I played the part of a gypsy boy in a tent. In those days

5

we often sang a Sunday School song called *Tell It Again,* which told the story of a sick gypsy boy who was lying in his tent, dying. Someone came along and presented the gospel story to the little boy, which he received with joy before his life ebbed away. The refrain, being repeated after all five verses, said, "Tell it again. Tell it again. Salvation's story report over and over... Nobody ever has told me before." As the children sang the song, I had to come in at the right time to sing those words of the refrain. Also, every year we had a Sunday School picnic with games - running races by age or class - and a bar-b-cue supper. Along with the regular church meetings, I received a good background in Bible teaching.

From my earliest years I heard the Gospel faithfully preached and was so concerned about going to heaven that one Sunday, after arriving home from morning services and Sunday School, I told my father that I did not want to be left behind when the Lord returned. I was changing from my "Sunday" clothes when he explained that all I had to do was ask the Lord into my life and then follow Him. I was just four and a half years old at the time and was standing in my underpants. I asked Dad, "Should I should go and get dressed first?" He replied, "No, come just as you are," using the thought from the old gospel hymn, "Just as I am!" And so I did, right there in our family room we knelt by the couch and I asked the Lord to save me. I have never doubted my salvation from that time or regretted that decision. I am ever thankful to my parents for their example as believers, which was a major part in my preparation for following the Lord and serving Him.

In my home there was laughter, fun, games, and much more. My two sisters and I got into mischief and always seemed to find ways to annoy our parents. Some of the great memories of those growing up years were the times spent with my 34 cousins, many of whom also attended our church. One cousin in particular, Jim Lucas, was the same age as me and we have been best friends all our lives. I spent many summer holidays with dad's sister Aunt Kate at Saratoga, where there was bush all around and beside the Brisbane waters that formed a salt-water lake with access to the ocean. Saratoga was an ideal place for a boy with plenty of fishing, swimming and just places to walk and hike in the bush. I had great fun exploring and being free from the city of Sydney. I learned much about life in general during those times.

When I was seven years old I came down with Rheumatic Fever. This serious illness caused my heart to dilate some three and a half inches. At one point the doctor told my parents, "If Ian lives through the night, he will probably be in a wheelchair the rest of his life. I do not want to frighten you, but you should be prepared." My parents contacted the church elders and that night there was much prayer on my behalf during the regular prayer meeting. Miraculously, next morning I was on the mend. Two years later I was playing rugby football at school with no heart problems whatsoever. Whenever I was not living as I should as a Christian, my mother would say, "The Lord didn't raise you from that bed of sickness for nothing; you'd better straighten up!" I always remembered that, even when I knew I was doing something not pleasing to God.

Education

Oh yes, there was also school to attend. This was not especially my favorite activity because I would much rather have been out and about exploring, even though I did do my lessons and I did learn. My peers, who did not hold the same values as our family about regularly attending church, continually challenged me. On Sundays I would hear about what God expected of me and then through the week I would find that it was very challenging for me to live the life that those "spiritual" older people expected. I was always getting into mischief of some sort as I found life too much fun to be so serious about those more important matters. But I learned the verses for Sunday School, knew the Bible stories as well or better than my contemporaries, and in spite of my fun-loving exuberance I continued to slowly grow in God's ways, even if I did not realize it much at the time. God was beginning to remove the rough edges and to form the arrowhead.

Attending school just three blocks from our home, where I not only studied the usual three "R's," - readin', ritin', and 'rithmatic," (spelling always was a problem!!!) school continued to be a daily challenge. I simply did not like having to sit still for such long periods of time. Games and running around always seemed much more appealing. I managed, without too much effort, to pass my exams and move up a grade each year.

In sixth grade the high school sports coach decided to give gymnastic classes to my grade level. I became one of the captains and really enjoyed the sport. I continued with gymnastics on through high school and later joined a gym club at the YMCA. At school I also enjoyed playing on the cricket team as a bowler (pitcher) and batter in the summer, and played rugby football in the winter, as well as running track and swimming. In seventh grade I won the 100 and 200 Meter sprints, and then in the summer, that same year, I won the school diving championship. I excelled in most sports.

Consequently, in my eighth and final year, I managed to find other activities that hindered my attendance at school. On a beautiful sunny day, the ocean and the surf off the coast of Sydney were far more inviting to me. By that time I had my own spear gun and could often be found in the water off one of the ocean reefs, spear fishing with another of my schoolmates. Some of the winter days we might go to the movies in the city, something that would have been frowned on by my parents and the "brethren" leaders at church.

This behavior, of course, did not help me academically and I was struggling to keep up my grades. Even when I was in school, I found ways to make my learning experience much more interesting. There was one teacher in particular who just did not quite know how to manage a room full of 14-year-old boys. My geometry teacher was Mr. Gardener, who very naturally soon had the nickname "Spade." One day I tore up an old three-inch thick phonebook and filled my bag with paper airplanes. I made sure that many of the other boys had a supply and when Spade turned to write on the board the air suddenly became full of planes. He could not tell who had thrown them as they were coming from so many different directions, so he just accused me. Me, of all people! I think he was just prejudiced! There was another "Christian" named Bruce in my class; his father was a Baptist minister. One time Bruce was made to stand at the front by the chalkboard as punishment. Spade drew a triangle on the board and when he turned to explain to the class Bruce grabbed the eraser and wiped it all out. When Spade turned back to the board, he was confused, as he thought he had drawn the triangle, and so he drew it again. After this happened a few times, he finally figured it out, grabbed his three-foot long cane and soundly whacked Bruce. The class erupted into total disarray. It

8

was obvious that Spade had no control over the class at all.

Then there was the time my mother was called to see our headmaster because of her wayward son missing too many days from school. During the conversation she mentioned, "I think Mr. Spade might be part of the problem as he seems to have it in for my son!" Mr. Edwards replied, "Mrs. Taylor, I think you might mean Mr. Gardener, but that's not what I was wanting to talk to you about. You see, Ian has missed 20 days of school over the past two months and I think we need to address that situation." My mother was not too happy when I arrived home that afternoon. After a royal roasting she concluded her very illuminating remarks with, "The Lord didn't raise you from that bed of sickness for nothing; you'd better straighten up!" I do not remember how many times she said that through the years! Neither did the thought ever occur to me that God might wish to use me in some way to serve Him. Mum had the gift of "the laying on of hands," which she used that day in an effort to drive the devil out of me! I am also sure she prayed earnestly for me to follow God in a true and faithful manner.

Mum and Dad at their 40th Anniversary

Consequently, I did not finish High School as I preferred to get a job and start earning money so that I could at least buy some new clothes instead of all the hand-me-downs I had been wearing. An older cousin worked at a shipping company in the city and told me that it was a good job. So, when the school year ended, in December 1954, just four months before my 15th birthday, I went into the city. Walking down George Street I found the Union Steam Ship Company of New Zealand. I told the clerk at the enquiry desk that I was looking for work and she sent me to be interviewed by the accountant. I told him I was 15, the age when many with an Intermediate Certificate left school for either technical school or to work. I must have made some sort of an impression as he hired me on the spot and I began work in the mailroom. I was only there for six months before being sent on to the accounts department; then to the traffic section which had to do with the movement of the coming and going ships as well as taking bookings for the people who wished to ship their cargo. This was followed by other areas of the shipping company such as the claims department, where we had to assess and pay claims for damaged cargo, since we carried our own insurance; the customs department, which involved clearing the ships at the Maritime Customs Offices; and working on the waterfront in the export section, which handled the cargo manifests. Next was the stock department, where all the ships' supplies had to be ordered, invoiced and an inventory of all the stocks kept. I was receiving a very good orientation in every department, which was the main road to management. Little did I know that this was really God attaching the arrowhead to the shaft, preparing me for other work on the mission field.

Unlike today in North America, and many other countries, most students in Australia left formal education after the eighth grade level. It was not expected that all students would go to university, which was considered preparation for skilled vocations such as medicine, engineering, the sciences, etc. Young people not wishing to pursue those degrees went to technical school or directly into the work force for on-the-job apprenticeship training. This was the path I chose.

A Commitment Made To The Lord

At the age of 15,I soon came to realize that I had a very important life decision to make. Either I was going to keep going along with the crowd and living life for myself, or I was going to make a commitment to follow the Lord in all of His ways and live my life for Him. I decided to give up smoking cigarettes and told my mother that if I could smoke a cigar, I would get sick and that would help me

10

give up smoking. I had been smoking cigars as well as cigarettes, but I wanted to make a point. I smoked the cigar in the backyard of my home, with my mother's tearful eyes watching out the kitchen window, then I told her I would never smoke again. I think that was a happy day for her. I was making a major decision, a life changing one. I spoke to one of the elders in my church and told him I wanted to be baptized. The following week after my baptism, I became a part of the local church fellowship participating in the remembrance of the Lord, in the breaking of bread worship service. Thankfully, I chose to really commit my life to the Lord and have never regretted that decision at any time since. It was the best decision I ever made. From then on I put all my energy into serving Him as He led me along. But I still had no idea all the plans God had for me, or how he had "sharpened" my life to this point of being able to surrender my life to serving Him.

For many years I sang in the Royal North Shore Hospital Choir every Sunday evening. We went around singing in several wards and then there was usually a short message by one of the older men during the song time. At the age of 18, I began handing out gospel tracts during my lunch hour on the streets of Sydney with one of my church friends, Brian Tizzard. One such day, while distributing tracts to the people sitting in a little downtown park eating their lunch, we saw the OAC (Open Air Campaigners) VW van equipped with a special platform, microphone and speakers. One of the OAC workers was preaching the gospel to the lunch crowd. We started giving out our tracts to those standing and listening as well as those sitting in the park. When the message was done, the worker came over to us and suggested we get a message ready for the following week. That was a challenge, but we were ready to try. Brian and I started our preaching there in the streets of Sydney helping the OAC preachers and getting some very important experience. God continued to sharpen my skills; the arrowhead was taking shape.

Brian and I frequently met during lunch hours at the Everyman's Center lunchroom in the city (it had been a Christian center for servicemen during World War II). We had a quick sandwich and then used a six-by-eight foot broom closet there to pray together about gospel work. As a result of our prayer times over several months, and conversations with some key people in our youth group, we decided to start a youth-group band in our church. We spoke to several of our contemporaries with musical abilities. After practicing solos, duets, quartets and group songs on Thursday evenings, we approached the elders in our church and asked them if we could start a youth meeting on the last Saturday of each month. These men were very sympathetic and gave us their blessing. We organized a band, including a double bass, my sister Norma played a piano accordion, cousin Jim Lucas played the trumpet, another person played a saxophone and I played a harmonica. My younger sister Anne also had a good voice; and together with Norma and a number of others from our youth group we became a really good singing and musical group.

The first night, we had several vases of flowers on the front of the stage, and we set up spotlights to shine on the group, (that sort of thing was unheard of in our church in those days!) With a sound system working we were really on the cutting edge. This was in 1958 and in a very conservative church, so we were a bit nervous when we had our first meeting. And so, with our young people and the older church members attending, we "jazzed up" the old well-known hymn, "When The Saints Go Marching In," as well as other contemporary songs from the Blackwood Brothers, and John W. Peterson. We then finished with either a gospel film or one of us preaching the gospel. The older men of the church thought it was a good effort and encouraged us by asking all the older folk to attend each time. Several months later, word had gotten around, and we started to get phone calls from different churches in the metropolitan area asking us to reserve seats for their young people. As we began reserving seats we had to kindly ask the older church members, "Thank you for your encouragement, but please stay at home and pray for us, as we need the seats for all our visitors." The church was by then packed with young people, some standing outside the doors or looking through the windows. It is a blessing to say that there is still a strong young people's work continuing to this day, in that church in Sydney. This is a real testimony to what God will do with people who are committed to serving Him.

The Chapel we were using was in the suburb of Greenwich and soon we had up to 150 young people coming to our youth meeting that we called GFC, Greenwich For Christ. We began receiving invitations to take our team to different churches, one invitation from 100 miles away in Newcastle. Brian, who was two years older than me, did most of the preaching, but I also had many opportunities to preach. We were kept very busy, especially when OAC later asked us to do the music for their Tent Campaigns.

During this same time I was also the leader of a boy's club at our local church, teaching the 14-17 year old boys Bible at each club meeting, along with tumbling, games, and special outings. I was one of four young men who were responsible for putting together a monthly magazine called Overcomer, each one of us working together as editors. This publication included articles, news of events as well as news from missionaries abroad whom our churches supported. We would work together each Thursday night and sometimes into the small hours of the morning preparing this paper for printing and distribution around Australia, New Zealand, and other European countries. This was my first introduction to writing and publishing. I loved being busy for the Lord and found much blessing in doing it. Once again, God was adding to my skill set, but I did not know why. I only knew that there was blessing in serving the Lord and, as noted from my youth, I needed to be active.

With my two cousins, Jim Lucas (L) & Bill Corson (Back)

2

FIRST TRIP TO SEA AND STAYING THE COURSE

I very much enjoyed working for the Union Steam Ship Company and was assigned at the age of 16 to Captain Harrison George's office. Captain George headed the Marine Department and had the responsibility of hiring and firing the different ship's officers as well as auditing their wages, including their overtime, and making sure they could spend the regulation days off for "home port" days while in Sydney. We had many ships in the fleet. Some carried cargo plying the Pacific route to Portland, Oregon USA to collect timber, or carrying cargo to Vancouver, Canada and returning with sockeye salmon, timber and other commodities. We had a few passenger lines and I was working with several of the captains of these "deep sea" ships to the USA, as well as ships on regular trips around Australia and to New Zealand. My job was to assist Captain George in his record keeping. Our office was on the waterfront overlooking Pier 14 in Darling Harbour in Sydney. The cargo ships' officers usually came into the office when in port to check with their "boss" Captain George, and I got to know them pretty well, especially those on the ships plying the Australian coastal trade.

One of the Chief Officers, Ian Craig, suggested I sign on to his ship some time as Purser and do one of the round trips along the Coast. A Purser on a cargo ship is an officer and generally handles the business side of things. He organizes the manifests of the cargo, so that copies are ready at the discharging ports; and also is the person who is responsible for the legal papers and finances, including the crews' wages. This sounded like a pretty good idea as my annual holidays were coming due. I spoke to Captain George,

15

who gave me permission, so I made arrangements for the next trip of the M.V. Kootara.

When the time came for me to sign on, I made the trip to the Mercantile Marine Office located on Harrington Street, right beside the pylons of the Harbour Bridge. Ian Craig came with me and I officially signed onto the ship's crew log as Purser. I went to my parents' home in Naremburn to pack my bags and then caught the tram back into the city, crossing the famous Harbour Bridge, and headed down to Darling Harbour to board the ship. This was really quite exciting and I tried to carry it off as I thought a "mature" seaman (crew member) would. I boarded the ship and moved into the Purser's cabin. The Chief Steward came to welcome me and brought me a cup of tea with some fresh scones the cooks had just made. "Wow, this is the life!" I thought.

The ship's horn sounded three times telling other craft in the area that we were backing out of the Darling Harbour pier. Suddenly the engines stopped and we were drifting. I was up on deck and could see that the wind was blowing us across the harbour towards the

MV Kootara

piers at Piermont on the opposite side. I was quite surprised at how the wind could move this 3,000-ton freighter so fast across the harbour! I believed we were about to crash into the wharf, but thankfully the engines finally turned over and we gradually moved on our way, turning out of Darling Harbour. We sailed under the Harbour Bridge, on through the beautiful harbour with the sun setting behind us, moving out of the calm waters, through the Sydney Heads and on into the open Pacific Ocean. I stood on the deck watching the coast slip by as we headed north on a short hop to the Newcastle Steel Mills. We arrived in the middle of the night, tied up and began loading steel and coal for Launceston, and Hobart, Tasmania.

The next morning, while the ship was loading, a representative of the BHP Steel Company came on board and invited me on a personal tour of their large facility. I was shown inside a huge blast furnace that was being repaired, and then to other areas where the furnaces were functioning and the molten steel being poured into huge buckets. I was then shown the process of pouring the molten steel into molds to cool. This allowed the steel to be made into many other forms such as I-beams, reinforcement rods, rebar, corrugated iron and finally extruded into wire, as well as bolts and nails. It was a really interesting process and gave me very useful insight when involved in construction projects many years later.

Finally the ship was loaded and we set sail after lunch for Launceston, a three-day trip from Newcastle. At about 2:00 PM, Ian Craig called me to come up on the bridge. I did not need a second invitation and when I got there he asked me, "Would you like to steer the ship?" (Remember I was only 16 years old at this time).

"Yes, that would be great!" I replied, trying to sound self-confident.

Ian Craig turned to the seaman at the wheel and told him, "You can have the rest of your shift off."

The seaman, happy with the extra time to himself, left the bridge and headed for the seamen's quarters.

"Now," Ian continued calling me over to take the huge wheel, "All you have to do is keep the compass there, right in front of you, on 156 degrees south and adjust your course if it begins to stray. The bearing is on the chalkboard in front of the binnacle in case you forget."

I had never steered anything larger than a row boat before and expected Ian would be there to consult as we sailed south about six miles off the coast of New South Wales. However, with those few words he left the bridge and I was left completely alone on the bridge steering this valuable, 3,000-ton ship down the Coast of Australia. My heart, after about five minutes, began to slow down somewhat, which is when I noticed the compass had moved off the mark turning the ship a little toward the Coast.

The waves were coming from the southeast pushing the bow of the ship to the starboard (right) side. I turned the wheel just a little to adjust our direction back onto the course, but nothing happened. I turned it a little more and still nothing happened. The ship was still pointing off course, so at this stage I thought, "I had better get this ship back on course or we will be wrecked on the coast." I turned the wheel a good full turn and suddenly the bow began to swing to the Port side with the coastline fast disappearing from my peripheral vision on the right. Now we were pointed to New Zealand and still turning. By this time I was perspiring; sweat poring off my forehead as I spun the wheel to turn the ship back toward the starboard side. Thankfully, it began to turn back to the course, but it kept on going so we were then pointed directly at the coast again. I spun the wheel in the opposite direction with the same overwhelming result of the ship suddenly swinging back to face directly east.

At this point I was in complete panic mode! I continued to make these wild turns for what seemed like an eternity but probably was not more than about 20 minutes. About that time Ian Craig came back to the bridge and, with a smile on his face, he gave me some very important instructions about gently turning the wheel into the waves and then quickly going back to "center." With his instruction we soon had the ship back on course. Then he said, "Come over here to the wings of the bridge with me. Now take a look back up the coast. What do you see?" I looked and could see the wake of the ship zigzagging up the coast behind us.

With my heart almost beating normally again, I returned to the wheel and continued steering until the seaman starting the 4:00 PM watch arrived to relieve me. By this time I was more than ready to return to my cabin, take a shower and put on some clean clothes before the bells sounded for dinner.

I arrived at the dining room as the steward was sprinkling water on the tablecloth between the knives and forks as well as under the cups and condiments. "Why are you wetting the tablecloth?" I asked.

"The sea is beginning to get a little rougher and the wet cloth stops the plates from slipping off the table," he replied. I thought that was clever, and remembered this was also the reason why the table and chairs were bolted to the deck.

18

The officers and engineers arrived and we all stood around the dining room chatting, until the Captain and Chief Engineer arrived. When they sat down, the others sat at the table in their prescribed order. The Captain was seated at the head of the table, the Chief Engineer at the other end; First Officer, Ian Craig, on the Captain's left, then second and third officers, then me - the Purser - to the right of the Chief Engineer. Along the other side of the table were the four engineers in their respective order.

The stewards had served the soup and the next course was placed before us. As we began the main course, the Chief Engineer spoke to the Captain, "I say, Captain, did we get orders for a change in our destination today?"

"Not really, Chief, why do you ask?" replied the Captain.

"Well I just happened to look out my porthole this afternoon and noticed that we seemed to be heading back to Sydney. Then it looked like perhaps we had orders to go to America as we seemed to be going due east."

At this point my face was getting red with the option of turning purple.

The captain responded, "It might have been the rough seas, who knows, what gave you that idea?"

"Strange, strange," went on the Chief, "I can't understand it, the weather has really been mild."

By this time I felt I should slide under the table. Everyone broke out into laughter and I realized they were all in on the joke at my expense.

This was another valuable life lesson in training for the mission field! When I recall this experience I see it as a symbol of our lives. Circumstances may take us on different courses but if God is in control it is good. If we are in control (like I was at the wheel) it could mean disaster by being off course. Another good lesson, was learning that it always helps to have a good sense of humor! It is always good to be able to laugh at yourself.

Purser On The SS Waipori And Visits With Friends

In 1959, at the age of 19, I arranged for a four-week trip to New Zealand. I had the company's permission to sign on to the SS Waipori, which would leave Sydney for Christchurch, New Zealand.

It was a four-day trip across the Tasman Sea on a ship, which had a reputation for not only rolling, but also corkscrewing in the ocean waves.

It was a pleasure sitting in the dining area listening to the ship "working" and hearing the sounds of the ship as the metal plates and inside bodywork moved and creaked with each roll of the ship. I also spent much time on the bridge watching the waves hitting the bow and crashing over the foredeck.

We finally sailed into Lyttelton Harbour in the South Island, a deep volcanic crater, on the north western side of Banks Peninsula surrounded by beautiful mountains. As it took several days to unload cargo, load other cargos for the ongoing N.Z. ports, and return to Sydney, we had several days in Lyttelton. The company manager had arranged for me to sail the same night on the Hinemoa, an inter-island passenger ship, for an overnight trip to Wellington where the Union Steam Ship Company had its Head Office.

The following morning in Wellington a company representative met me. He had been assigned the responsibility of giving me a tour of the company's buildings, offices, shipyards, and even to check out our own tugs for helping berth the larger passenger ships. I also saw our computer floor where the company computer was working the old punch card system. It occupied the entire floor with quite a few punch card operators feeding the computer with the data coming in from our companies in many countries. This was most interesting, as I had worked in our accounts department in Sydney and every different item being bought or used had a code number, which eventually came to this computer. (My smartphone now has more data storing capacity than that old style machine.)

The company had arranged and paid for my hotel with a large comfortable room. They were giving me the "royal" treatment. I had brought a contact phone number for someone connected with our churches, so I called George Cassels who invited me to his parents' home for dinner. Little did I know he would one day marry one of my cousins, Beverly Corson.

I sailed back to Lyttelton on the Maori, another inter-island ship. On board was one of my friends from Sydney who had accepted a full time job as Purser. His father was a preacher and Mark was, or had been, a practicing Christian. However, it seemed that he had

20

fallen to the temptation of so many of the seamen, being involved with wine, women, and a fast life. What I saw and heard that night was one of the reasons why I later refused what seemed like a wonderful opportunity. God uses many ways to sharpen our skill of discernment so that we can be more useful to Him.

From Lyttelton, the port for Christchurch, we sailed to Timaru just a hundred miles or so down the coast. Robin Sides lived in Timaru and he had been to Sydney a couple of years before to attend one of our church's Easter Camps for young people. The camp was at Kurrajong Heights where I had been a study group leader since I was 16 years old. I had gotten to know Robin pretty well so I had let him know I would be in New Zealand and would contact him while there.

We had arrived late on a Saturday night, so early on Sunday morning I dressed for church and walked a couple of miles up North Street, to the Sides' home. Robin was surprised to see me and to-gether, with some others from his family, we attended church. The elders asked me to speak at the ministry teaching meeting, and then we returned to the Sides' residence for lunch.

As we were eating Robin asked, "Did you see my sister Ann when she stopped off in Sydney on her way to France? She was at one of the churches there."

"No, I don't remember seeing her," I replied, wondering how I could have missed a nice young lady.

He seemed to be a little surprised and could not understand how I could have possibly not seen his sister!

"Well, you know, a lot of people come through Sydney and per-haps she went to one of our other churches."

"She will be returning in a year," he went on to explain.

"Oh, that's nice, I will make sure I see her when she returns and will show her around Sydney," I assured him, thinking that I would not want to pass up this opportunity for sure. A fellow never knows when God may be sending that "special someone." We then moved on to another subject.

"How long will you be in port," he asked.

"We will have about four days."

"I can take a couple of days off work and show you around if you like."

21

"Wow, that would be great," I replied and we then began to make plans.

Robin gave me a first class tour of the area, which did not take too long; Timaru was not a big town. I really enjoyed my time with Robin over those few days, not forgetting the notice of his sister possibly coming through my area the following year.

We drove to some interesting places including a trip to Akaroa, a pretty part of a huge deep water bay that was once a volcanic crater. On another day we left for the long drive to Mount Cook, the highest mountain in New Zealand. Sir Edmund Hillary trained on Mt. Cook before being the first to conquer Mount Everest. Finally the Waipori set sail for Dunedin still further down the South Island.

I made arrangements to have a two day tour to Lake Wakatipu, a beautiful long lightning- shaped lake surrounded with The Remark-ables, a snow capped range of majestic mountain peaks overlooking Queenstown, a pretty tourist town. (Much of the movie, "*Lord of the Rings*" was filmed in that area.) After a beautiful drive in a tour bus, I unpacked at the bed- and-breakfast where I was staying, then went down to the docks at the Lake to take a cruise on the Ernslaw, an old ferry steamer. We sailed north on the lake to Glenorchy on the extreme north end of the lake, and had time to take a short walk into a beautiful fern-covered valley, before beginning the return ferry ride back to Queenstown. I took the bus back to Dunedin ready for the next leg of the voyage. We finally left Dunedin for Bluff, the port for Invercargill, and the southernmost port in New Zealand.

The SS Waipori sailed out of the harbour at Bluff, but as we steered west around the bottom of the South Island of New Zealand we ran into the "Roaring 40s," the very strong winds coming from the west and circling around these southern seas. I awoke during the night being thrown around in my bed. In order to stay on the bed, I had to brace my knees on the boards, which were about six inches higher than the mattress. I learned the next morning that one of the officers had been thrown out of his bed, across the space between him and his sofa, and landed on the sofa itself. It was almost impossible to take a shower as the water coming from the showerhead moved by gravity. This ship was not only rolling, but also corkscrewing, which meant the shower water was going in circles around the shower stall wall. I decided to take a sponge bath

22

from then on, and just a good dose of deodorant!

At breakfast there was nothing cooked, as none of the pots and pans would stay on the stove. We had toasted cheese sandwiches for the next two days. Walking along the alleyways and up the stairs was difficult, as I had to hang on or go flying. I climbed the stairs to the bridge and stood at the chart table, legs spread apart for balance and leaning on the table itself. There was a pendulum on the wall beside the door to the bridge and I saw that the ship was rolling 45° from side to side along with the corkscrew motion.

I moved out onto the bridge and stood at the windows looking forward and holding onto the handrail, which ran from side to side below the windows. I looked out and saw the bow of the ship plunge under the huge wave crashing towards us. The wave moved from the bow toward the bridge, and the bow began to rise as the wave crashed against the ship's superstructure below the bridge, spraying green ocean against the bridge windows. We began to rise up over the wave, climbing to the crest and I saw about 75 yards ahead, the next wave with a valley between us about 80 feet deep. We careened down that wave, and again the bow dug into the oncoming wave, and this constant action continued for two days. The waves had to be between 60 and 80 feet high. I often wondered how the seamen were able to hold the ship on course. There was no automatic pilot, no GPS in those days, and the course was held by dead reckoning until we came close enough to land for the Direction Finder, which received radio signals, to triangulate a course. As we came up over the horizon through the haze and rain, I was surprised to see the Sydney Heads, and the entrance to the harbor was dead ahead.

That trip, with the crashing waves rising and falling, was another illustration of the turbulence of life. There was nothing the seamen could do to calm those seas. But when our life is in turmoil God is there to bring peace and calm if we ask Him to help us. God may allow difficult navigation through life to cause us to call on Him, allowing Him to lead where He wants us to go. Our lives are always better when we allow God to be in control. As Proverbs 3:5,6 says, "Trust in the Lord with all your heart, and lean not on your own understanding; in all your ways acknowledge him, and he will make your paths straight."

An Offer For A Fast Promotion

Not long after my trip to New Zealand, the manager of the Union Steam Ship Company called me into his office and after the normal greetings said, "There is an opportunity for you to go to New Zealand to work on the inter-island ships, being trained for work on the company's ships as a full time purser. After that you would be assigned to one of the deep-sea ships. A few years working on them will speed up your career to become a manager. You will need to leave in two weeks. Would you like to do this?"

Well, this was certainly an interesting and exciting proposition. Management must have thought I showed leadership and advancement possibilities. Honestly, I was quite happy and fulfilled with the

At a Union Steam Ship Company's Event

job I was already doing; but, always one for adventure, this offer sounded quite exciting. To make any such life decisions, however, I knew that I certainly would need to seek God's leading first. So, I replied, "Thank you for the opportunity; can I have a couple of days to think about it, please?" I said this, of course, knowing that I would not only think about this possibility but also pray in earnest for God to make clear what I should do.

"Yes, but we need to know as soon as possible."

I left his office with my head in a spin and returned to the Claims Department where I was working at the time, and which I very much enjoyed. This position not only involved paying the claims to clients for cargo which had been damaged while in transit, but on other days spending time on the waterfront checking on the actual damage, assessing the damage and loss. Other occasions found me trying to work out how the stevedores were stealing items from the arriving cargo. This was MY kind of excitement - figuring out how the thefts were being carried out and then reporting it to the authorities for action to be taken. However, after the conversation with the manager, I returned to my office, thinking about how much I enjoyed doing what my present job required, but also thinking about what going to sea entailed. I had seen the lifestyle of the seamen, including the activities they pursued when in port. My thoughts returned to the time I was on the inter-island ship with my friend Mark, whom I had always thought was a person who followed Christ and lived a life which reflected that fact, but what I witnessed did not match what I expected. While it was exciting to visit many different ports and be out on the open seas, I knew this kind of life would not help me in my spiritual growth and I would not be able to continue much of the service for the Lord in which I was so heavily involved. This was a real challenge. I prayed about it and spoke to my parents, telling them only about the benefits of going to sea as a purser.

Dad's first comment was, "We really need to pray about it and ask the Lord to give very definite direction."

Mum came at it from a different angle, "You shouldn't even think about it. God has given you so much to do here at home! You have a good job and you have so many responsibilities in the local church. If you go to sea you will be away from the influence of the church and your friends here. It's a ridiculous idea! You just need to stay at home."

"Well thanks, Dot, I'm glad you don't mind letting people know exactly what you think." (I always called her Dot, not out of disrespect but in some ways it was more familiar than plain old "mum.") "Nothing like getting the Lord's will directly," I went on. "I'll pray about it and make a decision by tomorrow."

As I contemplated this major decision for my life, I remembered how I had enjoyed a couple of holiday trips on the cargo ships as acting purser. These were only for three or four weeks at a time and most enjoyable. However, I had also seen how the seamen lived, their immorality and their onshore pleasures in ports away from homeport. I realized that mixing with those officers, living with those types of fun-seeking men at the same time trying to live a different style of life for the Lord would be a difficult situation. Knowing myself, I have always been a fun-loving person and could easily fall under these seamen's influence and my Christian life would suffer. My ultimate decision was based on my desire to please the Lord and allow Him to arrange my advancement in the company.

The next day I phoned the manager's secretary to ask if I could see him, and then fronted up to his desk. "Sir, I have thought a lot about your offer and want to thank you for considering me for this work. However, for personal reasons, I want to let you know that as important as it is for my advancement in the company, I feel I cannot accept the position at this time."

"Well, I'm sorry to hear this as it would have been a tremendous experience for you, but it's your decision and thank you for letting me know so soon."

With the matter settled I left his office and returned to my desk, still wondering if I had made the right decision. However, I was just beginning to realize that God is in control and He has a plan for my life. This sharpening process can be uncomfortable.

3

A WIFE ON THE HORIZON

In December 1960 Ann Sides did arrive in Sydney after spending a year in France. She was returning from a year of teaching experience in France, a privilege she had earned through high academic achievement in her graduate studies.

One of the Bible teachers from my home church, Walter Lickley and his wife Ruth, had invited Ann to stay with them during her two-week stay. She was introduced at church the following Sunday and I suddenly remembered my promise to her brother Robin, on my trip to New Zealand the previous year. At the end of the meeting, with purpose, and as quickly as possible without seeming impulsive, I went up to her and calmly introduced myself.

"G'day Ann, I'm Ian Taylor. I visited your home in Timaru about a year ago and promised Robin I would show you around Sydney while you are here, so I would like to set up some times to take you around." As you can see, I did not waste any time in getting to the point.

Ann was a very pretty lady, obviously a few years older than me being only 20 years old while she, on the other hand, had her degree and experience teaching in France. When she spoke she had a very cultured voice and very friendly smile that made her whole face light up. Rather captivating! Nice, but probably out of my reach by age and intelligence! So I thought!!!

We arranged a time for site seeing and I took a day off work. We visited Taronga Park Zoo, had good Aussie meat pies for lunch surrounded by the animals and the lovely gardens at the Zoo. Then I returned her to the Lickley's home in time for dinner, and went home with all sorts of strange things floating around in my mind! A few days later she rode the train into the city and I took a two hour lunch so we could visit the nearby Botanical Gardens, right on Sydney Harbour. After eating our picnic lunch we chatted and walked around until I went back to work and she went off on her own shopping trip. Now it was becoming difficult for me to concentrate.

Since the end-of-year holidays were coming up, including Christmas, Boxing Day and the New Year, I arranged to take Ann to the beach where most of our church young people went as often as possible during the summer. (Remember, this is the southern hemisphere so Christmas is mid-summer.) We had a great time watching various sea creatures in the rock pools, the waves, and becoming more acquainted with each other and maybe holding hands a few times. After a full day of body surfing, swimming and baking in the sun I had huge blisters on my shoulders; but I was not about to miss a moment to encourage this friendship. It was becoming apparent that we enjoyed each other's company.

During that second week, Ann told me that another young man, a couple of years older than her – meaning he was at least eight years older than me – had asked her out. He seemed to want to start a relationship with her. Since I had not made any sort of commitment with her at that stage, I did not say anything. I suppose, as I now think about it, I had some feelings of jealousy, which made me also wonder what my feelings might really be. I thought, "I'm still young and don't want to rush into anything, but…what!?" A few years earlier I had enjoyed a couple of girlfriends, at different times, with relationships that had not ended very well. I broke those friendships off, not wanting to get too serious with the girls concerned. I had promised myself that I would not get serious with anyone else until I knew that I would want that person to be my wife.

A few days after the New Year celebrations, Ann was flying home to New Zealand. I went to the airport with a few of the young people from church, waved her off and went home with somewhat confused feelings. I liked her a lot, she was a great Christian lady, good looking, well spoken, intelligent, (that would help if we had children; hopefully they would get some of their mother's brains!), but was I ready to commit to such a relationship?

I arrived home and my parents asked how everything went. Dad began right away, "You know, Ian, Ann is a very nice girl and would make a lovely wife."

Mum then added, "She is so friendly and nice; you should keep in touch."

"Okay, Dot, these are things I have to decide myself; so don't put any pressure on."

A week or so later Mum again got started, "Have you written to Ann yet? You should do it right away."

I did not answer; I just walked away. In spite of their pressure, I really was thinking of writing, but scared of the thought of starting something I could not stop. After much prayer for God's guidance and vacillating for another two weeks, I finally plucked up courage and wrote. I can't remember what I wrote and thought that Ann would probably not answer this rough Aussie. Unbelievably, a week later a letter with an NZ postal stamp arrived. I did not know what to expect but it was a couple of pages long, thanking me for writing and thanking me for showing her around while in Sydney. She had a really fine handwriting and the letter itself was folded in such a way that it exactly filled the envelope. All of her letters were like that! She asked me to write again! My heart missed a beat and the next day I started another letter. The letters became more frequent with at least one letter a week and I really could not wait to get another one in the mail. She was so good at explaining herself, and the way she said things made me feel very special.

Now, here, I need to stop and explain something which came into play at that time: When I started work four months short of turning 15, my mother counseled me to start paying into the Commonwealth Starr Bowkett. This was a registered, not-for-profit money lending society, formed with a limited number of memberships available. New members were assigned a number and had to select the amount of loan for which they wished to apply. Members then paid a monthly subscription for a set time period, which was about 16 years. Once the society had accumulated sufficient funds from subscriptions, ballot meetings were begun and held on a monthly basis afterward. Loan recipients were chosen by random lottery. Once a member had received a loan, they paid back the loan interest-free, and any amount still owed on their original subscription commitment.   After about 16 years, everyone in that particular group received the loan, so this eventually would be a sure thing, even if my name were not randomly called. I had been paying into it for several years already and had really forgotten about it; it was just another few dollars a month into a savings account.

I still felt some reserve about marriage. About June 1961, I began to pray, "Lord, if you want me to marry Ann, then you know I don't have a home; I won't live with my family, so I really need to be able to get a home before I can commit to marriage."

The very Saturday after I had prayed that prayer, I was sleeping in, and about 10:00 AM my mother came in with a letter. I thought it might be from Ann so I was immediately awake and grabbed the letter. I saw right away it was not from her, but rather from this Starr Bowkett Fund. "Probably something to sign," I thought. I opened the letter and it was not a statement, but announced:

"Mr. Taylor, your name came out in the draw this week and you are eligible for an interest free loan of $12,000. Present this letter to arrange the loan." I jumped out of bed and ran to tell my parents. They were just as excited as I was. I told them, at that moment, of my prayer about not having a home and not wanting to marry until I could provide a home for my wife and future family. Back in 1961 the going rate for a three-bedroom cottage was anything from $18,000 and up. The Lord had very definitely answered my prayer, which gave me all the confidence I needed to think about a proposal.

The following Monday I visited a jeweler friend whom I had met through his travel with our company. His workshop/office was on the other side of George Street from where I worked. I walked up the stairs to see him and asked, "Jeff, I am interested in getting an engagement ring. Do you have any pictures or samples I could have?"

"I've got catalogues galore; here's a couple you can have. Why don't you bring her in and she can look at what I already have in stock."

"That won't work mate; she is in New Zealand."

"Okay, what you need to do then is send the ones you like, and also tell her to cut some string and tie it on her ring finger, make sure it isn't too tight, make a knot and send me the picture she likes along with the string. I can make it for you in a week or two. Tell me how much you can pay and I will make it to order."

"Thanks Jeff. I will be in touch," I replied with great excitement mounting and my heart beating a bit faster. This new chapter of life was opening and I was ready!

I wrote the next letter to Ann and included about eight photos of ring designs I had cut out of the catalogues and a piece of string. In that letter I asked Ann if she would marry me. No, this was not the most romantic way to propose, but being a man of action I wanted to get right to the point. Making a trip to NZ was very expensive and I did not have time off from work. It sure would have been nice to have today's electronic means of communication back then.

She wrote back very quickly that time and told me, "We were all sitting down to lunch when your letter came. I opened it at the table and saw all these little pieces of paper and thought, 'what's Ian up to now?' and then some fell out. In a split second I realized what the pictures were on the photos. I grabbed the pictures and letter, ran off to the bathroom, locked the door and read your letter. My first reaction was, 'I can't do this,' but then as I read your words I realized that the Lord was doing something; so here is the string with my ring size and the type of ring I really like, and yes, I would be thrilled to be your wife."

Her letter was thrilling also to me as I could see that the Lord was definitely directing, and Ann was a woman who would be a real companion and helper for me, and a wife who would be able to support and follow my leading as a Christian husband. Again God was showing Himself faithful in opening doors of opportunity. Had I taken the job offer to serve full time on ships at sea I would have missed this blessing of a mate provided by God.

My parents were delighted, as you can imagine, and I swore them to secrecy!

The number of letters per week increased radically over the next couple of months. By that time Ann was teaching high school French in Christchurch, NZ. Jeff made the ring; we decided that we would become officially engaged in August during the school spring break.

I made the plane bookings with Air New Zealand to fly to Christchurch. On August 20, 1961, I arrived to see Ann again after months of separation. This was very exciting after only getting to know something about her character through her letters.

We left Christchurch the following day for Timaru, Ann's home-town, for me to officially meet her family, and where we had two weeks together getting to know each other face-to-face. There were long discussions making arrangements for the wedding, set-ting dates, and talking about future plans for our lives together. We decided to get married on January 20, the following year.

Timaru, New Zealand, January 20, 1962

This meant we had another five months of letter writing; then, while Ann was arranging the wedding ceremony, reception, invita-tions, and the honeymoon site, I was arranging flights to New Zea-land for my mother and sister Anne, as well as my life-long friend and cousin, Jim Lucas, who would be my best man. We did not have the funds for my father or my older sister Norma to fly or travel by any means to New Zealand, which meant they were not able to attend. Therefore, not being the wealthiest man in town, I also did not fly but arranged to sign on to a ship as purser from Sydney, a four day trip to New Zealand. The only ship that suited the dates was the SS Kuro, a sister ship of the SS Waipori, both known for their rolling and corkscrewing in the heavy seas. Because this ship was going only to Wellington on the North Island I had to also ar-range to take the overnight inter-island ferry, the MV Hinemoa, to

Christchurch. Finally arriving with a day to spare Ann and I went to the Christchurch airport to meet Mum, Anne and Jim, then we drove together to Timaru for the wedding a day later.

It was a small wedding party; Jim was my best man, and Ann had her friend Janice Hansen as her bride's maid. Janice would later marry Ann's brother Robin and become our sister-in-law. The wedding was held in the small meeting room of the Oddfellows Building, which was the room that the local church also used for their meetings. After the wedding service, we had the reception in a school dining area not too far away.

The officiate for the wedding was Jock Watson, a well known teacher/preacher among our church circles, and he spoke from Deuteronomy 22:8 *"When you build a new house, make a parapet around your roof so that you may not bring the guilt of bloodshed on your house if someone falls from the roof."* He emphasized the importance of the husband making sure that the family home was a place where the Bible would be taught and its teachings practiced. That would be the way to build into the lives of the children a strong love for the Lord, and establish a desire to follow and please Him. This would be a constant protection from the many evils and pitfalls in life and in the world around us.

Ann's brother Eric had a car sales yard and gas station, so he very kindly loaned us a car for the week we would have for our honeymoon. After the wedding, Ann and I took off toward Christchurch and stopped half way at a small Bed and Breakfast for the night. The next day we continued on to Akaroa for the rest of our honeymoon in New Zealand. Ann had arranged for a very small cabin on the hill overlooking the beautiful deep blue waters of the Bay formed by a volcanic crater. We spent a lot of time near the waters, enjoying long walks, a tourist ferry around the Bay, and a couple of picnics in the hill surrounding the Bay.

Sadly, this blissful time finished in a hurry. Ten days after the wedding found us setting off for the overnight trip on the inter-island ferry to Wellington along with several suitcases of Ann's belongings. The same afternoon in Wellington we boarded a very large passenger liner, the Johan Van Oldenbarnevelt for the trip from Wellington to Sydney. This trip would only take three days, as the passenger ship was much larger and faster than the old cargo ships on which I had traveled previously. We enjoyed the wonderful meals, sunbathing on the upper decks, and sitting one evening at the Captain's table for dinner.

There was a good crowd of friends and family waiting to greet us on the pier in Sydney. As soon as we had cleared immigration and customs at Circular Quay, we headed home to my parents' house in Naremburn where we would stay temporarily, until we could find a suitable home. We checked out the advertisements in the newspaper and, about a month later, found a three-bedroom brick cottage at Lane Cove West, which would suit our purpose. Quickly, I went to the office of the Commonwealth Starr Bowkett and made arrangements to use the interest free loan as a deposit, then arranged for a second mortgage through a company of lawyers, as we needed an additional loan of $12,000.

As soon as possible we moved into 9 Lihon Street, Lane Cove West, a suburb on the North Side of Sydney, and began setting up house. With only a mattress on the floor, a couple of chairs, a card table, and boxes storing our personal effects, it became home to us. An old wood/coke burning stove in the kitchen helped warm the house in winter, and was also used to heat the water for showers and the kitchen. The property had a pretty front yard with roses along the front fence. The back yard had a wide and deep lawn, with a raised vegetable garden along the back fence. I soon had tomatoes and beans growing along with the clump of banana trees and a large orange tree already growing there. I eventually lined the edges of the flower gardens around the perimeter of the yard with stones and built a 15 x 8 foot fernery on the east side of the yard, closest to the house. It was a lovely home in which to begin married life and perhaps begin a family.

Life Settles With More To Learn

Ann applied for a position as a French and English teacher at Hunters Hill High School, just a couple of miles away. She began teaching immediately, as it was the beginning of a new school year. With her salary we quickly paid off the second mortgage, and with my salary bought food and furniture for our home. We did not have a car at that time so a search began. I noticed a for sale sign on an old green 1945 Ford Prefect which we finally bought and Ann could use to get to school each day.

I usually caught the bus, which began its route just two blocks away, for the 40-minute ride to the City. It was at that time that I really began reading a lot and usually got through six or seven books a month. As I was usually the first on the bus, I had my favorite seat, and an "old" man who got on at the next stop usually sat next to me. His name was "Nobby" Clarke and he was the Librarian at Crows Nest High School. "So, what are you reading today?" he often asked. I had been reading most of Ann's classical novels by Charles Dickens, Walter Scott, Alexander Dumas and many others. She had received many of these as rewards for being the top scholar of her school. I also read many westerns, or war stories, and I read my first James Bond books on the way to work. One day Nobby asked me "What sort of things are you interested in?" He already knew about my work and some of my church activities.

"I like to study the Bible and enjoy getting to know about the background and historical things that happened in Bible times," was one of the topics I mentioned.

He then asked, "Would you be interested in archeology? There's a lot of history being dug up which could be a help in getting background for your studies."

"That sounds interesting, but I don't really have any archeology books."

"Not a problem, I am the librarian and can take books out without question, and as I see you every day, I know you will get them back to me."

Nobby fed me dozens of books on archeology over the next year or so. I studied the Sumerian, Mesopotamian, Egyptian, Old Roman, and many other Middle Eastern cultures. He also introduced me to other classical literature. Looking back, I think he was taking a special interest in educating this young fellow, and I still remember Nobby with a high regard for his friendship, and for helping me grow in my own understanding of life through the many books he loaned me. As I learned on the ship I steered zigzagging along the coast, I can say that God was in control of all these events and sharpening me in ways I could not comprehend at that time.

About this time, Ann and I thought, and prayed, about starting a family. In December 1963 Ann and I, together with my sister Norma and her husband John and their two children, went down the South Coast to Sussex Inlet for a vacation. This was a beautiful spot on a river with the entrance just a half-mile away from the Ocean. We had a wonderful time there, fishing, swimming and enjoying the peaceful environment of that area. When we arrived home after two weeks of vacation, we found that Ann was pregnant with our first child. This was really exciting and we began to get the second bedroom ready for the new arrival.

Wednesday, August 19,1964, Ann's contractions began, "I think we need to get going," she said, and off we went to the Royal North Shore Hospital at about 4:00 PM. I checked Ann in and sat in the waiting room until finally a nurse came out and said, "It will probably be awhile."

In those days the fathers were not allowed anywhere near their wives during the birthing process and I was not going to sit around there waiting. I did not smoke cigars like they always showed the fathers in waiting rooms doing in the movies or cartoons. So I told the nurse, "I will be going to my parents' home which is much closer than our place, so please call me when anything happens. The phone number there is JF-2829." With that I went to my parents' home, had dinner and at 10:00 PM went to bed. I was sound asleep at 2:00 AM when the phone rang. Jumping out of bed and I caught it on the second ring. By that time my parents, bleary eyed, were standing at their bedroom door, my younger sister Anne came flying out of her room, and I was told in a perfunctory way, "Your wife had a baby girl." Then the phone went silent.

Hugs and cheers all round. I dressed quickly and headed to the hospital about 15 minutes away. They would not let me in to see Ann at that time, but after another half hour I was taken to a room to see the new baby girl whom we named Diane Lee, all wrapped in her soft flannel baby blanket. After a while they told me I could see Ann for only 10 minutes. She was in a ward with about four other women in the beds around her with dividing curtains around each one, which provided some privacy. I was then told, "The visiting hours are… you can come back later." Not a very pleasant way to treat a new father! Thankfully the process is much better these days for mothers and fathers to be alone with their baby to rejoice, hold, pray and love as a family.

I had always enjoyed little children and having our own little girl was one of the most fulfilling experiences of my life. Watching her grow, learning to eat, then when first words began I was really enjoying that enchanting experience. Buppa, as the grandchildren called my father, made a baby-safe swing, under the frangipani tree just outside our back door. I had an eight-foot diameter plastic blow-up pool where Diane would play for hours. By the time Diane was nearly three years old, Ann was again pregnant and we were a really happy family enjoying our lives together, heavily involved in the local church, now at North Ryde, where I continued as the leader of the 14 to 17 year old boys' club.

However, it was around this time that I announced to Ann that I had been really concerned about my commitment to the Lord. Then I dropped the bombshell, telling Ann that I thought the Lord might be directing us into missionary work in Colombia! - - How did I come to this conclusion? Where did I get that idea? What made me so sure? Perhaps the arrowhead had been sharpened and was ready to be attached to the shaft and put into service. But what about Ann and the family; how would this work? Only God could show the way.

4

THE CALL

Luke 14:26-27 *"If anyone comes to me and does not hate* [love God more than family or self] *his father and mother, his wife and children, his brothers and sisters—yes, even his own life—he cannot be my disciple. And anyone who does not carry his cross and follow me cannot be my disciple.*

As seen in previous chapters, my life had begun to take shape, and serving the Lord with a wonderful wife and family was a great blessing. "My plan" had been to work diligently, save funds, then retire at an early age, in my mid-50s, with a good pension. Then I could serve the Lord full time visiting churches, preaching and teaching at my own expense.

One day the thought came into my mind, "Am I really fully committed to the Lord?" I had to work my way through that idea and came to realize, yes, I was serving the Lord, but I had my own plan for life. Actually, I was only doing my own thing and not allowing the Lord to control my life.

After some months ruminating over this I finally came to the place where I could say, "Lord, I am totally willing to be completely committed to you." It was at that point that I realized that GOD's plan was somewhat different than mine, which He showed me through a very direct illustration. During my lunch hour one day I was walking down the street and saw a bum picking up cigarette butts, trying to get a final puff from them. The thought came to me as though God was speaking: "That's what you want to give me, the butt end of your life, but I want ALL of your life."

I then made a real commitment to the Lord and had peace about that decision. Several months passed when finally, wondering why the Lord had challenged me to make those decisions, I asked the Lord, "What do you want me to do?" In my mind the thought came:

"Would you be willing to give up your job? Leave your family (parents and relatives) and go where I want you to go?" This was a much more difficult decision and it took several more weeks of prayer to work my way through that idea. I finally gave in and could honestly tell the Lord, "Yes, I will do whatever you want with my life." After months of thinking and praying about this idea, I reached the point where I asked the Lord, "If you want me to leave Australia, as a missionary, where would you want me to go?"

I had made that prayer the same week we had an editorial meeting preparing one of the monthly *Overcomer* magazines. This was a publication I had been helping to edit for several years with three other men, which included Bible teaching articles for believers and missionary news from around the world. One of the letters was from a missionary in Colombia, South America, telling of the difficult tasks he had trying to meet all the needs there. In the middle of that letter came the exclamation, *"Surely God is preparing young people somewhere to come and help with the work in Colombia!"* As that letter was read I was immediately challenged. Is this what the Lord wants? It became, for me, a real "Macedonian call." (Acts 16:8) I did not know any Spanish and did not have a clue where to begin. The next day, on my lunch break, I went to a building in Sydney where the Berlitz School of languages had an office, to check the possibilities of Spanish classes. Coming in the opposite door was my friend Andrew Rothlisberger who was another editor on the magazine. We asked each other, "Why are you here?" and each replied that we were challenged by the same letter and felt that the Lord was calling us to missionary work in Colombia. I didn't even immediately know where Colombia was and had to get an atlas to check it out!

"Is this just an emotional bubble?" I asked myself. For my daily Bible reading I was in the habit of reading five pages each day from four different sections of the Bible. With this approach I could read through the Bible in a year and reading from different sections, I wouldn't feel bogged down getting through some of the "heavier" books. A couple of days after being challenged by that missionary letter, and just before my daily reading I asked the Lord to give me a verse that would help me understand if going to Colombia was what He wanted. The first section I was reading that day started in Deuteronomy 11. In the earlier part of the chapter it spoke of the Lord taking Israel to a land of mountains and valleys, a land for whom the Lord cared. I knew by then that Colombia has plenty of mountains and valleys! When I came to verses 26-27 the verses just jumped out at me. In the old KJV it began, "BEHOLD, I AM SETTING BEFORE YOU today a blessing and a curse" There was blessing for obedience and a curse for disobedience. That hit me like a sledgehammer! Was this verse something that the Lord had arranged for me to read at that precise time?

I decided to pray about it, which I did for a week. Then a week or so later I asked the Lord, "Please give me a verse to confirm the first verse!" I did not want to be carried away by a coincidence! I was reading that day in Jeremiah 21 and when I got to verse 8, I was slammed between the eyes with another "BEHOLD." When God says BEHOLD, you had better listen! "BEHOLD I AM SETTING BEFORE YOU the way of life and the way of death." This one started off with the same *behold* phrase. Was it a just another coincidence? Now I was getting concerned! My prayer life was taking on a different dimension; it was becoming more of an intimate talk with God. Three days later I said to the Lord, "Lord, is this a coincidence or are you really telling me something. Please give me another verse!" That morning I was reading in Revelation 3 and I thought, "Well I don't think I'll get a verse today!" UNTIL... I reached Revelation 3:8, "BEHOLD I HAVE SET BEFORE YOU an open door that no one can shut." Three strikes and you're out, as the baseball players know! I also knew that Gideon had asked God two times for confirmation to move forward, so rather than being "out" I was being brought "in" by God to a service for Him. All this was much more than coincidental and I had to just bow my head and thank the Lord for such direct confirmation.

"Okay Lord, I give in. I take it you want me to go to Colombia, and I am ready and willing." At that point all my doubts and fears were settled, but now came the hard part! I had the task of breaking the news to my wife telling her what I thought the Lord was directing us to do. Being a typical man, up to that time I had not shared with Ann all the prayers and challenges of the spiritual journey through which I had passed during the past year. She was really happy with life as it was. We owned our first home; I had a good job; we had a cute little two-year-old daughter, Diane, another baby on the way and we were together enjoying participation in the activities and fellowship of the local church. When I stated, "I think the Lord might be calling us to go to Colombia as missionaries!" she just about had a conniption. From one moment to the next she was no longer living in her pleasant, comfortable, secure world. It was now being torn apart. "What?!!!" "Where did that idea come from? What put that idea into your head?"

All I could say was, "Well, I'm sorry I haven't shared all that I have been thinking over the past months. I had no idea it would all lead to this point." Then I went on to explain the journey that I had traveled up to that time and how I came to this seemingly odd decision. I felt pretty bad about my lack of communication and had to back off for a while to allow Ann to deal with all that would be involved in such a move. The Lord had not spoken to her yet (although she was always looking for ways to serve Him) and it was quite a shock for her to hear what I had to say. It took a few days to get her back down to "sea level!"

I had to let Ann work her way through the missionary challenge for herself, but the Lord was also working in her. Every now and again she would read an article in the newspaper about something happening in Colombia. A bus went off the mountain killing all on board, or the terrorist guerrillas had killed people in a town she had never heard of. She would turn on the radio and the first news item was about a truck carrying pesticide and flour into a town. There must have been a leak in the barrels as some of the pesticide had mixed with the flour and when the local people ate the bread they died. It seemed there was never really good news, but Colombia was coming in loud and clear!

One evening I was heading out to a local meeting where missionary Elaine de Russett was speaking. She had been in the Congo in the early 60's during the Simba uprising and had been kidnapped, abused and held for many months. She had a slide picture presentation and would be sharing her experiences. I had known Elaine and her family, having preached with her father at Manly Beach on various occasions. As I was leaving for the meeting, I said to Ann, "Well at least we won't be hearing about Colombia tonight!" It was a very challenging night and at the end I went over to speak with Elaine. Her first words were, "Hello Ian, isn't it wonderful that they are preaching in the streets of Bogotá again? I just had a newsletter from the field director in Colombia, Pat Simes, telling us about it." Talk about feeling weak at the knees! When I told Ann about this conversation later that evening she also became convinced that the Lord was calling us even though she personally did not have a real sense of the Lord's calling to Colombia. She said, "It's obvious the Lord is calling you, and we are one flesh, so that includes me!" She had a great attitude, and she was to become a wonderfully gifted missionary wife, mother, teacher, and a true example to so many. The ladies would love her and be truly thankful for her ministry among them as well as in the training of Sunday School teachers and many other activities.

After many months of praying and talking with people who could mentor and counsel us, we thought it would be wise for me to make an exploratory trip to Colombia to check out the work and see if this is what we should do. But when and how was God going to make this happen? The very week that we asked the Lord to make it possible for me to travel to Colombia to see the work and make sure that this was where the Lord truly wanted us, I was again helping at one of the *Overcomer Magazine* meetings. This time there was a letter from missionary Grant Steidl working in Jamaica, inviting someone to represent our Australian churches at an international missionary conference to be held there. I immediately thought, "That's how I'm going to get to Colombia." I knew I could include a stop in Colombia and the timing was just right. The only major concern was for funding, as we did not have the money for the plane fare. Our second baby was due in several months, which would involve extra expenses.

However, God had a plan: About a year before reading Steidl's letter, the manager of the shipping company told me he wanted me to start working in the Travel Department. I had worked in every other department in the company and especially enjoyed the outside work on the waterfront, meeting passenger ships at the Sydney Harbor Heads, boarding the ships, working on the piers, watching ships loading, checking damaged cargo for our claims department, and clearing the ships prior to departure with the maritime customs office. I told him I would rather not work in the travel department, but he insisted, stating that he wanted me to have experience in every department if I was one day planning to be a manager. I reluctantly began working in the Travel Department, booking people on our passenger ships, planning air travel for other travelers and writing their airline tickets. Now, thinking about the missionary conference in Jamaica, I called Pan American Airlines to ask if I was eligible for a discounted plane fare. They told me that I could have a 75% discount if I had been selling air tickets for 12 months. When I checked back to the time I started in the Travel Department, the 12-month deadline was exactly two weeks before I would have to leave for Colombia and Jamaica. The Lord had carefully placed me where His purposes would work out. I found out His sharpening process is always precise.

"The LORD will guide you always; he will satisfy your needs in a sun-scorched land and will strengthen your frame. The LORD will guide you always." Isaiah 58:11

I spoke with the elders in our church telling them about the missionary conference and also about the way the Lord seemed to be guiding us to go to Colombia as missionaries. They were very happy for me to go as the Australian representative to the meeting in Jamaica as well as visit Colombia. On the Thursday one week prior to my departure, Pan American Airlines called to tell me that I needed to pay the 25% fare and write the ticket. I told them I would do this on the following Monday. The elders had arranged a special meeting for prayer and encouragement the Sunday afternoon before I was due to leave. This special meeting went well. Many prayed for me, for the trip, for the contact with the missionaries and for the Lord's guidance. They gave me a letter with greetings and introduction for the different churches I would be visiting both in Colombia and Jamaica. Meanwhile I was thinking, "I wonder what they would say if they knew I did not have the money for the fare?"

After the usual refreshments that always seem to follow these church special fellowship meetings, I was saying my goodbyes to all the folk there. As I shook hands with each one, many of them had a piece of paper in their hands. I put them in my pocket and shook hands with the next one. This continued until Ann and I were ready to drive home. When I arrived home and emptied my pocket, there was the exact plane fare! This was another wonderful lesson and confirmation that the Lord was doing something very special.

He was showing me that if I was prepared to step out in faith, He would provide for me. The following Monday I paid for my ticket and set out for Colombia and Jamaica on the Thursday. I was just 27 years old and really excited about seeing Colombia, and getting to know personally the many different missionaries whom I had come to know through their letters to our magazine.

First Visit To Colombia April 1967

The flight was via Honolulu then on to Los Angeles where I stayed with Will Missen and his wife. He had been a missionary in Colombia and at the time of my visit was the editor and president of *Good Tidings Publishers,* a Spanish publication ministry.

On Monday Will Missen and I flew to Cali, Colombia just in time for their Semana Santa (Easter) Conference. Jorge Berney, a Swiss brother who had been working for many years in Argentina, was also at the conference and translated much of the messages for me. I met the missionary who had sent the letter with the "Macedonian call," Alden Poehner, and was impressed by his love and devotion for the Lord. A few days later, I went by taxi to Ibague with Esau Parra and his young family, traveling over a road that went up to 11,000 ft. I was enthralled by the beautiful mountains and the scenery. The local church in Ibague had a school whose director was Elsa Barolin, a missionary from Argentina. It was obvious there were many doors open for evangelism and church planting, and the Colombians were very friendly and open. Everything I saw and heard on that visit was so positive that I was confident this was where the Lord wanted us to serve Him.

However, there was one glitch in the visit. During the Easter conference I received a telegram from Australia saying, "SON BORN [five weeks] EARLY IN DANGER – STOP - ANN DOING WELL - STOP." Even though I enjoyed the rest of the time in Colombia, there was a dark cloud continually hanging over me.

There were no cell phones, Skype, or other means of quick communication in those days. So at the back of my mind the entire time I was wondering what had happened to my new baby boy. It was a time when I had to begin to learn that I could trust the Lord even though I could not understand what He was doing or allowing. Apparently this arrowhead needed a bit more polishing and refining.

I flew on to the missionary Conference in Jamaica with Will Missen, Jorge Berney and Alden Poehner. There was another telegram waiting there for me, telling me that our son Alan was out of danger and doing well. That was a tremendous relief and for me a real answer to prayer.

The missionary conference was a tremendous experience, meeting so many missionaries face to face. One of them was Bill Van Ryn who was serving the Lord in Puerto Rico. Bill and I quickly became close friends, a friendship that would last to the present day. After the week long conference, I flew back to Sydney and went to the clinic to see our new son; he was still in an incubator, as his lungs had not completely developed when he was born. A week later his lungs were normal and we brought him home. His big sister, Diane, was ever so excited to have a little brother.

As you can imagine, Ann and I had some very long discussions about our future plans. "When do you think we should plan on leaving?" Ann asked.

"I don't think we should rush this; we need to be very sure of the timing the Lord has in all this," I replied. "At the conference I met an older brother from Holland who is full time in the ministry. He told me that his daughter and son-in-law (Annemarie and Peter Nunn who were living in England) had felt the same call to Colombia having read the same letter published in our magazine that challenged me. They were planning to go to a Spanish Language Institute in San José, Costa Rica. Perhaps we should consider going there also. He had suggested that if we were going to minister in a foreign country, then we had better be able to speak the language fluently. I think that is something worth considering." We prayed about the language study and I wrote a letter to the Spanish Language Institute asking for information and the cost for a year of intensive language study. Since this was in the days of snail mail, it was about a month later when a packet arrived enclosing an institute catalogue and an application form. The cost was to be around $4,000 for the year for our studies. We would have to rent an apartment, arrange for a Costa Rican maid to mind the house, who would also look after the children and prepare our meals, all at our own expense. This would free us to concentrate on our studies so that we could be totally immersed in Spanish.

46

Baby Alan had arrived and those expenses had been met so we made a real effort to save as much as possible that year to help toward our move, as well as for our language study and travel expenses to Costa Rica, and then on to Colombia. I had a meeting with the elders of our home church and they were happy for us to plan to go to Colombia and they would be free to commend us to the Lord's work as missionaries. After visiting many of our churches in Australia, I took some time off from my work, and as a family we went to Timaru in New Zealand, to visit Ann's family and let them know what we were thinking. We included visits to the many churches in New Zealand, telling them of our challenge and asking for their prayers. That visit was positive in every way and the believers were encouraged by our plans; they also gave us financial help that we included with our savings for the Institute fees and our travel. Our churches did not have a mission board and we knew we would need to depend on God to provide all of our support as He directed others to give, a practice that continues today.

We had much planning to do during that year, getting the Institute enrollment organized and talking with the family about our home. Should we sell it? What should we do with our belongings? I wrote to the missionary in Colombia asking about what we should do with our household goods and he told us to bring as much as we could. That meant arranging storage while we were in Costa Rica, then shipping to Colombia once we moved there. My father retired at this time and we decided that he would sell their house and move into our place. He and my mother would then have our place to live in and the sale of his home would help financially with his retirement. Then maybe, at some future time should we need to leave Colombia, we would have a home to which we could return.

I made a booking with the Sitmar Line to sail on their ship the "Fairsky." The departure date was for April 1968, just one year after the Jamaican missionary conference. The ship would sail from Sydney to Auckland, New Zealand, then across the Pacific Ocean to Tahiti, then on to Panama where we would disembark, and fly to San José, Costa Rica. The time came to give the company my month's notice. When I sent my letter of resignation the manager called me to his office. I was a little nervous, but took a deep breath and knocked on his door. "Ian, I have this letter, but I want to know what you are thinking about? Why are you thinking of leaving? We have trained you for 13 years and you are in line for management. Do you want more money?"

"No, it is not about money, and I have enjoyed working here all these years, but I have had a calling that is much stronger, and that is to be a missionary in Colombia, South America."

"That's ridiculous, why would you want to give up a decent life here to go to a country like that?"

"Well, as you may know, I am really committed to being a follower of the Lord Jesus Christ and I have had a very distinctive call to missions. I believe God wants me to serve there and feel compelled to do this."

"Well, there's plenty of missionary work in this country I'm sure, but if you are not inclined to change your mind, I want to wish you all the best, and I will have a letter of reference for you before you leave."

I thanked him and left, "Whew!" Now there was no turning back!

The 13 years I spent at the Union Steamship Company, working in every department, was a tremendous preparation for me. All that I learned during those years had given me a wonderful preparation for the mission field. God had used some of these tools to prepare this arrow for service.

My parents had moved into our home and the day we were to leave for the ship, my father, as always before any journey, said, "Let's commit you to the Lord for all that's ahead." He began to pray, but suddenly he was quiet; I looked at him and tears were rolling down his cheeks. I had never seen him cry before and that brought a heavy sadness to my heart as well. We might never see each other again! I didn't know what the future might hold and the reality of leaving became a sudden fear. "I am going off into a complete unknown. Amen to Dad's prayer, Lord, we are in Your hands."

We were at the Pyrmont docks in Sydney Harbour, our luggage had been taken down to the ship the day before, so we boarded, found our cabin, had another little prayer and after about an hour the loud speaker boomed around the ship, "All visitors ashore! All visitors ashore! The ship will be departing in 15 minutes. All visitors ashore!" There were hugs all round and my parents, sisters and other family members walked down the gangplank to the pier. We stood along the rail and began to throw paper streamers from the ship to family on the wharf. They held on to the ends of the streamers - our last contact before sailing off into the unknown. The ship's lines were shortened and then the last lines were cast off and the Fairsky began to slowly move away from the dock. Finally the streamers broke. The last physical contact with our loved ones was lost and, with tears in many eyes, along with shouts of, "Goodbye. The Lord bless. We love you. Don't forget to write." etc., we moved out of earshot. The ship began to turn to go under the Sydney Harbor Bridge, continuing past the Opera House still under construction, and along the most beautiful harbor in the world, to Sydney Heads, then out to sea. This was to be a 21-day voyage to finally arrive in Panama City.

"Goodbye family, goodbye friends, goodbye former life. We are on our way to the mission field."

File Photo

Ann, Diane, Alan and Ian in San José Costa Rica

5

LANGUAGE SCHOOL IN COSTA RICA

Jeremiah 29:11 *"I know the plans I have for you,"* declares the Lord, *"plans to prosper you and not to harm you, plans to give you hope, plans to give you a future filled with hope."*

On The Way

Of course, being on a ship was quite comfortable for me, but never had I experienced the excitement of encountering so many unknown places and activities. God had so obviously prepared me for this journey by giving me a spirit of adventure and a willingness to go forward, a loving wife to share in this direction in life, and a deep sense of honor to be used of God to proclaim the gospel. This arrow was honed sharp and ready for service - or so I thought.

The Fairsky sailed between the Sydney Harbor Heads and out into the Pacific Ocean. There was a gentle swell and the ship then began to gently tilt one way, then the other, as we moved across the incoming waves. We stayed at the rails looking back as the coast of Australia began to sink below the horizon, our emotions in a some-what similar state. The water took on a darker blue as the ocean floor dropped away into the deep. We went back to our cabin to change our clothes, and then took a walk to explore the ship. There was a children's area with all sort of toys with slides, swings and a see-saw, all on a nicely carpeted enclosed area so that little ones could be left there to play while the adults did other activities. The ship's stewardesses were there to care for the children.

Soon it was suppertime and we had to decide how to handle a difficult situation. Children were required to be fed in a separate area while the adults, without the children, dressed up for a formal meal. We were scheduled for the second meal, which allowed us to take the children for their meal, bring them back to the cabin and lock them in while we went off for our meal. Our cabin had two sets of bunk beds and on the lower one, where one-year-old Alan would sleep, the steward had hung a heavy rope netting (the sort used to hold cargo being lifted and transferred ship to shore) so that the baby would not fall out if the ship was rolling. It could also be used as a "prison" for the baby while we went for our meals. We were not too happy about leaving them, but we had to comply with the ship's rules. (This would only be the first of many challenges in juggling parenting and missionary service.) The food was good and we enjoyed the ambience of the ship's dining room. The captain had a special table and during the course of the twenty-one day voyage, each adult would have the opportunity of eating with the captain.

Three days after setting sail, we arrived in Auckland, New Zealand, and were met by the Jolls, believers from one of our churches. They drove us around Auckland sightseeing. We returned to the ship by late afternoon as the ship only had a twelve-hour stop scheduled there. Once again, we were back on the Pacific Ocean, now headed for the French Polynesian island of Tahiti.

One day during that nine-day section of our voyage, we stood at the rail and watched dolphins swimming and diving alongside the ship. Every now and again, a couple of the dolphins would come close to the bow of the ship and "surf" in the bow wave. Another day, we watched the flying fish jump out of the water and literally fly about fifteen yards before diving back into the deep blue. There was always something exciting for us to do. Our greatest fear was for one-year-old Alan, who always crawled everywhere. On one occasion we grabbed him after he had crawled under a lifeboat and was lying there looking over the side at the water washing past. From then on, we made sure he always wore his harness with a leash whenever we were on deck.

On one of those days at sea the entertainment officer arranged some sort of a dress-up party. We found some cardboard that I shaped and painted to look like a tortoise shell, which we strapped on Alan's back. We then had a real live tortoise romping along beside us in his harness and leash.

The ship's daily newspaper had informed us that Tahiti would be coming into view the next morning, so we made sure we were on the deck to catch the beautiful Island coming up over the horizon. What a wonderful sight! We berthed at Papeete (Pa-pé-te) and had twelve hours to tour as much of the island as possible. There were many Polynesians on the docks, many dressed in their traditional Pacific Island garb and giving the children seashell necklaces and other trinkets. All sorts of interesting fishing boats, catamarans, larger deep-sea fishing boats and a couple of tankers were moored further along the harbor. We hopped into a beat up old taxi and drove around for about two hours followed by a typical meal in one of the tourist restaurants. There we drank coconut juice and tasted other marine life, crab, and fish along with some interesting tropical fruits including sour sop that we had never eaten before. As the sun began to set, our ship sailed away from Tahiti for the last leg of our journey to Panama. As we left Papeete, and sailed on the emerald waters surrounding those Islands, with the lush mountains of the Island of Moorea on our port side, we felt as if we had seen one of the most beautiful places in all of God's creation.

For the day we crossed the equator we had been warned of some special activities. This was supposedly a really dangerous day, as "King Neptune" did not appreciate people taking the crossing of his equator for granted. He came aboard from the depths, with his crown in place and his trident in hand. Several passengers were put "on trial" and judged guilty, tied to the mast and punishments meted out. One young lady in her swimsuit had a huge bowl of spaghetti, with plenty of sauce, poured over her head. Another man had chocolate pudding poured all over him. The unsuspecting ship's Purser, who was conducting the court, had someone come up behind him and pour a bowl full of raw eggs over his head. This didn't really enhance the official look of his white uniform! I am glad I never had that type of "fun" when I was a Purser working for the shipping company.

Land finally hove into sight as we approached Panama. Upon anchoring near the bridge across the entrance to the waters leading to the Panama Canal, some passengers disembarked on the Western side of Panama. A door on the side of the ship was opened as a ferry tied up alongside. The baggage was discharged onto the ferry first, followed by the passengers who boarded the ferry by using a slide-out gangway to board the vessel and move off to the nearby city. We remained on the ship because we were due to get off in the American zone on the eastern side of Panama.

The next morning we got up early so that we could experience the journey through the canal. Later that day, the ship docked. Having made sure our luggage was among all the bags being brought up from the hold, we disembarked and headed for the customs shed with our passports in hand, along with our Institute papers to show we were going on to Costa Rica.

An older man from one of our churches in Panama met us at the dock. He took us out to lunch and showed us around the city. At lunch this dear old black brother took out his teeth to eat his lunch and put them in his pocket. "The brethren kindly sent me the money for these teeth," he explained, "and I don't want to wear them out." Our three-year-old daughter Diane could not take her eyes off him. He was the first black man she had ever seen. Suddenly she burst out, "He has a pink tongue!" We tried to squelch any further comments and went on with the meal.

Our plane was scheduled to leave the following afternoon, so we were booked into a hotel in downtown Panama City. The next morning as we were looking out our third floor window at the street below, we saw crowds of people running from soldiers armed with shields, guns, and batons. As we watched with our mouths open, soldiers fired tear gas at the crowds. "We really have arrived in Latin America!" I said to Ann. We didn't know that it was an election day and that the riots were apparently normal for such a day.

We were happy to leave Panama later that day and after a short time our plane touched down at the San José International Airport, in Alajuela, Costa Rica. Students who were halfway through their study program met us, and would be our "big brothers" to help us get settled. They were there to ferry us through customs and take us to the Language Institute. These wonderful helpers had already located an apartment for us about a block from the Institute and, after dropping off our luggage, took us to meet the Institute director, Dr. Coble.

Because of the timing of our voyage we were late starting our courses. The trimester had begun two weeks earlier. After meeting the director, we went back to the apartment to unpack. The maid was already there and was preparing our supper, so we tried as quickly as possible to get settled. Classes would start the next morning. Nervously, we left one-year-old Alan with this maid about whom we knew nothing. We could not even speak to her at that stage. Diane had been registered to attend a school for the students' children and after dropping her off we headed to the Institute to begin our Spanish classes. This proved to be another of the challenges of juggling parenting with missionary service. But our trust in God reminded us that He was in control. While the trip to Costa Rica had been another exciting adventure it was now time to get to the task at hand: learning to speak Spanish fluently.

Classes Begin

The first thing we were required to do was to take an assessment test, which was designed to ascertain our language ability. The test took about forty minutes after which the director told both Ann and me that we could skip the first trimester of classes and join with the second trimester students. This was an encouragement and came about because Ann had her Masters' degree in languages, understanding French, English, Latin, and Greek. I had my two years of high school French. Consequently, she received top grades ahead of those who had completed the whole year. I had to work hard the whole time learning the grammar, vocabulary, and phonetics.

Sometimes, when translating from the Spanish New Testament, I would come across a difficult word and say to Ann, "I just can't work out this word." She would ask, "What is it?" I would pronounce the word and she would reply, "There is a word in French ... and a similar root word in Latin that means... So it probably means..." I would then look it up in the dictionary and she was always right! I think the Lord brought Ann and me together knowing I would need a real linguist as I prepared for missionary work in Colombia. Ann's linguistics expertise was invaluable to me later as she proofread every tract, book, and monthly magazine I wrote, edited, and printed in Colombia.

By the end of my second trimester at the Language Institute, my proficiency in Spanish had grown quickly and I went out regularly on student outreach activities. These included doing door-to-door visits selling the New Testament Dios Llega al Hombre, (Similar to *Good News for Modern Man* in English), which was helpful with conversational Spanish. On one of these door-to-door visits we were in a rather rough area of town when I knocked on one door and a young lady invited me in. As I walked in, I noticed there were a lot of cubicles on both sides of the hallway. Then she asked me, "Would you like a thirteen-year-old?" I suddenly realized where I was, gave her a New Testament, and ran out hoping that none of my Christian student friends had seen me coming out of that place!

During my second trimester a Baptist Pastor, Adrian Gonzales, taught a special preacher's class. This was a great help, knowing that teaching and preaching would be one of my main activities in Colombia. I also had a composition class that used a book written by a Catholic priest, refuting evangelical teaching. We had to disprove his arguments, which at the same time helped us learn much about the major religion we would encounter in Latin America.

Every few weeks we had an orientation class for living in another culture, and occasionally, Dr. Cabezas from the San José hospital came to give orientation classes particularly related to caring for our health in the tropics. He spoke of the need to eat a lot of fruit, but also how important it was to wash all the fruit before eating it. Some of it would no doubt be collected from under the fruit trees, which in many areas was the main bathroom for the country folk. He also told us that if we wanted to eat lettuce we should soak it in iodine over night or boil it. Why? In some areas the country folk put urine on the lettuce to make it greener!   OK! No more lettuce! (I never really liked it anyway, so that was no hardship.)

Other orientations were by businessmen, clergymen, or professionals who could give important pointers to help us understand the Latin mind and therefore be able to reach them with the gospel

Me, For President?

Between each trimester we had a one-week break, and during the second and third trimester break, a number of students approached me saying, "Hey Ian, some of us want you to run for Student Body President next trimester."

"Me? Why me?" I wondered what had given them that idea. They continued to insist, so I said, "All right, I don't mind if you want to nominate me." I didn't think any more about it until I noticed that another student, who was also a candidate, had flyers and posters tacked up, with people running around wearing signs on their clothes supporting him. Others were handing out papers with my rival's wonderful accomplishments, his great character, his strong Christian spirit, as well as his captivating personality.

I thought, "Well, that's all very interesting, but why all the hoopla?"

Later that day several of my "sponsors" came to ask me why I had not started my campaign. "Why haven't you put up any posters or prepared any flyers?" The problem was that in Australia, the political system was vastly different. Any advertising for the next Prime Minister was advertising for the party, not necessarily for the leader of the party. If the Labor Party (equal to the US Democrats) won, then the leader of the party became the Prime Minister, and if the Liberal Party (equal to the US Republicans) won, then their leader became Prime Minister. I had very little knowledge of the millions of dollars that were spent in the United States by individuals to get elected. Unlike the USA, the voters just voted for the party they favored. So I thought the whole idea of spending money on advertising to become Student Body President for my last trimester at the Institute was a lot of nonsense.

I told my supporters, "Well I don't intend to do anything like that; if the students want me then they already know me and can vote for me if they like! If not, I'll lose and that's all right by me. I don't intend to try to eulogize myself and make all sorts of egotistic promotional maneuvers just to win." They probably thought I was a bit strange at that point. The day for voting came, along with a lot of speeches from the other party's followers, and by the late afternoon the time for the count arrived. All the ballots had been cast and the committee reached their final count and came to me to tell me that I had won comfortably.

With this news, I had another visit from my now very happy and excited sponsors, "You need to call Bob, the defeated student, and thank him for running a good race." I thought, "That's nuts, why all the hoopla?" But I did call him, and many years later I came to realize they were just replicating the craziness of American politics. I still cannot understand why millions of dollars are used in campaigning when this money could be put to better use helping the poor and needy.

Ann did not take any courses the last trimester, as she wanted to stay at home with the children. We finished the year well and Ann had the best scores for grammar and general Spanish. I had a better score with conversational Spanish, no doubt because I did not wait to speak until I could say something perfectly, as Ann did. We both excelled in the areas where we would be most useful in our later ministries. We were looking forward to leaving in a few weeks to begin the work God had so clearly called us to do. To be the straight and sharpened arrows bringing the gospel to the lost and hurting people in Colombia.

6

A NEW AND UNWELCOME CHALLENGE

Alan Andrew Taylor

Alan Andrew Taylor - 2nd Birthday
3/25/67 - 4/3/69

Looking back over our year in Costa Rica, it is easy to recall the night our pattern of excitement and blessing changed. All had retired for the night, and as he often did, little Alan awoke in the

59

middle of the night, came into our room, climbed into bed and lay on my chest, arms gently hugging my sides. As I savored the moment, a thought stole unbidden into my consciousness: "Would you be willing to give me your son? Abraham was called to sacrifice his son Isaac; would you, like Abraham, be willing to do the same?" I recoiled at such an idea. Even as tears began to burn my cheeks, thinking about losing one so precious, it persisted. I finally answered, "Lord, I could never do that, but if that is what you want, then you will have to give me the strength for it." Thus answered, the silent messenger left, and this conversation with God was forgotten until several months later.

We were just a few weeks from graduation, Easter, 1969. On Thursday I went off with a group of students, leaving at 2:00 PM, to an area where the Volcano Arenal had erupted some months before. Many people had been killed in the town nearby and we planned to visit the homes of the survivors to talk with them, offer New Testaments, and share the gospel with them.

Ann, together with Diane and Alan, was at the door of our apartment to wave goodbye as the bus pulled off for the Language Institute where I would meet up with the students. I didn't realize that this would be the last time I would see little Alan alive. We had just celebrated his second birthday two weeks before.

It was a four-hour drive from San José. First we went to the area where the volcano had blasted pumice and ash and had blown out mostly on one side. The devastation was incredible! There was nothing green left growing and the trees had been turned to charcoal, if not totally consumed by the intense heat that had spread out over the countryside. As we walked back to our base camp after surveying the damage, one of the students came running to me and said there was a phone call for me. There was only one phone in that area set up by the search and civil defense teams just after the eruption. I picked up the phone wondering why anyone would call me there.

It was a fellow student on the phone who was obviously very nervous as he hemmed and hawed, then finally said. "There's been an accident."

"What happened?" I asked.

"Well a stone fell on your son."

60

I was wondering what sort of stone; was it the cover off the toilet water tank?

"What stone fell on him?"

"It's not good; I'm afraid it killed him."

He didn't offer any other explanation and I just told him, "I will leave right away for home," and hung up.

One of the students had a Jeep and offered to drive me back to San José. It was one of the longest journeys I have ever taken. I kept on wondering what had happened. I just couldn't believe that my little boy was dead.

"Lord, what are you doing? How could you possibly allow something like this to happen?"

We finally arrived back at the apartment in San José. The apartment was full of students, the director, Dr. Coble, and other teachers.

I came in and hugged Ann asking, "What on earth happened?" All the visitors who were there to be with Ann until I arrived back home, left so that finally the two of us were together just holding each other and weeping. Ann then began to explain what had happened. It was Easter Thursday, they had waved me good-bye when I left for Arenal, and Ann told the children she was going to make a nice surprise for supper. She told four-year-old Diane and two-year-old Alan to play in the enclosed veranda outside the back door while she prepared the treats.

The Full Account

The Wednesday before Alan died, Ann took the two of them for a walk to a shop to buy some Easter eggs. They walked down by the train line and watched one pass, much to Alan's delight. He just loved to watch the trains, tractors, and anything that moved. They couldn't find any Easter eggs but Diane had one that her teacher had given her, so she shared it with Alan. She was generally pretty good with him. One of her baby sitters remarked on how much she loved him. When Alan would tear one of her pictures or booklets, she would just say, "Oh, it's all right; he's my baby."

When they got home from the shop, Ann prepared their supper. Then they listened to all the audiotapes, which had been sent as gifts, until 8:30 PM. These included all the Christmas tapes, stories, and Diane's birthday tape. It was a lovely evening together. Alan had a nap earlier so wasn't tired.

On Thursday morning the children played out in the back yard, as it was a lovely sunny day. Alan had his little soldier doll and Diane had hers. At one stage when Ann looked out, Diane was sitting on the step and Alan was lying with his head in her lap looking up at her. Ann cooked a tray of biscuits (cookies) and a chocolate slice (cake) that Diane enjoyed so much. Soon after, Alan disappeared. When we found him he was hiding in the back room in one of the corners with the whole tray of chocolate slice, having a wonderful time! They had a rest after lunch and after I left for Arenal they played inside all afternoon. Diane was painting and Alan was playing with his magnetic train. He then pinched one of Diane's brushes and started painting his blocks. He kept calling out to Ann, "Painting, painting!"

Ann started getting supper ready; and told the children to play out on the back-enclosed porch for a while. She had bought two special eggcups as a surprise for them. The cups were little chickens with head and feet etc. Ann was going to boil eggs and paint faces on them. Diane and Alan played happily for quite a while since their toys were in this enclosed area, including a small play table and chairs where they played having tea and cookies. Meanwhile, Ann was making some cupcakes in the kitchen just inside the door from the veranda. Up against the wall beside the back door was a bookshelf, on which there were a few more toys and some children's books. On the top was a two-inch thick marble slab. Just above the bookshelf was a window from which Ann could look out onto the veranda and keep an eye on the children.

Alan, excited about his surprise, climbed up onto the shelf as he had done many times before, when somehow, we don't know how, it fell. The heavy slab of marble landed on top of him. He was instantly with the Lord, beholding the One whose Name he had so recently learned to say. Whenever he heard anyone say it, whether in prayer or conversation, he would say "Jesus" in his sweet little voice.

Diane screamed and Ann came running. Ann rushed next

Diane and Alan - Arrow points to the marble shelf top

door but couldn't raise anyone there, but some passers by saw her and came in to try and ring an ambulance or a doctor. They couldn't raise anyone, as it was Holy week before Easter; everything closes up, as it is almost a sacrilege to do any work. With all the noise, a fellow student, Will Thiesen who lived next door, came running in. He lifted Alan in his arms, started giving mouth-to-mouth and his wife took charge of Diane. Ann and Will, with Alan in her arms, borrowed another neighbor's jeep and they took off for the hospital. He had police chasing him as he was breaking every rule of the road, through lights etc. and wouldn't stop for police. One bike pulled alongside and seeing Alan he gave them an escort with sirens sounding. They made a fast trip to the hospital. However, Alan had died instantly.

After the hospital confirmed to Ann that Alan was dead Dr. Coble took her home. In next to no time all the students heard the news and there were groups who stayed with Ann until I got home, at 11:30 PM. I came in and hugged Ann asking, "What on earth happened?" Ann went on to tell me all about it and that, when she returned from the hospital, she found the students who had heard the news had already cleaned up the area where Alan had been killed. It had taken two men to lift the marble slab that had been on top of the shelving, which weighed about 100 pounds. Ann had, with superhuman strength lifted it off of Alan herself.

As Ann filled me in with all the details she kept saying to me, as she wept copious tears, "I'm so sorry, I'm so sorry. I should have been with them." I had to reassure her that I did not blame her for what had happened. The accident was not her fault; in fact she was the perfect mother, just preparing a lovely surprise for her two little ones, a special Easter treat. Diane later told us that she saw the stone falling and ran back, so we thank the Lord for sparing her. Everything possible was done for Alan but the Lord had taken him instantly; it was all part of His plan.

We had to discuss the funeral with the Institute Director, Dr. Coble that night. At 1:00 AM he also attempted to put calls to Australia and New Zealand, through the long distance operator, which we had to use in those days. This was always a tedious procedure, certainly not as easily done as it is today. No one was answering so we waited until 2:00 AM, Dr. Coble having left already at 1:15 AM.

We praise the Lord for the right people being at the right place to be of help that day. Of course, I was away on the humanitarian trip with other students when I received the devastating news. One of our neighbors, Bob Burtis, went with another neighbor, a lawyer and Government official to the main police station to get word to me. Bob stated, "The police said, 'There is only one phone there, and it is too difficult to try to get through. The lawyer fellow said in good Spanish, 'Listen here, sport, I'm Mr. X, so you just get cracking.' The policeman saluted and gave him the phone number; so the message was sent through to me on their phone." This lawyer traveled throughout Central America and wasn't home very often.

Charles Moore, millionaire turned missionary, heard the news report on the radio and went straight to the hospital. He was a ham radio operator and the one who sent the messages, which eventually reached each of our families in Australia and New Zealand. It took three or four hours on the air before he finally got through to Australia. The operator there told Charles that he couldn't pass on messages as it is against the law, but that if Charles could speak to someone in New Zealand then the operator in Australia might be able to listen to him and make some sort of contact with families. (This was kind of like eavesdropping on

64

purpose.) By this time Charles had twenty other operators from North and Latin America, including HCJB (the Missionary radio station in Quito, Ecuador), searching different bands for someone in New Zealand. Finally someone was found on the air, a Mormon missionary in North Island, New Zealand. This man said that he couldn't pass on any messages, but to tell him all about it as he just might know us. So Charles gave him all the information including telephone numbers in Australia and New Zealand. After the man said he didn't know us, Charles said, "Well we had better send a cable." to which the Mormon missionary replied, "Well I wouldn't if I were you, it could be that someone has overheard us, who knows the family." As we found out later that operator did ring Robin Sides, (Ann's brother) who then rang the police in Australia. Robin knew to tell them that my folks were attending a Bible conference at a community hall in Sydney. The police in that suburb went to the conference to tell my parents in person. Ham operators were crying as they spoke on the air and some asked Charles to pray for them. Another gave his testimony over the air of how the Lord had given him strength and grace in a similar situation; others said they would be praying for us. Special prayer was made in churches all over Latin America as the news got around. Many missionaries in Latin America had been to the Institute so there was a missionary grape vine, throughout Central and South America. Charles also got in touch with the Poehners in Colombia and Will Missen in the USA so the churches there would know about this incident. The Body of Christ in many churches was pulled together by a little two-year-old boy and his tragic death.

Charles wrote to me recently, when I shared my writing of this account, and gave me some facts that I had either forgotten or did not comprehend because of the pain and heartache at that time. He wrote:

> *"When I rushed into the emergency room I saw Dr. Coble and then saw Ann in her pink dress, heavily splattered with blood. She ran to me and hugged me saying "He gave him to us and He took him from us."*
>
> *I told Dr. Coble that I would assume the responsibility for Alan and suggested he take Ann home.*

Little Alan deserved all of the respect that I could give him. I wouldn't let the hospital attendant pick up his little lifeless body and rent a cab to take him to the morgue. Instead I picked up that sweet little boy, wrapped in a white sheet and carried him to my car. The attendant accompanied me. Again I did not allow the attendant to carry Alan from my car into the morgue. I would've wanted someone to have done that for one of my precious children.

Ian, you and Ann were able to stand at the door of the language school and console each of us as we walked out of the door. [On the day of the service.]

Sunday afternoon after our two families had eaten at the Hotel Royal Dutch we went over to Elizabeth Strachan's home, then a widow of several years, where you (Ian) told us the following story.

You said that upon awakening that Saturday morning of the funeral, both you and Ann did not believe that you could even attend the service. But you knelt down together beside your bed and God made his presence known to you in a very real way.

That Sunday afternoon at Elizabeth's home you said that you and Ann would not change anything that had happened in the previous days if it would cause you to lose the relationship that you now had with your Savior.

The story of little Alan continues today bearing fruit for our Lord. Many times I have repeated what you and Ann testified to that afternoon in Elizabeth Strachan's home. It is a living testimony that God's grace IS sufficient." (signed) Charles

We had broken hearts and cried so much that we dropped into an exhausted sleep until 5:00 AM when the milkman rang the bell; he came early, as it was Good Friday. At 7:00 AM Friday two little boys from nearby came with a bunch of red roses saying, "For the niño who had died." 8:00 AM Friday morning the night watchman from the car sales room next door came to see if it was true. He

66

asked several times if it was the little "marcho" (blond boy,) who spoke to him every day. He was crying there at the door. Alan used to call out to him "Migo" (amigo - friend) after he had waved Diane and me off.

Locals whom we had never seen before came to see us and to sympathize with us. An Australian lady, a diplomat, who lived around the corner, took Diane home with her after the accident and Diane stayed there for the night. We had all our meals taken care of by the students who either cooked them or sent it around to our home, or to the home of others who had us over for a meal. Someone was there all the time to answer the phone and the door and make coffee for those who visited.

. Diane came home Friday morning and told me there had been an accident. I told her that Jesus had taken Alan to heaven to live with Him so that he wouldn't have any more bumps or hurt any more. She wanted to know how he opened the sky to let him through and asked a lot of questions about what Alan might be doing up there.

Friday night Diane received the Lord as her Savior after I had read John 14 to her. She had wanted to know where Alan would live so I told her Alan was in one of the little places the Lord had gone to prepare and so she wanted to be sure she would have a little place with Jesus too. She slept with us, as her room was too lonely for her. We told her the Lord might give her another little brother or sister, but she said with a little tear in her eye, "But I want a little two-year-old brother." She was really missing him too.

Friday morning Ann and I had to go to the morgue to sign the death certificate. I wanted to see little Alan and also take his white and blue "onesie" for the funeral. We watched the men pull him out of the refrigerator, put the little PJ's on him and then brought him over to where we were standing. When I kissed his bruised face it was hard and cold but even that could not spoil his handsome little face. My heart was broken.

I called Adrian Gonzales, the teacher I had for preaching class my last term, and whom I thought so much of, and he came with us to the morgue. He was a tower of strength in that time of need. We then purchased the small "caja" coffin; the outside was lined or covered with a white fur-looking material. It had a lid with a glass window underneath so that when it was open you could see Alan's face under the glass.

Different students came to us with verses, hugs, tears and words of comfort. Unfortunately, we discovered that some people could be utterly stupid when trying to speak to grieving people. One missionary stated, "It's just as well he died, or he would have been a vegetable." There certainly was not much comfort in a statement like that.

During Friday afternoon we had many visitors, at one time there were 24 from the little church at Zapote. That was where I had done most of my practice preaching. They were terribly upset and promised to care for the grave for us, which we appreciated. In fact they arranged to pay for the small headstone and any other construction needed after we left for Colombia. They are all poor people so their offer really touched our hearts.

Dear Alan had touched so many lives, and as one man said, "It is possible that by this early death he will do a greater work than if he lived another 40 years." It certainly had a profound effect on the missionaries there at the school. We had breakfast at the neighbor's house on Saturday morning then read the cables and received the flowers, cakes and food. One ex-student, a non-Christian, sent around a big bag full of the most expensive brands of soups, tinned meats and chocolates. It was so that we wouldn't have to worry about cooking too much. We had four families home for supper Saturday night to help us eat the food, which wouldn't keep. Many of them gave us money, which just about covered the cost of a trip to Puerto Limon on the Caribbean coast, which we took later. Everybody gave themselves to us and we thank the Lord for such friends at that time. One of the Tica ladies (Costa Rican) said we certainly had a very precious offering given to God in baby Alan. Her daughter sometimes babysat for us.

We cried on and off, even waking up crying during the night. But about lunchtime Saturday, praise the Lord, we experienced a complete peace and joy in the Lord. He Himself had completely filled the void that Alan left at that time. By Saturday noon all the pain left us along with the heartache so that, we were overshadowed by the Lord Himself who gave us a peace that was really

68

tangible and difficult to explain. We had peace, a profound peace, even a joy, that the Lord had counted us worthy to suffer for His name. Now we were beginning to understand that it was for the fulfilling of the Lord's purposes that Alan died and we were seeing something of the results of it already. This had drawn us so close to the Lord and each other that we could honestly say we were thankful for the way the Lord had led us. From time to time on the Christian radio station they announced that the "niñito" (little boy,) Alan Taylor, son of Ian and Ann, had gone to be with the Lord. They gave the time of the service, requested prayer for us and finished off quoting the verse, "Precious in the sight of the Lord is the death of His saints" Psalm 116:15. Just think, the Lord loved him more than we did. He also knew the path ahead for us and chose to take our sweet Alan to be near His throne.

Being the Easter weekend, the funeral was to be on the Saturday in the Spanish Language Institute Chapel. We went to the chapel at 1:45 PM; the casket was at the front with white flowers all around it. White flowers are the custom there for children. We had another look at him there. I took some photos of the chapel then we went back home until 3:00 PM when we returned. The news of Alan's death had been reported in the San José newspaper and, as I was the Student Body President, I had met different business people in the community, such as the bank manager where most of our students changed their dollars into Colones. The chapel was full, and overflowing into the classrooms at the back. Over 200 were present. All the students and teachers were attending, many folk we had not even met from the community as well as some of the business people I had met. We walked down to the front, the lid was open as is the custom, so we had another look with calmness hard to imagine. A ray of sunshine came down and shone on his face, his eyes were half open, like a tired little boy, and it seemed to us both, "looking off unto Jesus" Hebrews 12:2.

The pastor of the Zapote Baptist Church had the opening message and spoke from 2 Samuel 12 about David. During this message he said, "Most of you at the Language Institute are missionaries, pastors, etc. and as a result of what has happened your lives and your ministry will be enriched." He delivered a very comforting message. Adrian Gonzales followed with the main message.

It had been a very overcast day, clouds then sunshine. Toward the end of his message the sun came out and shone through the skylight right onto the face of little Alan in the open coffin. There wasn't a dry eye in the chapel... except for Ann and me. Why? We were experiencing a tremendous and tangible peace that was inexplicable. Many had been praying for us, both overseas and in San José. As Adrian was finishing his message I signaled him, letting him know I would like to speak. He invited me to the pulpit.

I stood in front of a full chapel with Ann at my side, and began my first message in Spanish to a large gathering. "Today I can say that the Lord is true to His Word. In John 14:27 He told his disciples, *'Peace I leave with you; my peace I give you. I do not give to you as the world gives. Do not let your hearts be troubled and do not be afraid.'* Even though our hearts are aching, my wife Ann and I have been given a tremendous sense of the Lord's peace. Dear believers and friends, today is a day of sorrow for us and our hearts are full of sorrow, but also there is within our hearts a peace and a joy, which could not be found outside of Jesus Christ. Our deepest prayer is that every person present would be able to say that one day they will see Jesus face to face, just as we are going to see Jesus face to face and be united again with our son." After the message we finished with the hymn, "Face to Face With Christ My Savior."

We then waited at the door and shook hands with everyone; well really it was more Latina style, as the men and women both gave us a big hug, which is a really warm expression. The five university students we had been working with were at the funeral service and when they came out I said to them, "Miren, amigos, (look here, fellows) all the philosophy and the material things of this life and world just couldn't give the peace and joy which we have in moments like these. I do pray that you will find Jesus Christ as your personal Savior very soon."

Another missionary, a Wycliffe translator, came up to us and said, "The seed that has been sown here will bear fruit in all of Latin America." What he meant was that there were over 180 missionaries at the Institute. This event had a profound effect on

70

all of their lives and God was going to use this as they completed their studies and served the Lord in Latin America.

The burial service was at the Zapote cemetery, and we all drove there. It is a beautiful site situated looking toward the mountains.

Don Tomás, the pastor at Zapote, preached from 1 Corinthians 15. He said the proof of the resurrection was seen in the great number of people who hadn't believed that the Lord had risen, but who saw Him later on, and because He lives we shall also live. It was a good message (again everything was in Spanish and for this reason everything was more meaningful, and we appreciated what was said). But this sad time touched us deeply as we laid little Alan to rest in the Lord, to await the Lord's shout of command, and the voice of the archangel, followed by the wonderful time when all His own will be united, to be forever with the Lord. The lid was open during this service and at the end I put a little posy of red roses on the glass and shut the lid. He was laid to rest until we are all caught up to be forever with the Lord. Walter Lickley (my youth Bible class teacher) sent us a verse, which we really appreciated John 13:7 "Jesus replied, 'You do not realize now what I am doing, but later you will understand.'" It was a real comfort to us. We left the cemetery as they were filling in the hole and returned an hour later to see it laid out with the flowers.

I wrote home to my family: "Please don't grieve; we have a real assurance and peace about everything."

On Sunday morning Ann and I had communion together and that Easter remembrance was really lovely; we appreciated the resurrection of Jesus Christ so much more that day. Charles Moore, at the end of the funeral service, had asked me if I would speak at his church the following Sunday, to which I agreed, and after sharing the same message at the First Baptist Church of Alajuela that night an 18 year old girl, Marta Solano, gave her life to the Lord. Even though Alan's death was a real "Body Blow", it was also a confirmation that the Lord was in control and confirmed to us that He had us in His hands and would be with us in the soon coming days in Colombia. This was the first fruit of my Spanish ministry, in a way a result of Alan's death. I say that because his death had done something to our lives that we wouldn't have had otherwise. It was a nearness to the Lord, which was truly wonderful.

God does not promise that our lives will never be without trials or testing. He only promises, that "I will never leave you or forsake you." And "My grace is sufficient for you." These verses hold true in every circumstance of life, and we called on His Grace many times.

Charles took us out to lunch that Sunday and we had a nice time together. Later Sunday afternoon we had afternoon tea with Elizabeth Strachan whose husband Ken Strachan, had been a missionary in Costa Rica and director of the Latin American Mission. He introduced the "Evangelism-in-Depth" ministry.

http://www.bu.edu/missiology/missionary-biography/r-s/strachan-r-kenneth-1910-1965/

Monday morning we were still at peace but exhausted physically from lack of sleep and the strain, and of course our nerves were shot. Considering all of this Dr. Coble had suggested we get away for a few days and it seemed a wise thing to do. Since some students had given a love gift, we had the funds for such a trip. As we waited for the train I wondered if I was going to make it; I was bordering on the shakes and felt like running – anywhere, but just run. We boarded the train from San José to Puerto Limón on the

Caribbean side of the country. As the train got going we unwound a lot, the movement and the scenery were just what we needed. We were in the last carriage of the train – saloon class – it cost a couple of dollars more but was worth every penny to sit at the back, in the fresh air, and enjoy the scenery. Betty Gonzales, wife of the preacher, had a sister in Puerto Limón who met us at the train and drove us to the hotel. It was a very nice room overlooking the ocean and only cost $10 per day. We still didn't have any appetite, and got to bed at 7:30 PM sleeping until 7:00 AM. We could walk to the beach where I went body surfing for a while then sat with Diane, swam a little and visited the open market. It was a difficult time with the weight of what had happened still sinking in.

Betty met us after lunch and took us up to a beach called Playa Bonita, (pretty beach,) which certainly lived up to its name. It was like what you see on post cards of the tropical deserted beach, with palms along the shore and clean breakers rolling in. She had two of her friends with her who also had kids, so Diane had about eight kids to play with; she really enjoyed herself. I stayed in the water most of the time, as it was just right, which meant I had at least three hours swimming in the afternoon, that further helped me to relax. You wouldn't believe it; the locals didn't swim in the afternoon, as it was too cold!!! The temperature is around 90°f, which I thought was wonderful. Arriving back at the hotel about 5:30 we all enjoyed our dinner, our appetite had returned. We were really feeling relaxed again after all the physical exercise at the beach and we were thankful to the Lord for everything.

Our four days in Puerto Limón were really important as it allowed Ann and me to be able to "regroup," as we had plenty of quiet time to read the Word and pray together seeking God's mind as to our future. We boarded the old train and enjoyed the several hours journey over the hills and the beauty of this tropical paradise.

The last two weeks in Costa Rica were extremely busy, and having heavy hearts didn't make it any easier. I had finals coming up before graduation and had to "hit the books," while Ann was at home with Diane packing up, getting everything ready for our flight from San José to Cali, Colombia. Ann had already taken her finals several months before and had topped the class, including all the students that had been there the full year. While she may have had top grades with grammar, my grade for conversational Spanish was higher. This no doubt was because she was a perfectionist when it came to speaking; everything had to be grammatically correct in conversation. I was too anxious to speak, and spoke at top speed, something I still do when preaching!

On the day of graduation, all the students were excited to be finishing this segment of their training for missionary service, but we

Ann and Ian - Graduation Spanish Language Institute, April 1969

noticed their demeanor was not just excitement; there was a seriousness because of the "unknown" when going to their fields of service. Alan's death had made all of us realize that while we are doing God's will, there is always the possibility of death, sickness or tragedy of many kinds just around the corner.

With only a few days remaining after graduation, we had already sent ahead most of our belongings and arranged our airfares to Cali, Colombia. But now what to do?

Some people suggested that we should not go on to Colombia after this tragedy. That was never an option; we did not have any guidance from the Lord that we should change the course on which He had put us.

Dark thoughts came into my mind that I shared with Ann. I had felt I was in the center of the Lord's will, was preparing for missionary service and that nothing like this could happen to me or my family. My first feelings were of a loss of confidence in God. Satan suggested that as God couldn't care for my family in Costa Rica, how could He possibly care for us in Colombia? The emotions ranged from this feeling of despair, to a feeling of utter peace as the Lord again and again confirmed His love and will for us. We prayed about these thoughts and I had to recognize where they came from and push them out of my thinking. We had seen how God had prepared us for this missionary endeavor, providing for us in every way and directing us to this time. "We have to just trust him and keep on going, and doing what He wants. We still need to live by faith and trust Him to keep us," I said, and Ann agreed.

We really had experienced a wonderful year in San José, meeting so many missionaries whom we would remember for years to come. They represented many different denominations, but we all had a common cause - to serve the Lord and help one another - in spite of the practical differences that might exist.

Satan had brought tragedy into our lives and he continued to play on our minds. We went from pure joy in our growing knowledge of the Lord, to depths of sadness, fear and bewilderment, as we left San José for our field of service, Colombia, in early April 1969.

In the months and years to come, we could never understand the reason for the Lord allowing Alan to be killed, but we found strength and peace in submission to, and acceptance of, God's will for our lives, in the good as well as the difficult times. As Ann and I talked about our loss in Costa Rica, we came to the conclusion that perhaps the Lord had allowed this tragedy to help us empathize with the Colombian families where the infant death rate was high at that time. We soon found that in other cultures the value of life is not the same and some Colombian believers sought to encourage us by saying, "Don't worry, I have had six children; two have died and you can always have more." But we still grieved the loss of sweet Alan as we began the ministry in the country where God had sent us.

Now the arrow seemed to be broken, but being wonderfully repaired to be ready for service. The arrowhead was sharper than before, with the knock aligned and feathers to guide it straight. The sharpening was needed to carry the gospel to many who needed the Lord. An arrow can only be shot by pulling it backward; so when life is seemingly dragging you backward with problems, tragedies or difficulties, it probably means that it is going to fire you into something great.

PART TWO

BUILDING AND WATERING

1 Corinthians 3:5-9 "What, after all, is Apollos? And what is Paul? Only servants, through whom you came to believe, as the Lord has assigned to each his task. I planted the seed, Apollos watered it, but God made it grow. So neither he who plants nor he who waters is anything, but only God, who makes things grow. The man who plants and the man who waters have one purpose, and each will be rewarded according to his own labor. For we are Gods' fellow workers; you are God's field, God's building."

Part Two relates the various mission activities in which we were involved.

Diane and pet monkey - Paco - Pto Boyacá

Transport to Cachimbero

Public Transport Near Puerto Boyacá

78

7

ON TO COLOMBIA

The Target Is In View

With a mixture of emotions ranging from excitement for a new chapter in our lives to begin, to the heaviness of our recent loss, Ann and I, along with our daughter Diane, arrived in Cali from Costa Rica. We were joining two other new missionary families who had already arrived. They drove us from the airport to the Casa Evangélica (House of Evangelism) in Cien Palos, a suburb of Cali. At this church there was a large chapel with a three-bedroom apartment over the chapel area. Alden Poehner, the missionary who had written the letter with the "Macedonian Call," lived in the apartment and had purchased the homes behind the chapel in the next street. Those two homes served as a place for the new missionaries to live.

During the two months we lived in Cali we were able to pick up the baggage we had forwarded from San José, as well as get our cédulas (identification papers) and start the process for a resident visa at the offices of DAS, (Administrative Department of Security). We were also able to get our driver's licenses while in Cali.

The Herbert De Ruiter family had arrived some months before us and they had decided to move to the area of Pasto, in the South, to work with a church there. Peter and Annemarie Nunn, (the couple from England) whom we had come to know in San Jose, at the Language Institute, had already been in Cali for three months. By this time they knew their way around the region and had been visiting different areas where we had churches, or preaching points, as we called the groups that were the beginnings of new churches. However, they had not made any definite arrangements as to where in Colombia they might settle. Visiting these places with them, I had the opportunity to preach in Spanish just about every night. We enjoyed our time with the Nunns in Cali, getting to know them better, and they came to be very close friends over the years, a friendship that continues today.

I asked Alden where there was an area that might need us, and he told me about a town in a jungle area situated on the banks of the Magdalena River. The Magdalena River runs almost the length of Colombia from the south to Barranquilla on the north coast, where it empties into the Caribbean. The town was Puerto Boyacá, a farming area and an oil town.

Alden and I decided to make the nine-hour trip by car to Puerto Boyacá. Leaving Cali early one morning we drove up over the Andes on a road that climbed to 11,000 feet on the first leg of the trip, to Ibagué where our churches had a school. Elsa Barolin, a missionary from Argentina, was the principal whom I had already met in 1967 when I made my first trip to Colombia from Australia. I was asked to preach at the church meeting that evening. We stayed in the guest room overnight, leaving early next morning for the four-hour drive to Puerto Boyacá.

As we continued north, the heat became more and more oppressive going to well over 100°F with high humidity. After we crossed the river at El Dorado, we were down to 200ft above sea level. Much of the countryside had been cleared and there were fields of cotton and ajonjolí, or sesame seed, as well as Brahman cattle, popular in these hot steamy areas. Being so close to the Equator, the sun usually rises between 6:00 and 6:30 each morning, and then sets between 6:00 and 6:30 each evening all year round. Coming home from one of the preaching points one evening, we actually ran over a very large snake that was crossing the road. It was about ten feet long and had a girth of about five inches in diameter. "Strange speed bumps you have here, Alden! No doubt about it, Puerto Boyacá is really close to the jungle," I remarked. He laughed and had a few stories about snakes, ñeque (a rodent of unusually large size) and other animals he had seen.

Driving towards Puerto Boyacá I saw a dead eight foot long alligator on the side of the road. "The road kill is a bit different here," I said, "I'm more used to seeing kangaroos or rabbits in the outback back in Australia."

"You'll be surprised at the different wildlife over here," Alden replied.

After visiting some of the preaching points during the two days we were in that area, we eventually arrived in Puerto Boyacá having spent many hours on dusty unpaved roads. Some of the roads had been sprayed with untreated oil from the many wells in that area which at least kept the dust down, but became like driving on ice as soon as it rained. Stopping there we got a room at a very rustic local hotel. There was no air conditioning, but we did have a ceiling fan, which helped in the oppressive heat. Then we went to the chapel to visit some of the believers.

The school at Puerto Boyacá

Jesús Guizao was a full time church worker in that area and was living in an apartment beside the chapel. It was a modest apartment with a small kitchen, an all-purpose front room for table, chairs or couch; also a bathroom and a very small room, that would be good for an office. Upstairs there were three small bedrooms and a bathroom. Jesús offered for us to have this apartment for our family if we decided to stay to work there. Alongside the chapel there was also a school as part of the complex, with three classrooms that were used for grades one through eight. There were several grade levels in each classroom and the chapel itself served as a classroom. I spoke again that evening at the church meeting and most in the congregation were excited by the thought of a missionary coming

81

to live there. The expressions of friendship were very encouraging.

Alden and I returned to the hotel and showered to cool down a little, although there was no such thing as cold water. The cold-water tap produced warm water, which refreshed even though it did not cool. We sat on our beds where I was thinking about what we had been seeing that day.

"What do you think about what you have seen so far?" Alden asked.

"It looks like it could be an interesting place to serve," I remarked.

"You need to know that there have been some difficult problems here, mainly because of the background of the older believers in the fellowship, and some other difficulties related to the school."

"If we are to come here, I need to know as much as possible about the people as well as these problems you mentioned." I responded, realizing that a missionary cannot come in and make immediate wholesale changes or try to "fix" past issues.

"A bit of history will help," he began. "Two missionaries with their wives came to Colombia in the early 1930s and planted a number of churches in the areas of Pasto, Cali, and Pereira. Lester Morgan was in Pasto where there was a lot of persecution by the Catholic Church at that time. After a few years they somehow put ground glass in his food and he died as a result."

Alden went on to tell me of other missionaries who had come to help. "Will Missen was mainly working further north and, while there was some persecution, he continued until it was time for a furlough when he left to return to New Zealand. Returning to Colombia via the USA he applied for a visa and found that he was declared a persona non grata and could not get back in. He then went on to Puerto Rico where he continued his missionary work for a number of years. Eventually he took over the work of Good Tidings Publishers, *(Editorial Buenas Nuevas)* from Mr. Crabtree who had taken over from Robert Grant who started GTP back in 1876." He continued, "As you know Will is still heading up that Spanish literature work." This was information that would later have an effect on my work.

Alden continued to tell me that, as there were no missionaries, the believers in the churches they had established began to wonder how they could continue without the missionary leadership. The leaders decided to become a part of some of the evangelical

82

churches. After a couple of years there was a meeting of the original national leaders, who realized that they really didn't have the same liberty in the formal denominations and decided to form their own denomination.

They called themselves The Fundamental Church. Along with this impressive title they formulated 10 statutes that any new members would have to sign at the time of their baptism. One of these "statutes" was that the only way to pray was by kneeling. Another was that women should only wear dresses with sleeves to the elbows. This was so that men couldn't look inside their sleeveless dresses. There were other similar strange rules. He commented that, "Most of the older men in the church here are from that group and are still practicing some of those 'statutes.'"

I replied, "Alden, I really wondered what was happening this evening when we walked into the chapel. Everyone was kneeling beside the benches and a voice from nowhere was praying. It was a bit creepy. Then the brother stood up after he had finished praying from behind the pulpit. That's really stupid! His voice was muffled and it was difficult to hear what he was saying. That has to put people off if they come into a meeting for the first time and someone is hiding behind the pulpit praying."

Alden agreed, "Well, that's one of the problems here. They are very legalistic about a lot of those sorts of things."

Driving back to Cali, Alden and I had uninterrupted conversations about the work in the local church, as well as issues that could be problematic with the school. Some of the people in the church, and some of the small church groups scattered around, needed pastoral care.

In spite of the problems I was hearing about, I thought it would be a good place to start my ministry in Colombia. We returned to Cali arriving late at night, so I just went to bed. The next morning Ann and I had a real heart-to-heart conversation about Puerto Boyacá. We prayed asking the Lord to help us to know for sure that this was what He wanted. After some time that day of just talking and praying, we decided that in spite of the problems, we could probably be a real help. Ann would be able to help with the school organization, and I would be able to give some good basic teaching refuting some of the teachings of the "Fundamental Church," and be an influence in moving onto a more Biblical basis in those areas of legality.

Ann and I went over the whole prospect of moving to Puerto Boyacá, some of the inconveniences such as virtually no electricity, as well as the over 100°F constant heat and humidity day and night. Also there was the need to encourage Juan Ayala and his wife, who were teachers at the school. We also thought about some of the potential dangers in that rather wild oil town where there were gunshots just about every night, a couple of murders each week, and a very problematic local church.

After much prayer and a lot of thought and conversations, we decided that the Lord was opening up an opportunity for us to be helpful in a place that really needed it. We also talked it over with Peter and Annemarie Nunn who by then were thinking of moving to the city of Pereira. Ann and I met together with Alden who was really happy with our decision. Remember, it was his letter saying "surely the Lord is preparing young people somewhere to come help with the work in Colombia" that was our missionary call. He offered to take all our luggage in his Toyota Land Cruiser. Then Ann, Diane and I could fly there to avoid the long journey by road. He would then meet us in Puerto Boyacá after helping the Guizaos move their things and clean up the apartment to be ready for our arrival.

Corporation For Missionary Funds

During those first few months in Cali, Colombia there were three new missionary families who came, joining three others who had been there for a number of years already. We were receiving funds from churches and individuals overseas, which were sent for the work and we thought it was important to organize a not-for-profit corporation. All the missionaries would be able to access those funds for their respective ministries; for construction of church buildings; the purchase of vehicles or even homes; and in this way separate taxable personal funds from those of the ministries. Herbert de Ruiter, one of the first of this young missionary group to arrive in Colombia in the late 1960's, headed up the legal work to establish the CORPORACIÓN MARANATA (Maranatha Corporation). We elected him president, with the rest of us serving as officers.

84

We held regular bimonthly meetings, usually in Bogotá, which was a central place and easily accessible. Each time we met we had prayer about some of the problems and issues confronting us, discussed the work in general, planned activities such as camps and conferences, and decided how general funds should be used. These regular meetings were also an important means of building strong relationships among the missionaries.

In 1974 Herbert with his family moved to Peru to work with the Peruvian churches with whom we were affiliated, and I was elected president of the Maranata Corporación, a position I held until I left Colombia.

Our small backyard in Puerto Boyacá

8

PUERTO BOYACA

First Mission Area to Work

The following week we booked passage on a flight to Medellin. We spent the night in a hotel, and then the following morning boarded an eight-seater twin-engine plane for Puerto Boyacá.

Medellin is set in a valley with high mountains surrounding it. Arriving and leaving, the plane must circle down into the valley before landing and circle up over the mountains when leaving. As we circled, we had a lovely view of the city, and once over the Mountains we could see for miles down to the wide lowlands along the Magdalena Valley.

We were met at the small local airport and driven to the chapel where we found our things waiting for us in the apartment. There were wall cabinets above the kitchen sink and a refrigerator nearby. Upstairs there was a single bed in the second room and a double bed in the main room. Because there were no closets for our clothes, we needed to purchase some metal closets and a desk at the local hardware store. Interestingly, in spite of having a fridge, there was no electricity during the day. At night, the local power company made some effort to provide power for this growing oil town. The amount of power that came to us was so little that it would not start up the fridge and when we turned on the house lights, we had to actually look up at the light bulb to see if the filament was even glowing.

After unpacking, we settled down for the first night and that was when we began to realize just how hot and humid this town was. Lying on the sheet, no need for covers, I remember the perspiration building up on my chest and trickling off down the sides. I tried moving my arm to a cooler place on the sheet, but found it was even warmer than where I had been. It was cooler where the perspiration had been evaporating, so I just didn't move! In the morning, the wet outline of my sweaty body was on the sheet.

The following day we walked to the shopping area to get some groceries and meat. Because it was too hot to grow any quantity of spinach, green beans, or lettuce, we bought good quantities of the tropical fruit which we would either cut up to eat, or turn into juice. We weren't all that hungry with it being so hot, so the fruit juices became a staple diet for us. We were really impressed with the meat market! As we walked along the rows of booths in the open air, the butchers had their meat hanging on hooks connected to a rail just under the tin roof over their stalls. Sitting on the roof were very large black vultures with their bald heads and necks, just waiting for a piece of meat or scrap to fall from the butcher's table. As our fridge didn't work, Ann had to go to the market every morning at 6:30 to get any meat we needed for that day. The idea was to point to a chunk of meat that looked more or less fresh, and then say, "I want two pounds off that piece!"
Another day she spotted some spinach in one stall and quickly purchased it. She soon found out that another lady always beat her to the spinach because she had some rabbits! Most Colombians in that area would never eat greens, so Ann always hoped she might beat the other lady as we really missed our greens. Ann mentioned this in one of her letters home, and a couple of months later a package arrived in the mail with a number of packets of dried peas. These were a real luxury for us and we only cooked them on special occasions.

During the first two months we did not have a vehicle so I purchased two bicycles and "Mum and Dad" would pedal off to town, only about a half mile away, to pick up our mail at the shop that acted as a post office. Ann would use hers to get to market every morning. Fortunately, Dr. Cabezas, in his orientation classes at the language school in Costa Rica, had prepared us for culture shock. So, even though we were feeling that living here was crazy and things were better back home, we realized that we were experiencing typical culture shock and adjusted to it pretty quickly.

Some funds had come for us to purchase a vehicle. A month after settling in, I flew via Medellin to Cali where, with Alden, I went to the Ford company sales room and put in an order for a Ford F-100 pick-up which, after importation from the USA, would be converted into a van with seating for about eight in the back and three up front. It was arranged that I would borrow missionary Ton Oostra's jeep until my vehicle arrived from the USA. Ton and his family, originally from the Netherlands, were living in Ibagué and with some public transport there, he kindly lent us his four wheel drive Jeep. He realized that my travels would be in difficult areas in the surrounding countryside around our new home.

Later that year I purchased a Ruston Diesel, which was a two phase Generator. Alden, an engineer who loved building things, arranged for a small cement block shed to be built in the far back corner of the school yard, which had barred windows and a steel door to keep thieves out. Inside they built an eight-inch solid cement base onto which the generator was bolted. There was a ten-foot wall, topped with broken glass, around the whole chapel, school, and apartment premises, and a large steel two-door entrance wide enough to drive a truck into the yard.

Alden's worker, Segundo Ignacio Parra, installed the two-phase wiring so that the apartment had one of the phases and the chapel and school had the other. This meant that we could run the generator for the evening meetings, which was a real improvement from the hurricane kerosene lamps, which we used in the house and in the chapel. The kerosene lamps only added to the heat. We also started the generator for a few hours each morning and afternoon in order to use the refrigerator and fans in the house. The generator made a tremendous difference.

If homesickness was an issue it was no use thinking about it. Letters to Australia and New Zealand took about three or four weeks each way, so news from the home front was always slow and out of date by the time it arrived to us, and another few weeks before answers returned. Nevertheless, I tried to write a letter to my parents every week and Ann also kept up regular correspondence with her family in New Zealand. The only phones in the town were at the office of Telefónica Telecom. It usually took about a half hour just to get a call to another town or city in Colombia. Calling overseas was out of the question.

A Missionary On A Pedestal,
Or Just One Of The Boys?

I had not been in Puerto Boyacá many weeks before I felt that the locals were putting me on a pedestal, thinking that I was better or more important than they were. When discussing matters with those who seemed to be leaders in the local church they would wait for my opinions before stating their own thoughts, and then only agree with what I said. This made it difficult for me to understand their real thoughts or opinions. It also created a disadvantage in being able to correct some of their beliefs or understandings about the true meanings of Scripture, especially as it related to their background in the "Fundamental Church." I was quite concerned about this problem and was looking for a way to subtly rectify the situation without making an overt announcement.

One solution came when I found out that every now and again, on a Saturday, some of the men would go hunting. They would head out of town to either hunt around cleared farmland or go deeper into the jungle for some of the wild animals. I had done some hunting in the outback in Australia as a teenager and found it fun. In conversation with two of the church members, Esau Parra and Juan Ayala, I told them I would really like to join them sometime. It gave me opportunity to just be "one of the fellows" in a friendly activity not related to the church work. Esau explained I would need to go to the army base in Puerto Salgar to get a license to own and carry a gun, and then purchase a weapon and ammunition at the base.

We made arrangements to travel to Puerto Salgar, near La Dorada. Along with Esau and Jesús Guizao who also came with us as I needed two people who could act as references to my character - that I was not a sicario, *(an assassin or a guerrillero, a revolutionary guerilla).* We arrived at the army base and were ushered into the office of the captain who would issue my license. The paperwork was done and then the two witnesses had to sign the papers. Guizao being the oldest, and a black man, was about to sign when the captain asked him, "What is your relationship with Mr. Taylor?"

Guizao came back with, "He's my brother."

The captain's head jerked up from the paperwork to look at Guizao then at me with a very disconcerted look on his face. "Your brother?!!!"

"Yes, my brother in Christ, I can recommend him. He's a good man."

The captain laughed and quickly signed my papers.

We went out to the armory and I chose a Remington 12 gauge shotgun and a Spanish model Starr semi-automatic pistol. I also bought a cartridge belt to hold about 15 shotgun shells and ammunition for the pistol, along with a belt holster for the pistol. Ann made a bag to have over my shoulder to carry pistol ammo, as well as snacks and water on our hunting trips.

Over the next couple of years a number of men would go hunting on alternating Saturdays. When I finally had a vehicle, we could go further into the jungle areas to hunt. We had plenty of time to talk and become friends, breaking down the distance that had existed because I was a missionary. I often made grammatical mistakes and told them to always correct me. Since I was still learning vocabulary and current idioms, their help was invaluable at the same time as I was enjoying and learning about jungle hunting.

It was about this time when the men from the local church really bonded and we learned to work together. We could discuss some of the doctrinal problem areas, not on the basis of a missionary telling them what is right or wrong, but just as friends discussing matters on the basis of Scripture, and showing why some practices and traditions weren't really Biblical.

There is no better way to really get to know a person than when walking together in swampy land with water up to your waist, holding a hunting bag and gun up over your head, and looking out for snakes, alligators or other wild animals. Each one looked out for the other, and strong friendships and trust were established. I believe that these hunting trips were as important as preaching and teaching in the chapel. The men were ready to listen, share and discuss matters with a missionary who just became one of them.

We hunted ñeque, monkeys, tapir, ducks, one time a goose and other wild fowl, along with snakes whenever we saw them, alligators, and even iguanas. There was a strange assortment of weapons, starting with Esau's gun, which he called a Chisboom; a homemade muzzleloader. When the hammer hit the cap to fire the powder in the barrel there would be a hiss as the spark moved down the tiny channel to the powder, then the bang. "Chisss, boom!"

A few times when we had no success finding any of the usual animals or birds, we went to a small river with a pond off to one side - something like an Australian Billabong. There were some really good fish - bocachicas, or small mouth bass, that would come up to the surface and as their mouths hit the surface, a small ring would expand on the water. We would then shoot the center of the tiny growing wave with my 12-gauge shotgun, and then plunge into the water to grab the headless fish before it sank or was washed away.

As flocks of macaws, or Guacamayas were flying over, one of my "good friends," told me that those birds really made a great meal. I shot one and took it home for supper that night. We kept the beautiful tail feathers for Diane who tied them together and hung them on her bedroom wall. After cooking this bird for a suitable time, we sat down to eat the cooked Guacamaya with its grey flesh. When we tried to cut or chew it, it was as if we were chewing car inner tubes. The meat was hopeless and impossible to eat. The following day, after the morning services, I found Esau and Juan Ayala and said, "Hey, that bird was terrible. There was no way we could eat it."

Juan replied, "You have to know how to cook it."

"What did we do wrong?" I asked.

"Well, you need to cook it in the pressure cooker and put a small round river stone in with it. When the stone is soft, it is ready to eat." Laughter broke out all around and I realized I had fallen for another of their jokes at my expense. The importance of all this was that now I was accepted as one of them, someone they could pull pranks on, but also someone they had come to respect.

First Encounter With Demon Activity

Several months after our arrival in Puerto Boyacá, Alden had arranged to take me on a visit to a town that was in a remote jungle area at that time, called Carare. We left our home at 6:00 AM, drove for quite awhile on dusty and sometimes muddy roads, past small farms where land had been cleared providing some pasture for the Brahman cattle that were well suited for that type of terrain and climate. Arriving at another town farther north on the Magdalena River, Puerto Berrío, we left the vehicle with another Christian who would make sure it wasn't stolen in our absence. Then we went to the railway station to wait for the train that would take us to Carare a couple of hours still farther north. Back in 1969, there were no roads connecting these towns in the jungle, so most of the time the train trip was through jungle with occasional small farms along the way.

We finally arrived at the Carare stop, which wasn't a railway station, anything like I was used to seeing. It was just a shed beside the tracks that had a small office for selling tickets and taking delivery of goods being shipped there for the local townspeople and farmers. It also had a small storage room for incoming and outgoing cargo, a platform about 6 inches higher than the tracks, and a roof for shade. We alighted on the side that had no platform and the heat was overwhelming. It had to have been at least a very humid temperature of 115°F with the waves of heat reflecting off the hard earth as we walked along.

However, the heat was not the thing that affected me most. I had a feeling of extreme anxiety; I felt that I had to just run and get out of there. Thoughts began to flood my mind that my daughter Diane, back in Pto. Boyacá, had been attacked or kidnapped, that there were no phones or means to make any contact with the family, and there was no way out until the following day when the passenger train would come through. There were similar thoughts to those I had after Alan was killed. "If God could not look after your little boy in Costa Rica, you have no idea what's happening to your little five year old girl, Diane, in Pto. Boyacá. You know there are shootings every week and people breaking into homes, killing the occupants and stealing everything they own. Something terrible has happened to Diane!" I thought I was having a nervous breakdown. Anyone who knows me would realize that I do not have anxiety attacks and circumstances do not easily scare me, but my own feelings were that I should just run and get away from that place.

Alden and I walked about two hundred yards to the home of a brother named Ismael. When we arrived at his home, made from sheets of plywood board and tin, his wife came out to meet us.

"Hola hermano (hello brother) Alden. I'm sorry, but Ismael is very sick with a high fever."

"So sorry to hear that, can we come in a pray with him?"

"¡Claro, que si! Siga adelante." ("Of course; come on in.")

Ismael was perspiring profusely. He obviously had a very high temperature, and was tossing and turning on the bed. He did recognize Alden who then introduced me, "Ay, hermano, I'm so sorry to see you like this. I have brought Hermano Juan (Brother Ian), a new missionary who is now living in Pto. Boyacá. He will be working now in this area of the Magdalena. Perhaps Juan you could read some verses for Ismael and pray for him and the family."

Now, I was still having these horrible feelings of anxiety, of dread, and wanting to just run. This brother was seriously sick with malaria, probably with a temperature over 104°, and I really didn't feel like ministering to him, but because I had been asked there was no excuse for not reading a portion and praying. I opened my Spanish Bible to Psalm 90 and began to read the wonderful verses. *"Lord, you have been our dwelling place throughout all generations. Before the mountains were born or you brought forth the earth and the world, from everlasting to everlasting you are God..."*

*Immediately a fantastic peace enveloped me that w*as so real it was tangible; it was almost something I felt I could reach out and touch. I then remembered the peace the Lord had given me at my son Alan's funeral in San José, Costa Rica, and realized at that moment that my feeling "crazy," wasn't a nervous breakdown happening in my head, but rather an oppression coming from an outside source. I realized this was a demonic oppression!

I knew that demons cannot possess a born-again believer, because we have the Holy Spirit dwelling in us. I knew the Holy Spirit would not share his "temple" with a demon, and as 1 John 4:4 states, *"You, dear children, are from God and have overcome them, because the one who is in you is greater than the one who is in the world."* The interesting thing was that even though the oppression continued the entire week I was in Carare, every time I opened the Bible to study and pray with people in their homes, or when I stood at the pulpit to preach, that same peace flooded my whole being. This helped me to realize that I had to learn not to trust my feelings, but to trust the Lord who had brought me to this country. Something difficult to explain is that in spite of the oppressive feelings I was experiencing, at the same time I had come to a place of quiet inner peace as I trusted the Lord, and so, could continue on with the visit to Carare throughout that week.

When I arrived home again, I have to say it was a great relief to see that all was well; nothing untoward had happened in my absence, and Diane came running to give me one of her welcoming hugs. You can be sure what happened on that first trip to Carare was a lesson that helped me in many difficult circumstances in the following years.

It was so good to hear Ann ask after a welcoming kiss, "Well, how was your trip into the jungle?"

"It was OK," I replied. "I really enjoyed my time there."

Later that evening I was able to tell her about the struggle I had experienced, and how the Lord had confirmed once again, through a miracle of peace, similar to that which we had both experienced in Costa Rica at Alan's funeral. *"Peace I leave with you; my peace I give you. I do not give to you as the world gives. Do not let your hearts be troubled and do not be afraid."* John 14:27

Special Guests At A Baptism!

After almost a year in Puerto Boyacá, the school was functioning well and the local church was growing. Having received the necessary funding I was able to purchase a large Ruston two-phase power generator, which provided lights for these meetings. This also encouraged attendance and the chapel was pretty full each night. There were a number of professions of faith so I began baptism classes with those who wished to take that step of identifying with the Lord Jesus in His death and resurrection. The classes were held once a week for six weeks and were important as most of the Colombians had a Catholic background and the inbred teaching that baptism is needed for salvation.

During that time I had the opportunity to teach the basics of Salvation so that their faith was not placed on the works of baptism or anything else, but the work and blood of the Lord Jesus. I included teaching on man's two natures and the spiritual struggles, as well as the priesthood of all believers with the fundamentals of church doctrine. By the end of the classes I knew if they were truly saved, that they understood the step they were taking, and the fact that they were now part of the local church body.

At the conclusion of a particular set of classes there were five ready for baptism, including a lady about six months pregnant. The date for the baptism was arranged for a Saturday afternoon and many of the church people, plus other interested folks from the town, set off on foot for a small lagoon about two miles down the road. I drove my Ford F100 with Ann, Diane and a couple of the older folk. It was a very happy time with almost a picnic atmosphere as we arrived at the banks of the lagoon.

We began by singing several hymns; then I entered the water and called for the first to be baptized. As each one came up out of the water, the believers, with their hymnbooks open and ready, sang a verse from the hymn "Que Mi Vida Entera Esté, consagrada a Tí Señor", ("Oh That My Entire Life Might Be, Consecrated To You Lord.") A very fitting hymn for a baptism.

As the last one to be baptized, the pregnant lady came out of the water, I stood there in the water with my hand on her shoulder. The last verse was sung and I closed that very happy time with prayer. We stood around talking for another half hour and then in small groups the people began to walk back to the town.

Later that evening at the dinner table we were half way through our meal when five-year-old Diane spoke up. "Dad, did you know a crocodile came up behind you at the baptism?"

'Gator attends a Baptism - Puerto Boyacá

"A crocodile? No, it was probably just a log or branch of a tree floating there," I replied.

"No, daddy, the second time it came up it opened its mouth and it

96

had really big teeth! Eunice was beside me and she saw it too."

"What!? Why didn't you yell and let me know?"

"Well, you were praying and I didn't want to interrupt you while you were praying," she replied in all her innocence.

The next day I spoke to Esau and Juan Ayala telling them what Diane had told me. So, that same evening they went to the lagoon and shot two seven-foot alligators in the lagoon. That was one of those occasions, I believe, when God closed the mouths of the "lions" - alligators in that instance.

Visiting Jungle Churches - Blessings And Struggles

Ian's First ride into Cachimbero

Ann was able to meet with the two school teachers regularly to counsel with them as well as giving some lessons to the children. This, along with ladies' meetings she had started, gave her a full-time ministry. Diane was in first grade and doing well. She had been in a missionary kids' class in Costa Rica and had started speaking Spanish faster than her parents.

Ann's activities at home left me free to make trips to some of the areas fairly close to Puerto Boyacá, and the first of these was to an area called Cachimbero. Together with one of the men from the church who knew the area well, we would leave home at about 4 AM and drive a couple of hours to a place called Kilómetro 17, along the main road which eventually ended at Puerto Berrío. It was called a main road but was unpaved, and in many places had deep mud holes from side to side. We needed the four-wheel drive sometimes to get us out of the holes.

On one of those trips we came to a standstill as two cowboys with their lassoes around the horns of a very stubborn cow were trying to move the cow to a nearby field. The cow had its hooves firmly planted and would not move in spite of the rope around the saddle horns and the horses trying to pull it. Domingo, a believer sitting in the back seat behind me, said, "Hermano, pull up to the side of the cow." I slowly moved up the right side of the animal, "A little bit more," he said. He then grabbed the cow's tail, lifted it up to his mouth and gave it a really hard bite. With that the cow took off at a run with the cowboys and horses galloping along, now behind the cow. They waved their thanks as they moved off the road and into their farm, and we continued our journey. This reminded me of a verse in Hosea 4:16 *"The Israelites are stubborn, like a stubborn heifer,"* which later gave me a good illustration for preaching, especially with legalistic believers who just dig in and want to stick to their traditions and unbiblical practices.

Arriving at Kilómetro 17 there were a few thatch-roofed homes at the side of the road, a small shop that sold gaseosas (soft drinks), and a small one-room building that was the chapel. The chapel was also used as an all-grades school for about 15 children living in that area. One time brother Maecha was preaching in that little chapel. The walls were made of unfinished boards loosely nailed together and as he was preaching a snake crawled between the boards and started to slowly crawl up the space between the boards. All eyes in the audience were on the snake and brother Maecha's back was less than a foot from where the snake crawled. One brother called out, "¡Hermano, hay una culebra atrás!" (Brother, there is a snake behind you!) Moisés Vázques jumped up from his seat, knocked the snake off the wall with his boot, stomped on its head, and then took his seat again. Maecha had not stopped preaching and went on saying, "Don't be distracted by a snake. That has always been Satan's method of distracting people's attention from God and causing sin. Now you need to forget the snake and listen to the word of God and the message of salvation through Jesus Christ."

After a quick visit to a family about a half-mile farther along the road, it was time for us to drive back to Kl. 17 where the Perez brothers had organized mules for us to ride into Cachimbero. We mounted and trekked into the jungle. The first leg of the journey was across low swampy land and then we followed a track into the hills as the jungle began to close in around us. We went up and down steep inclines, through knee-deep muddy areas and finally the jungle began to open out into a clearing where brother Pablo Emilio Huertas

Snakes on the way

lived with his wife and family. He invited us into his home, a typical home made from the jungle with walls made of straight two-inch thick poles bound together with rope and jungle vines and standing upright. There were a couple of rooms walled off inside, in a similar way. The kitchen was at one end of the house under a sort of lean-to, all covered with a thick thatch roof made from palm branches. Pablo kindly asked if we would like some lemonade or coffee. I opted for coffee. I knew the lemonade was made with water from the creek nearby, where people bathed and the cows drank, with only some lime juice added for flavor. I knew that would be refreshing, but I also knew that the coffee would at least have been boiled. Therefore it was less likely to infect my intestines with amoebas!

I had been previously told that this brother had been part of a group of roving bandits during the time of the La Violencia (The Violence, a civil war). During that time an amnesty was given to those who would lay down their weapons and return to normal life, and

Daniel Perez farm Cachimbero

Pablo took that opportunity as he had come to know the Lord Jesus as his Savior. He married and left for the jungle, as many others did. By the time I met him he had become a strong leader in the local church in that area.

We had a short Bible Study and prayer with the Huertas family then left for the farm of Aladino Perez and his family, not too far away. They had already finished lunch, but there was some fruit and coffee to keep me going. I was age 29 on that first trip and had a lot more energy and stamina than in later years. We had a similar visit with that family and then continued again through more jungle and, as evening was falling, arrived at the farm and home of Daniel Perez. We were to have a church meeting there that evening as people from some of the nearby farms walked the jungle trails, sometimes an hour or two, to be at the meeting.

These were wonderful times for me as the people were hungry for the Word and usually thought a preacher had "run out of gas," if he didn't speak for more than an hour. The idea is that you just forget you have a watch; time doesn't matter, simply enjoy sharing and expounding Scripture.

After the meeting, Daniel's wife had prepared a hot chocolate drink for everyone and also some food for our group, which was all the more enjoyable as I hadn't eaten real food since breakfast.

After eating and visiting I blew up my air mattress, placed it on the kitchen table and hung my mosquito net from the rafters over the table. At about 11:00 PM it was good to finally lay down for a good night's sleep.

About 4:00 AM, a nearby rowdy rooster startled me out of my sleep. Daniel's wife had already begun stirring the ashes on the stove to start the fire and make some coffee and prepare breakfast. The stove was like a table with four legs and a solid top; the 6-inch border around the top was filled with dirt. Above the fire there were wires hanging from the ceiling beams where a pot could be hung and an elevated flat metal sheet could also hang over the fire on which the arepas could be cooked. Colombian arepas are a staple food, especially for breakfast, throughout the country. They are easy to prepare, consisting of cornmeal, water, some butter or fat, and if you want to enrich the flavor shredded mozzarella cheese can be added. This would be similar to a quesadilla. The following day I watched as two of the young girls worked with a stump that had been hollowed out from the top to form a large three-foot high mortar and the pestle, which was a three-foot pole that had a rounded club-shaped end. With this they added corn and pounded it to prepare the cornmeal for their arepas.

The next Sunday we went off to one of the neighbors who had built a chapel in the jungle. It had no walls and was about 15 feet by 15 feet, with a typical thatch roof made from the palm branches that abounded in the jungle. The benches were lengths of eight-inch diameter round logs fastened into the ground, with rough-cut boards resting on top and nailed to the logs. There was a home-made table at the front, which was used as a pulpit and also for the remembrance of the Lord's Supper (communion service). The emblems were a large arepa and a glass with red raspberry soda. These were wonderful reminders of the Lord Jesus and His sacrificial death for us on the cross at Calvary. The men participated with prayers of worship, choosing hymns that reminded us of the Lord's character, worth and work, some related Bible readings, and then the partaking of the emblems.

This was one of the most wonderful times of worship I had ever experienced. Just listening to the simple folk opening up their hearts in worship, thanksgiving and praise. The hymns were sung, usually

Preaching Jungle Chapel Cachimbero

in a sad minor key, along with the macaws, screeching as they flew over, and the many other jungle sounds adding to a natural praise for such a loving Savior. I visited this area many times over the next few years and each time there was something new and enjoyable

Sometimes I carried my shotgun on these trips also, and the locals always appreciated the fresh meat if I was able to shoot a howler monkey. Normally they would buy meat in the market, then bring it back to their farms and cut the meat into thin slices and heavily salt it. Then they would hang the meat on a wire in the sun to dry and preserve it, as there was no electricity and therefore no refrigerators.

Making one of these visits, we were passing an army check-point prior to getting to Kilometro 17. The soldiers asked if we had any weapons and I showed them my shotgun. "Mire, look, you had better not carry this into Cachimbero this time as we have a patrol out there somewhere. There have been guerrillas in the area and if they see you coming with a gun over your shoulder, they will shoot first then look to see who is carrying the weapon. You can collect it on the way back." I handed over my shotgun wondering if I would ever see it again, but on the return journey they handed it over without any trouble.

For another trip to a group of believers a few miles further north of Cachimbero, on the road to Pto. Berrío, a couple of us went by bus instead of driving the car. The church group in that area was next to a rather large ciénega,,a large marshy area with some deep pools of water, and surrounded by tall thick grassland. That evening after the meeting one of the boys, using his flashlight, showed me the many pairs of red alligator eyes out in the water and along the edges of the swamp. There was a large number of alligators in this ciénega and many small 'gators near the sandy edges.

I thought I would catch a small 'gator and take it back for the "museum" at our school in Pto. Boyacá. (We had a collection of stuffed and dried animals and birds secured on the chain link wire that formed the large classroom windows under the roof covering a walkway). One of the young boys who lived there decided he would help me catch one. We had a lot of fun dashing after the 'gators as they quickly ran into the water and disappeared. I finally caught one, about 18 inches long and, holding its mouth shut, walked up to the house. We tied its mouth shut with some string. It was just about time to catch the bus back to Pto. Boyacá, so I used another length of string to tie one end to its mouth and the other to its tail. Women have crocodile skin handbags so why couldn't I have an alligator shoulder bag?

I had my backpack and "shoulder bag" when we flagged down the bus. All went well until the alligator somehow got loose and started running up and down under the seats. You can imagine the confusion as ladies were screaming and I was dashing up and down the aisle looking for my pet 'gator. I finally caught it again and we got back with no further incidents. I let it loose in our enclosed tiny back yard for a couple of days and finally it found its way to the museum where it still possibly hangs today. It seems that missionary work can also be fun at times.

Monte Loro

"Monte Loro" translated Parrot Mountain, was another area where we had a small church that I visited a number of times. It was a couple of hours away from Puerto Boyacá and on a very primitive road that was mostly two tracks where the wheels of the cars had hardened the soil. After leaving the farms around Pto. Boyacá there was a river to cross with a very old bridge that was falling apart. The cross beams were still intact, but the surface planks on the bridge were loose, and most were missing. Therefore someone had to walk ahead of the vehicle, moving the planks into place, so that the wheels had something on which to ride. Soon after the river we had to drive through very dense jungle, now and again passing little farms, and finally coming to the tiny village of Monte Loro. It wasn't much of a village, a few thatch-roofed homes alongside the road, but the believers there had built a chapel where there were regular meetings. I usually made a one-day visit to this church, as there really was nowhere to stay overnight.

The people there were solidly entrenched with the "Fundamental Church's" errors, which I had been warned about when we first arrived. The believers had become not only traditional-minded but also legalistically entrenched. You will remember that one of the "statutes" they had to sign when they were baptized was that the ladies must have sleeves to their elbows with the purpose of making sure the men didn't surreptitiously take a peek inside if they wore a sleeveless dress. During those visits I had been trying to give teaching to show that their type of legality was causing the church in this area to stagnate and grow cold.

One time as I was preaching one of the sisters began to nurse her baby. Now I do not have any problem with that; better a fed baby than a crying baby when you are preaching. After a while she switched sides but did not cover the first side. Now that is a bit disconcerting when you are preaching, but I kept my eyes on every other person and continued. Finally the baby finished on the second side and the lady just left both breasts uncovered, which is even more disconcerting as there are only so many people to make eye contact with as you preach in a small congregation.

"So, what's the need for long sleeves?" I thought.

There was another more problematic inconsistency as a new family came to know the Lord and began attending the church there. The new sister questioned their insistence on several of their "statutes," which caused the folk from the older group to make life difficult for that new family. One of the things they did was to place broken pieces of glass in the muddy track that their children used when going to the creek for water.

104

Not only that, one of the ladies in the older group told the new lady's neighbor that her husband was having an affair with the new sister. A few days later the neighbor stabbed the new believer in the back several times and left her bleeding in front of her humble dwelling. It was a long way to the nearest hospital in Pto. Boyacá and this sister would have bled to death, but the Lord had prepared for the situation. A medical doctor, who hardly ever went out to that area, just "happened" to be driving by. The dying woman's husband ran out and begged the man to take his wife to the hospital. The Doctor did what he could to stop the bleeding and then rushed her to the hospital where her life was saved by the surgery that followed.

The believers came to our house to tell me about the problem and I was able to visit the sister and made arrangements for the family to come live in Pto. Boyacá. The husband was a carpenter and was able to make a living there along with the help of our local church.

I was very upset by the actions of the believers at the Monte Loro church, so I made a trip there the following week. I called the group together and after reprimanding them all for such disgusting behavior, challenged them as to their even being true Christians acting the way they had acted with the new family of believers. No one confessed or even said they were sorry for what had happened. Their attitude was, "If you don't accept all our statutes and traditions then, they basically deserved what they got." At that stage I declared that this wasn't a functioning church, which they should disband and not try to meet as a church until they were acting according to Scripture. We could no longer consider them as being a part of the fellowship with our churches. Thankfully, this was the only time I had to do anything like that, but their behavior was a real disgrace and dishonor to the name of Christ.

Brother Jorge Berney from Argentina visited Pto. Boyacá on one occasion and when he heard about the requirement to kneel for prayer he began his message with, "Before I start, let's pray." Many began to kneel by their benches and at that moment he called out, "No. No. No. Everyone stand up; we are going to pray standing up." Everyone stood and this helped us very much in Pto. Boyacá. He read Scriptures referring to the many bodily positions for prayer that the Bible clearly mentions. We had no further struggle with that error, but all sorts of other problems persisted.

The situation in Monte Loro and the many other legalistic and "Fundamental Church" attitudes brought me to the conclusion that I should "not be building on someone else's foundation," Romans 15:20. These many problems and inconsistencies confirmed my thoughts that I should wait on the Lord as to the possibility of moving to an area where we had no churches, in order to start up new churches with solid foundations built on the Lord and Scripture.

Our time in Puerto Boyacá had been a time of tremendous learning experiences; not only working with difficult situations, and making lifetime friends, but also coming to understand the culture. We understood more fully what depending on the Lord really means, along with building up my language abilities.

9

FIRST FURLOUGH

Reassessing Our Ministry Focus

The years since leaving Australia had been very busy and some-what taxing with intercultural changes and settling in a new country. First, the one-year in Costa Rica for language school ending with the tragic death of our son Alan just prior to arriving in Colombia. Then taking on responsibilities in the jungle area of Puerto Boyacá for almost three-and-a-half years. We thought it time to arrange a furlough to reassess what God was directing us to do. Since Ann had been unable to get pregnant again even after many visits to an OB-GYN we decided that we would love to have another little boy to help fill that void left by Alan, and we began the paperwork for an adoption, which would perhaps be accomplished while we were on furlough. Diane was almost 7 years old by this time, and in spite of the age difference, a little brother would be good for her.

We applied to an agency in Sydney Australia; and after filling out all the paperwork we finally had a visit from a representative of Bienestar Familiar, the Colombian social and welfare agency established to help families and protect children. The purpose of this visit was to check our family and our living conditions. It was quickly established that we would be suitable parents and we were given approval. The Australian agency contacted us and told us that the following year a baby boy would be designated for us and would be available. This was wonderful news. We planned to leave mid December 1971 so that we could enjoy Christmas with our family and commending churches in Australia. Thinking about carols in the park beside the chapel was something we would enjoy.

Several months before we planned to leave for our furlough,

however, George Berney and Elsa Barolín visited us and told me about some good contacts they had in the large city of Bucaramanga and were planning to visit after they left Pto. Boyacá. I decided to go with them. In fact, we used my vehicle for the trip.

The three of us arrived several days later as there were no direct roads to Bucaramanga from our place. First we drove to Ibagué, where we spent the night at the school where Elsa was the principal and had a guest room where George and I slept. The following day we drove to Bogotá where we had lunch, then continued on to Bucaramanga. After settling in at a hotel we went to visit the Santamaria family in their spacious home. The husband was an engineer and had contracts with the government, building roads; so the family was really well off financially. They had a large family and that evening the young ones played their guitars and sang some hymns followed by a Bible study.

I told this family that I had been thinking and praying about moving from Puerto Boyacá; at which time they warmly encouraged me to come to Bucaramanga where there were good opportunities for planting a new church. This sounded really wonderful, an answer to prayer. I had really felt that I needed to establish a work that was based on Scripture so that we could move forward and grow in a positive way. Spending so much time just sorting out other peoples' problems caused by legalism and unbiblical traditions had become a real burden for me. I explained my plans for a furlough but that, Lord willing, Ann and I would come back to Bucaramanga after our furlough.

By this time Anne and Andrew Rothlisberger had been studying Spanish in Costa Rica and were due to arrive in Colombia several weeks before our family was due to leave on furlough. I wrote to them about the opportunity to establish a new work in Bucaramanga and strongly suggested they not delay their time in Cali after getting their documentation organized, and that Ann and I would return directly to Bucaramanga after our furlough. They arrived in Cali a short time before we were due to leave and I flew to Cali to meet our old friends and traveled with Andrew to Bucaramanga to meet the Santamaria family and see the city. Bucaramanga is a city at about 3,000 feet so it has much cooler weather than where Ann and I had spent our first three years. Andrew returned to Cali and, with his wife Anne, made plans to move to Bucaramanga. It was a great encouragement to see how God was continuously directing our steps.

The week before Ann, Diane and I were due to leave Puerto Boyacá for our furlough, one of the church leaders sent a message to the local radio station inviting any and all to come to our farewell meeting on the Sunday night. His intentions were good but the result was not. On Friday, the day following the radio announcement, a truck with six soldiers stopped at the front double gates to our compound and knocked at the private gateway to our apartment. When I opened the gate they told me I was under arrest and walked me to the gate where I had to climb up on the back of the truck. They took me to the local police station.

I was totally surprised and wondered what was happening. I entered the police station where there were two police and another man with them. The officer at the desk stated, "This man here claims that you hit his son with your vehicle and he now has eye trouble and needs $1,500 pesos for doctors' bills. This was about US $100.00. Now, I did have this with me as I needed it for our travel in preparation for leaving on the following Monday.

"I don't know what he is talking about; I haven't caused his son to have eye trouble." I replied.

"Well, if you don't give him the money, we will have to keep you here and you won't be able to leave on Monday," the policeman said.

Now this was obviously a scam and they knew they had me "over a barrel." To understand how problematic this was you have to realize that, in Colombia, it is always difficult to do anything easily. In order for our family to leave, I had to not only purchase the plane tickets to Australia and New Zealand and then back to Colombia, but I also needed official permission stamped in my passport from DAS, the department of Security. To get the latter, the nearest DAS office was at that time in Ibagué, five hours drive away. I had received their "stamp" of approval for the dates shown for our travel and missing our flights would really mess up everything. There was nothing I could do, so I handed over the money; no doubt the cop was getting his share. Obviously, I was nervous the rest of the weekend hoping that they wouldn't come back with more "requests."

Wonderful Refreshment and New Baby

We did get away on time and had an enjoyable, restful flight back to Sydney. The first stop was Los Angeles, then Honolulu and on to Sydney. My family and many church friends were at the airport to meet us so it wasn't long before we were back in our old home at Lane Cove West. We had a special welcome meeting at the North Ryde Church, one of our sending churches, and I had a slide show ready to present to them about what we had been doing over the past four-and-a-half years. Diane, wearing a colorful poncho, sang a couple of choruses in Spanish; I was wearing a poncho, one of the typical Colombian hats as well as having a machete in its scabbard on my belt.

Everyone made a real fuss over Diane, especially at the church Christmas tree event for the Sunday School children. I was booked to visit churches in Sydney over the next couple of weeks. Then we went to New Zealand to visit Ann's family and friends, and back to Sydney for more presentations. However, there was also time to just enjoy the summer days at the beaches, my old stomping grounds.

Together with my sister Norma and her husband John we set off to drive 2,000 miles north up to Cairns and the Great Barrier Reef. We were away nearly three weeks enjoying the country, the beautiful beaches all along the east coast of Australia, and visiting many of the tourist sights. There were also churches that were supporting us to visit where I was able to share what the Lord had been doing in Colombia, and our future plans to plant a church in Bucaramanga. Several churches were in the Cairns area, out among the sugar plantations. We also made some boat tours out on the Barrier Reef and spent a Day at Green Island swimming, snorkeling, sightseeing in the glass bottom boat, and checking out the crocodile farm. It was refreshing to be back home, even for a short time.

While in the Cairns area we were staying with some of the believers from one of our churches. One evening I had a phone call from my parents saying that the adoption agency had called to tell us that our little boy had been born. It was the 11th of April, my birth date and now also that of my new son, the best birthday present I had ever received! The agency had arranged for a responsible family to care for our new little boy, whom we called David Robert, until we arrived back in Sydney. Obviously we hurried back to Sydney, arriving there in four days to meet our new son.

David was a real character; his eyes followed us as he listened to our voices. His hair was blond, about two inches long, and sticking up in all directions. It was a real blessing for us all to have this lovely little fellow and he brought real joy into our lives.

Training During Furlough

While on our first furlough Ann and I decided to do a little more training for the mission field. We had seen many sick people, and some serious injuries, like machete cuts to the arms and even one on a man's head; amoebas were very common because of the drinking water, while malaria and yellow fever were rife in most of the country at altitudes lower than 2,500 feet.

We registered at the Sydney University for a four-week tropical medicine course that was designed for people moving to tropical areas of the world. Among our student group were diplomats, oil company personnel, a couple of missionaries, and a few businessmen. The classes were from 9:00 AM until Noon daily. Ann took copious notes that were much more detailed than I could do, so I just listened and asked questions from time to time. We learned about filarial, life threatening worms whose larvae are transmitted to humans via mosquito bites. These are found in some African waters and enter the bloodstream by biting the legs of people who were walking or working in the water. Other diseases affected the eyesight causing blindness, and amoebas were a major problem in most third world countries.

After a week at the University, I said to Ann, "I think I will go to the Royal North Shore Hospital to see if they can give me some help with suturing serious cuts, and giving injections." In Colombia, at that time, a prescription wasn't necessary to buy any medications or antibiotics carried by the pharmacy.

"Yes, it's worth a try, why don't you go to the E.R. where they deal with a lot of accidents?" Ann readily agreed.

I drove to the Emergency Room at the hospital and spoke to one of the interns, "G'day doctor, I'm a missionary to Colombia, South America and have been living in a jungle town the last three-and-a-half years. During that time I have seen machete cuts as well as many accidents where stitches were necessary; but the people just had to wrap their injuries themselves because the local town doctor or hospital was too far away. They don't bother with prescriptions in Colombia so I am able to purchase antibiotics and any sort of medicine. I could at least give these people first aid and maybe even save lives."

"Hang on mate; I'll take you to the supervising doctor to see what he says."

I was ushered into the supervising doctor's office. He was probably in his 40's although his hair was greying around the sideburns. I repeated the same story to him and also added that I was doing a tropical medicine course at the Sydney University.

"Why don't you come back here tonight, and every night at 6:00, as that's when things start to get busy? We'll see what we can do to give you some training. Okay?"

"Thanks doctor, you can be sure I'll be here."

When I returned at 5:50 PM this same supervising doctor was still there, along with about four interns who were treating the patients.

"Here, put on this lab coat," the doctor said, pointing to a number of white coats hanging in a small closet.

I donned this official-looking piece of medical uniform, which even had a stethoscope in the pocket that I never used, and then we walked out to talk with the interns. He called them over and told them, "Mr. Taylor is a missionary in Colombia, South America, and needs some training to be able to give injections, and some practice suturing bad cuts. Start him off with the injections and tell him about the different types. Then show him where and how to inject a patient. He needs some detailed instruction, so make sure he knows what he is doing, then let him get some practice. After he knows how to give the injections, then we'll start on the suturing."

With that he walked back to his office and the younger interns began questioning me about Colombia. They were probably my age or younger and very curious about what I had seen and done. I was just thirty-one at the time. Finally they said, "Just hang around and watch for a while and then we can get you some practice."

After observing the other doctors and nurses giving injections and being shown anatomical drawings identifying the sciatic

112

nerve and other places to avoid giving an injection, I was instructed to help a patient in the examination room. The nurse had prepared her for the necessary injection; I entered, told her, "Good evening, this won't take long," and administered the injection. I then instructed her to get dressed and come to the front desk. With that I walked out of the room and the doctor gave me a wink and thumbs- up.

The next week was spent watching people being sutured and learning all the fancy stitches. My notebook was filling up with drawings of these as well as types of medicines and antibiotics I might use in the tropics. With the aid of a *Merck Manual of Diagnosis and Therapy for identifying various illnesses* and a large Pharmaceutical Resource Guide from the doctor naming every type and dosage of drug and medication, I was feeling much more prepared to help those in need when we returned to Colombia.

On one occasion two Spanish-speaking families came to the emergency room because their children had some sort of rash. The doctors had been searching their manuals and could not come up with any information. As a last resort they came to me to take a look at the rash thinking I may have seen it somewhere. Since these people were Spanish- speaking, the doctors probably thought that I may have seen something similar. At least I could communicate with these families easily. One intern stated that he and the others didn't want to have to ask the supervising doctor, but rather diagnose it themselves.

As a matter of fact Ann, Diane and I had this type of rash as well not long before we left Colombia. But I did not tell the interns this; instead I held my chin for a couple of moments and seemed to be thinking about it. I then said, "It looks to me like Scabies. They will need to take a very hot bath, then scrub their skin with soap and a bristle brush. After that they will need to apply ointment, (I forget the name of it now!), then repeat this for two more days."

These interns looked at me like I was a fully trained doctor; one of them ran into the office and checked out my diagnosis only to come back telling the others that I was exactly right. We all had a laugh and then they prescribed the treatment and sent the family home.

After several weeks in the E.R., a lady came in with a little boy, about six or seven years old. He had fallen out of his bunk bed, which resulted in a two inch split in his skull.

The intern came out and told me, "I have a job for you. There's a little boy with a bad cut on his head; I want you to deal with it."

"Thanks," I replied, then looking at a nurse standing close by, I said to her, "Nurse, could you come with me, please? I will need some sutures and Novocain."

We both walked into the room; the little boy was lying on the bed, looking pretty sad and frightened. "Well, my boy, what have you been up to?" I asked. The lady, who I took to be his mother, was on the other side of the bed. "He fell out of his bed and landed on a wooden block. He obviously needs a few stitches," she stated.

"Let's see what we need to do, " I said to the boy. "Well, that's not too bad is it? We'll fix that up before you know it."

"What's your name, son?" I asked.

"Rodney," was the tearful answer.

"Nurse, I will need to cut away some of the hair around the wound. Could you get me the scissors, please."

She brought the scissors. I carefully trimmed the long hair around the cut, then swabbed the area with alcohol to disinfect it. While working I continued talking to the little boy, especially while I was injecting the Novocain around the cut to deaden the area. "Do you play cricket?" I asked.

"Yes, Doctor, I play at school."

"Well, that's good. Are you a batter or bowler?" I asked, as I began to start suturing.

"I like to bat, but some of the other kids are better than me."

"Well, you are going to be a great bowler when I have finished with you because you will have a six-stitcher in your head."

For you folk who don't know anything about cricket, a six-stitcher is the type of ball used in cricket. It is just as hard and a bit larger than a baseball. It is a red ball with six rows of stitches around the circumference.

The little boy had a huge grin on his face. We talked a little more about cricket and then the job was done.

"There you are. It's all done now and don't forget, you have a six-stitcher that none of the other boys will ever have."

The lady who brought him in then spoke up, "Doctor I want to thank you for the way you handled this. I'm Rodney's aunt, and a nurse. I've seen many doctors working with kids, and none were ever as good as you. Thank you for chatting with him and calming him."

"Thank you for saying that. Bring him back in six days to get the stitches out. Have a good night."

It seemed the Lord had given me another talent of which I was completely unaware, "acting!" Thankfully, there was not much call for my services in the medical field when in Colombia, but the knowledge of helpful drugs was useful.

After that "training" the supervisor took me to the operating theater to witness surgery. Also he showed me firsthand how to find a vein for administering injections. "I wanted you to learn that, as you may have to give someone an I.V. (intravenous injection) sometime," the surgeon explained. From there I was taken to the maternity ward to observe deliveries of new life, created by God, in human babies. By now, Ann and I had completed the tropical medicine course and she had a notebook full of notes and my notebook full of treatments and drawings. Before I left, the doctor handed me a packet that contained a good selection of medical tools. Just a week later I finished my most enjoyable four weeks of "medical school" at the RNS Hospital.

Note to readers: I realize that in this day of "modern" medicine, and sophisticated legal requirements, what I was allowed to do at this Sydney hospital is quite unorthodox and would never be allowed today. However, at that time, God opened the way for us to receive very practical training for no charge. Practical first aid information is necessary to anyone who will be far from modern facilities and should be considered part of the missionary training program.

The Dental Hospital

The next week, following my "medical" training, I had a dental appointment for myself. In-between moments of having a pipe sucking air and saliva from my mouth, I told the dentist about my experience at the Hospital.

His reply was something I had not expected.

"I'm the director of the Dental Hospital where we train students for dentistry. I'm sure in a third world country there are many rotting teeth. If you like, I can set up a couple of days for you to come to the dental hospital and teach you how to pull teeth."

"That would really round off my medical training," I said. "What days will you be there?"

After checking his calendar, we agreed on the days I should come for observation. I arrived on time the first morning. The doctor first showed me a skull to learn where to administer the block needle to numb the jaw. After this he acquainted me with the various tools used in dentistry.

The students in the four-year course were working with patients who came for free dental work. Alongside were the instructors checking their work. At 11:00 AM, on my first morning, a lady came in and looking around came over to me. "Doctor, I would appreciate it if you could work on me as I'm scared that the students might do something wrong." She was about 40 years old and mistook me for one of the instructors. My dentist friend winked at me and nodded his head for me to agree.

"Yes, certainly. Could you go to that chair over there?" My friend had already indicated which chair to use.

I set her up with a heavy bib up to her chin, then put the suction pipe in her mouth and had a look inside her mouth. It wasn't hard to see which tooth was the problem on her jaw. The dentist handed me a syringe. I gauged where the nerve I was supposed to hit would be, then proceeded to inject. She jumped with fright. She would have jumped higher had she known who was sticking her!

Thankfully all went well, and with the dentist directing me, I gingerly wiggled the tooth back and forth and pulled it out. After placing the gauze compact in the hole and wiping her chin, I told her the job was done.

As she was leaving, she came to me and said, "Oh thank you doctor doing that for me, I feel so much better about it!"

I felt like saying, *"You have no idea, lady, I was probably more nervous than you were after my two hours of study and graduation from dental school!"* But I just nodded as she left and headed for the door.

Once again, I was given a complete set of dental tools and information, which would be of help to me.

I gave many injections over the years in Colombia and pulled a few teeth. Frequently I referred to my Merck Manual and the book of drugs, deciding which medicines and ointments I should recommend to someone. This made me always thankful for the help given at the hospital and dental school.

The way all these opportunities came together reinforced my faith in the One who is certainly in control. God provided the most elementary training for Ann and me, which could be useful and a great help to believers, while also giving openings to reach the lost with the Gospel.

P.S. The only sutures I gave in Colombia were to my dog after he was shot on the snout. I numbed him and stitched him up, so I did get to practice at least once.

Pescadero - Part of the main highway between Bucaramanga and Bogotá.

10

BUCARAMANGA

Returning From Furlough

Having enjoyed a wonderful time of refreshment visiting family, friends, and churches along with the joy of receiving our newborn son, we were ready to return to our mission work in Colombia. We believed we were ready to be the sharpened arrow God would use in His work.

Departing Sydney on September 8, 1972 we waved to the large crowd of family and friends who came to see us off. Thankfully, David slept all the way to Fiji where we stopped for two days, finally alone as a family after the busy time in Australia and New Zealand. For two days we spent time on the beach and in the tourist hotel; this was a blessing for us.

Travel as a missionary is often not only one flight directly to a destination, as there are people who may wish to hear of the work you are doing or encourage you along the way. So, leaving Fiji, we boarded the plane for the long trip to the USA, via Honolulu, going through customs in the early morning; then on to Los Angeles, and then changing planes for New York. Gus Kaschel had asked us to visit him in New Jersey on our way back to Colombia, which was the reason for our taking this route. He was involved in a missionary financial fund and wanted to hear first-hand the news about our work and the missionaries in Colombia. While there, we met numerous helpful people, were taken sightseeing in and around New York City, and had many encouraging conversations. While there I received a call from Andrew Rothlisberger telling me that he had been able to rent a home for us, which was on the same street and opposite his house in Bucaramanga. This was one of those experiences where we could see the Lord working for us. I told Ann and the lady of the house where we were visiting, then exclaiming, "Isn't that just like the Lord, to work things out so perfectly for us?"

The flight to Bogotá was uneventful and my cousin Bill Corson (who was also a missionary in Colombia with WEC, World Evangelization Crusade) and his wife Joy, along with Peter and Annemarie Nunn were there to meet us. We stayed with Bill and his family that night, leaving on an early morning flight to Bucaramanga the next day.

Andrew and Anne Rothlisberger were at the airport to meet us and took us to their home. They had been busy working with children in the neighborhood where they lived and had been able to get together a number of these street kids to come into the garage for a Bible class. Having our home opposite to theirs was very beneficial. We would be able to work with them using our garage also for the children's work.

During those first couple of years in Bucaramanga before the first church had been establish, we had gotten to know many missionaries from different denominations and often had fellowship with them. One such family became very close. John and Donna Duckhorn lived just around the corner from us and just about every Thursday morning we got together for coffee and to talk about the work in which we were both involved. They were from a different branch of the Plymouth Brethren and so we sometimes discussed the differences that we had heard about each other's fellowships. As it soon became obvious, we were really both on the "same page" and there was no real reason when we couldn't have full fellowship together. I would one day be living in the same state in the USA and we would be able to have a warm and closer fellowship than we even had in Colombia.

Need For A Church Building

Later that month, Jorge Ocampo, who was a truck driver by trade, arrived with all our furniture and goods from Puerto Boyacá. We settled in fairly quickly and it wasn't long before we also had many children coming to our garage Sunday School classes each

120

Sunday morning. Between the Rothlisbergers and our house we had more than 80 children attending the classes in our garages. Also the Sunday evening meeting attendance had grown to 70 people with about half that number being children. It was obvious that we really needed a large meeting room where we could begin church meetings. So we began looking for land.

Over the next few months Ann and I, along with Andrew and Anne, met together every Thursday morning for prayer. The need for the church building along with the many details we thought were necessary for the outreach work were high on our prayer list. We had many conversations about the types of things we would need

Sunday School class in our garage

for the new church building. Often we would follow up on some possible site, only to find that the land had been sold, or that local laws governing construction prohibited the building of a church on the lot. This, of course, was quite frustrating to us. However, God answered our prayer when one block of land, not far from where we lived, became available in November 1972, for $8,000. Much time was spent organizing all the legal paperwork, and on November 18, we were finally able to purchase the property. It was a good-sized space being fifty-nine feet wide and eighty-eight feet deep in an area suitable for outreach where we were already working. Once again, God proved faithful.

Our time was more than filled with keeping the church meetings going, along with finding and purchasing the land. One night Andrew and I were together at my house discussing the building project and he finally left at 10:00 PM. But right after he was gone there was a knock at the door. A man by the name of Mario P. was standing there. We had been counseling him because of his irresponsible ways, but he had eventually decided to straighten out. His wife and children were steadfast believers living for the Lord but his life had really been a mess. I invited him in and he sat down on the couch.

"Well," I said, "Qué hay de nuevo," ("What's new?") a normal greeting!

"It's just that I have committed some errors and I have come to confess them to you." The Catholic background gives people the idea that sin has to be confessed to a priest, or in this case, a missionary.

"That won't do you much good, because I can't forgive your sin, only God can do that. And if you're not prepared to repent and confess to God, then there's nothing I can do," I replied.

"Listen, I have done some very silly things, and I'm a mess," he went on.

"Oh, really?"

"Look, I have come here because there isn't another person in the world who can help me and if you can't help me, I'll leave here and do away with myself." At this stage the tears were flowing freely and I was rather skeptical about it all as he was half drunk.

As the story unfolded I found out that he had taken some Swiss watches that I had given him to be sold to provide money for his family. But instead he pawned the watches, gambled on pool games and was now in debt. Of course the debtor was demanding payment, which he did not have. Neither did he have money for his family. I was becoming very annoyed and concerned about how to help him.

"Please brother Juan, help me; it can be just between us. We won't tell Andrew or my wife or anyone, you can help me please do so," he pleaded.

"How much do you owe?"

"We-e-ell I lost $900 pesos."

"Ay, Ay, Ay. Tan estúpido! Last Wednesday you didn't have

the $30 pesos to get a health certificate for a new job. Where did the money come from? Have you still got the watches? Don't tell me you sold the watches and then gambled it away on Billiards!!! "What's become of the watches I gave you?"

"Well, I pawned all of them and got 400 pesos for them and one of the players is holding the others until I can pay the 300 pesos I owe him. You've got to help me or they will cart me off to jail. The guy holding the watches is looking for me. If I can't give him back the watches or the money, he'll have me arrested."

"When did you start drinking? I asked.

"Only this afternoon, things look so black that I didn't know what to do, and I guess the devil got in."

I didn't know whether he was serious about killing himself or not, as he had made one attempt before he was "converted" and I didn't want the responsibility of a suicide on my hands or conscience.

About that time Ann brought out some coffee and then retired to the kitchen.

"Drink some coffee, Mario, I have to do some thinking. I frankly don't know what to do."

After some time I suggested, "Look I'll tell you what I'm prepared to do. I will pay the 160 pesos tonight, but on the condition that you accompany me home and confess everything to your wife."

"But what about the other 300 pesos? If I cannot fix that up I might as well finish it all."

"Look, I told you I cannot use the Lord's money for this sort of thing."

He just shrugged his shoulders and looked sadder than ever.

"I don't know; I'll have to talk to my wife Ann about it all. We share in everything and if it's a matter of this sort of money, Ann has to know about it and also decide with me what to do."

"Okay talk to her and I will be forever grateful to you if you can help."

I called to Ann and we decided to talk it over. What swayed us was the uncertainty of his threat to commit suicide. We were primarily concerned for his wife and the children.

"Well, Ann has agreed, but we want you to know that it is for Beatrice's sake that we do it. She is going on well and has suffered a lot for what you have done, so it's for her that we are prepared to help. And remember that this is the last time we will ever use the Lord's money to help in this way. If it happens again you are on your own. There doesn't seem to be any accuracy about the amounts you mention so I will only give you 300 pesos."

"Aye, hermano, muchas gracias, you don't know how much you have helped me and I won't ever forget it," said Mario, now crying with emotion.

I went upstairs and got the 300 pesos then put my pistol in my belt and set off. We were going to a pretty bad part of town and I still wasn't sure about Mario. He was half drunk and could've been setting me up for anything. That's why I took the pistol.

As we got near the place where Mario's "friend" was waiting, I took the safety off the pistol and when he got out of the car to get his friend I took the pistol out of the holster and had it on my lap.

This was in a very rough section of the city. A young fellow came out of the dive, which was a billiard saloon and cantina, or a grog shop. He wasn't more than 24, but obviously a professional billiard player, or at least the type who hangs around these kind of joints.

He held out a piece of paper. "Give me the 310 pesos and here's your receipt," he grunted. I noticed he had added another 10 pesos.

Mario hadn't come out. "Where's Mario?" I asked. "Tell him to come out to see that I am paying you off, or the deal is off."

He went back inside to get Mario. I thought he may have tried to disappear at this point, but I was making sure he didn't get away again.

"Hop in the car, Mario," I directed, and as soon as I had paid the young gambler I accelerated off with Mario in the car.

"Okay let's get you home, it's now 12:15 AM and late enough."

"What about my briefcase with the other watches in it? They are in the hotel?"

"Well, I haven't got any more money to pay a hotel bill," I said, "And as you thought they were safe enough to leave them there all day while you wasted your time playing billiards, they can stay another night and you can collect them in the morning."

I think he was getting cold feet about facing his wife. Not wanting that to happen, I took off at top speed and was at his front door before he had time to think of an excuse to get out of it.

When we reached his house his 21-year-old son opened the door. He and his 19-year-old sister were studying for their university exams. They were about as surprised as I was when I first saw Mario. They woke their mother, Beatrice, who came to the front room. "Well, what have you been up to?" she asked Mario with a "Good grief" look on her face.

"I've committed some errors, mi amor, and Juan has been able to help me out. I want you to forgive me. I was overcome by the mountains of problems that I had," he stated.

Mario went on to explain that he had not been unfaithful but had gambled the money away. Beatrice was understandably unhappy, explaining that even their nine-year-old daughter was asking why her daddy did not come home. You can imagine how the conversation continued.

Finally I broke in and told him that Beatrice had every reason to cry and be upset. I followed by reminding him that if he had been following the studies we had in Ephesians the other night about a husband being a responsible head of the home, there would not be this problem.

Beatrice was able to forgive him and I left for home after 1:00 AM. Ann was waiting for me, not knowing what was going on, and she was concerned for my safety. The next day I took Mario to the hockshop, redeemed the watches and got the whole problem cleared up. Mario seemed to be very repentant and went to the job he had started just before his disappearance.

Purchase of Land for new chapel

November 18 was a very exciting day, what with the purchase of the land for the new chapel, and then the midnight fun.

Because we had included our thoughts for a suitable building in our newsletters, many had been praying for us. When they knew of this desire to build it was not long before some funds began to come so that we were able to begin the project.

Andrew and I made contact with an architect who was able to draw up some plans for the good-sized building we planned; not only to have a large space for the church meetings, but also a number of Sunday School rooms. Also there were plans for a kitchen we would eventually be needed for conferences, as well as a garage. We had included in the plans a sound and projection room at the back of the hall, and at the front a large area for a new bookshop on one side and an apartment for a caretaker on the other side.

Before we had the chapel bookshop I had hired someone to make a display stand where I displayed books and a few Bibles. This stand was put in the very front window of our house so that those passing by in the street could see the books. It wasn't long before many people were coming to our door looking for Christian

Bookstand in our home -front window

literature, so I purchased more books and Bibles and began to build up the stock to be ready for the new bookshop in the Chapel. It was obvious that there was a need for a good bookshop in Bucaramanga.

A man by the name of Edmundo heard that I had some books and Bibles so he came to see what I had and bought a Scofield Bible. He told me he had a friend who would be interested and a few days later brought the friend to see our small supply. After some talks about doctrine, Edmundo decided to come to our little garage Sunday School the following Sunday. He came with his wife who was about half his age, and three daughters aged eleven, eight and six. He appreciated our teaching of New Testament principles and invited us to take over a Sunday School work he was involved with in a new suburb in Provenza where he lived. We went there for the children's Bible classes the following Saturday and found about

126

38 children present. He also came with his family to our weeknight prayer meeting as well as the Sunday night gospel meeting bringing the total adults to 11. We were already beginning to see some progress. And in mid-October there were three people ready for baptism, one of whom was Sra. Moreno. She was a very poor lady with eight children who all lived in a hovel just out of the suburb. We had buried her seven-year-old daughter the week after we arrived in Bucaramanga, but she had come to know the Lord as her Savior and Guide.

By the end of December we had received a quote from the architect for the building of the chapel, which would be US $20,000 to $25,000. Andrew and I again made known the needs for this construction in our newsletters and soon funds began to come from churches and individuals in many countries. The need for a suitable building was becoming more and more urgent as the group of believers was growing, for which we were most thankful.

The Neighbor - Alan Tonkin

Around mid-year 1973 I had made contact with Alan Tonkin, a neighbor in his late 20s, who lived in one of the apartments just a block away. He was an Englishman who was teaching electronics at the university in Bucaramanga, working with CUSO, Canadian Universities Overseas (similar to the Peace Corps). He had a large black dog, which he walked past our house nearly every day. Eventually we learned from neighbors who had spoken with him that he made disparaging remarks about "these missionaries," and stating that they should give up trying to change the culture of the Colombians. He would say "hello," as he passed us sometimes, but we did not get into conversation with him very much at that time.

Ann and I had studied Spanish in Costa Rica with Heidi Reimer, a Christian missionary who had become the director for CUSO and living in Bogotá. We had planned for her to visit us but had somehow lost her phone number.

"I guess I'd better go and visit this guy up the street and ask if he has her number. I hope we don't get into an argument!"

Ann laughed and sent me off saying, "Watch out! He's bigger than you!"

Laughing with her as I walked out the front door I called back,

"Don't worry; I can probably run faster than him!"

He lived on the third floor and when I knocked he invited me in. He was very friendly, offered me a drink and found Heidi's phone number. He then went on to "interrogate" me.

"So why are you here in Colombia? What sort of work do you do? Are you just working in Bucaramanga?"

I answered his questions, asked about his work, and then after I had mentioned that every now and again I went back down into the jungle areas to visit believers and small churches there, he surprised me with, "I want to go with you the next time you go to the jungle. I've never been to the jungle and I want to see it."

How do I put this guy off? I certainly didn't want this sort of person tagging along. He swore like a sailor, having learned from his university students all the current swear words in Spanish. I could imagine him with some of the simple jungle believers letting fly with a string of words that they had given up when they got saved! They would look at me and wonder what sort of missionary was visiting them and what sort of company did I keep!

"Look, you wouldn't really be interested, because everywhere I go I will be conducting Bible studies, talking about the Christian life, counseling people about their spiritual problems and holding meetings every night."

"Don't worry, mate! I'll just block my ears and won't have to listen to all that stuff!"

I tried everything I could to dissuade him, "The temperature will be up to 115° (Fahrenheit.) We will have to tramp sometimes 6 hours at times in really difficult circumstances, ...there are communist guerrillas in that area..." Nothing worked! He just insisted on coming with me!

About that time, (I guess it was that "still small voice," of God) the thought came into my mind, maybe the Lord wants this no-hoper fellow to go with me so that he can hear the gospel. The Lord was using this arrow to strike Alan's heart to bring him to salvation.

"OK! I'll let you know when I have a trip planned. You will need to get a pack for all your stuff. Be sure to pack a light single air mattress, unless you want to sleep on the earthen floor with the snakes and other night creatures! Also, get a good mosquito net, unless you want to get malaria or yellow fever; a can of mosquito

128

spray, and snacks, as you probably won't want to eat monkey or snake meat."

Even with all of that information he still wanted to go along so I just said a little prayer, "Lord, he's in your hands! Help me!"

A few weeks later we set out and drove to Barrancabermeja, a city on the Magdalena River. From there we were able to board a train to head south to a town called Carare. The train could have been something out of an old Wild West movie from the USA. The carriages were very old, with wrought iron railings at the front and back of each carriage.

Alan's first culture shock happened in a hurry as we entered the carriage. People were mostly from the country and jungle areas. Some were carrying a small pig, or chickens, even a goat. The place smelled of sweat and dirty clothing, so we opted to stand on the small platform outside for most of the two-hour ride. We finally arrived at the Carare station. With our packs on our back and our machetes on our belts we went to the thatch-roofed home of a believer who had a small shop with a very small inventory of a couple of bags of potatoes, yucca, rice, coffee and some soft drinks. He offered us some Coca Cola and after chatting for a half hour or so, directed us to the trail that leads to another town some three-hours walk into the jungle.

Alan and I headed out of town but as we approached the trail to go to Capote, a farmer with an old tractor came chugging along heading in that general direction. He invited us to, "Hop on!" We were able to stand on the back with one foot on a small jutting part of the tractor and rode with him for about 40 minutes. This saved us quite a lot of time and we are really thankful for the ride. The farmer went off on another trail and Alan and I continued on a track that got narrower as the jungle around us became denser. We were talking about the different types of bushes, vines and huge trees that had canopies so thick very little sun reached the ground. However, this only made the sweltering heat and humidity more intense. At one point a man came off a sidetrack that led onto this main trail. As he walked along we noticed he had a string in his hand and something on the other end. It was a python about 10 or 12 feet long; Alan was totally freaked out.

"What's he doing with that snake?"

Anal Tonkin encounters a snake in the jungle

Remembering how Alan used to walk his dog down our street I replied, "Oh, he's just walking his snake."

It took him a few seconds to realize I was pulling his leg and then
wanted me to take a photo of him pulling out his machete as though
he was going to do battle with the serpent. The man was either

going to sell the snake at the town or take it somewhere to skin, which he would sell.

We eventually arrived at Capote and found Rafael Rodrigues' house. He gave us a royal welcome in his usual ebullient style, invited us to eat the evening meal with him and told us to get ready for the evening meeting he held in his home. At about 6:30 the people began to arrive and it wasn't long before we were singing some of the hymns in the Hymns of Faith and Praise book. The tempo was slow and the melody in a minor key which lent a sorrowful tone. I had the message for about an hour, then the attendees had a cup of hot chocolate and after about 40 minutes of chatting, they all left. Alan and I inflated our air mattresses in one of the spare rooms where we slept on the floor with our mosquito nets protecting us from the air-born invasion.

The next day we set off for Puerto Parra where there was a small farm with a family of believers. Very soon we were once again deep into jungle, up and down hills and crossing creeks and ravines on fallen tree trunks. That was when I learned that Alan was afraid to stand up on a log and walk across a ditch or creek. He would go on hands and knees, afraid of falling. We reached another creek, but there was no tree trunk or really narrow spot for us to get across.

"How can we get over this one?" Alan asked.

"Were you in the Boy Scouts?" I asked.

"No, I never did get into that."

"Well, what you have to do is go find a long fairly strong branch, or small tree, pull out your machete and cut it down, trim the pole and then we will pole vault over the creek."

"How do you do that?"

With that he went off and cut an eight-foot pole.

Taking the pole in my hands and holding it as though I was a pole vaulting champion, I gave a short run, then went through the action of jumping, and said, "Now, go back and run toward the creek, I will put my foot here where there is solid ground, you will place the pole in the center of the creek and jump from the spot where I have my foot, using the pole to carry you to the other side."

So Alan went back a suitable amount of space, and with his large pack on his back started his run towards the creek and my foot marking the last solid ground before the marshy ground and the creek. With the pole pointed toward the middle of the creek, he began his jump just as my foot lifted a little and he "unfortunately" tripped and landed face down in the mud and slime of the swampy area of the creek.

You can imagine the laughing at the sight of this six-foot some-thing, giant of a fellow getting up on his knees with the mud of the creek all over him. We were pretty hot and tired at that point and hadn't showered since we left Bucaramanga, so we both stripped off and laying our jeans and packs on the far bank of the creek, we sat in the creek and washed our bodies and shirts and cooled off. Putting on our wet clothes, we enjoyed the cool feeling as we con-tinued on, but that didn't last long as our clothes were dry in about a half hour.

A short time later, as we were nearing Puerto Parra, we heard a number of explosions. Puerto Parra at that time was an area where the FARC (revolutionary guerrillas) were known to be active. I told Alan that the explosions were either the guerrillas practicing how to make and explode bombs, or the Colombian Air Force were bomb-ing the guerrillas. I suggested that if we heard a fighter plane or chopper going over we should hit the deck as both of us had dark beards and could be thought to be guerrillas. I was just trying to put some fear into this unbelieving pagan!

We finally arrived at the farmhouse of the family we were visiting who warmly received us and showed us where we could leave our packs. The home was one large room about 12 feet square, divided into a sleeping and living area, with an outside kitchen under a lean-to shelter out from the thatch roof of the house. The floors were dirt; the walls were made of 1-inch thick-stripped branches tied together with vines and rope. Off to one side was a stand made from six poles in the ground supporting a platform about eight feet long by six feet wide, used to keep any corn or produce they had farmed five feet off the ground out of the reach of the jungle animals. It was also covered with a thatch roof.

Emilio, who owned the little farm, took the bags of corn down from the platform, so that we could have some space off the ground to sleep while there. We inflated our small air mattresses, set them up on the stand with our packs and set up the mosquito nets so that we wouldn't have to do this in the dark later. When we finally got up there on our air mattresses at night, we had a very unusual balancing act to be able to sleep. The thin poles holding us up swayed every time we moved, and when one of us turned over we felt like we were on a ship at sea. At least we were up off the ground out of the reach of snakes and other nocturnal creatures.

The next day, these very poor folk provided a lunch of some rice and corn from their very meager store of food. They only had four plates, a couple of pots and pans and prepared the food over their open air stove. This "stove" was comprised of a table-stand with the

Alan down for the night in our Jungle "Hotel"

surface surrounded by a six-inch wooden border and filled with dirt on which they burned firewood. Alan was really impressed with the love and care they showed us.

After lunch we set out with a couple of other men and women to another believer's nearby farm where we would have the evening meeting. When we arrived, there was a group of about 20 people and they had killed a small pig, which they roasted over an open fire pit near the house. Our visit was a real celebration; they didn't get too many visitors out in that jungle area. These farmers had hacked out some land with their machetes and were cultivating corn, platano (plantain), and yuca, along with papaya and other fruits.

As the sun was setting around 6:30 PM, we had all eaten, drank panela water or coffee and were ready to start the meeting. One of the men had a guitar and with our hymnbooks, "Fe y Alabanza" open, we sang for about an hour, then it was time to preach. The meeting room was an open area covered with a thatch roof, no walls. For light there were a number of cans with wicks and fed by oil, together with a number of candles scattered around among the folk sitting on planks of rough-dressed timber made into primitive benches.

I wasn't going to let Alan off the hook; he had said he could close his ears to my preaching, so I invited him to come up and hold the candle so that I could read my Bible as I spoke. As you can imagine there were literally thousands of bugs flying around our heads and the candle only attracted more. I had to be careful how to breathe and not inhale a few mosquitoes, moths or whatever else was cruising by. Alan on the other hand was swatting bugs and at the same time switching hands as the wax from the candle ran down onto his fingers. He was mumbling quietly under his breath and I was thankful nothing profane was forthcoming! I spoke for about an hour, normal time in a jungle church; they sometimes expected an even longer message. We sat around talking, answering questions, and just having great fellowship. The hosts served hot chocolate with arepas, a great evening snack.

Around 10:00 PM, together with three other men from that area, we set off to walk for about a half hour back to the farm where we would spend the night on our lofty platform bed. Each one of us had a flashlight, which was really necessary as the trail was very narrow at times with mud holes and slippery slopes beside the trail. At one point along the trail, as we walked through a very tall thick grassy area, the track became even more narrow. The grass was shoulder high and we were all in line with our flashlights on the path and on the person in front. Alan brought up the rear as we traversed that area and the men, who had by that time come to realize that the tall "gringo" had no idea about the jungle, started to talk loudly enough for Alan to hear.

"You have to be careful with the snakes at night. They seem to be attracted to the light!"

Alan's flashlight went out!

A couple of minutes later the other man answered, "Yes, but it's much worse if you don't see one and tread on it!"

Alan's flashlight went on again! The men had quite a few laughs at Alan's expense in the next few minutes as we continued on the path. I thought I would also try something, so as Alan was on his hands and knees crawling across a log over a deep ditch, I called out, "Look out there's a snake on the log!" Alan promptly fell off the log and into the bushes under it! Fortunately, we did make it back to the family farm where we would spend the night. It was difficult to sleep as we were rocking and rolling so much we wondered if the whole stand would come crashing down. Nevertheless, we made it until morning without any real problems.

The next day we made the five-hour walk back to the train stop, arriving hot and tired. We sat in a very large covered area where there was a kiosk to buy drinks. To quench out thirst we bought several warm bottles of Coca Cola and just sat resting while we waited for the train. I happened to notice that some soldiers were appearing. Two were off to the left at the corner of the building, then a couple more were behind us and I also noticed a couple on the other side of the building. I said quietly in English to Alan, "Listen carefully. Keep your hands on the table; don't grab anything out of your pack; and do not do anything sudden. We have just been surrounded by the army. Act naturally and pretty soon an officer or sergeant will come up to us and ask for our Identification papers." With our black beards we looked like a couple of revolutionary guerrillas just come out of the jungle!

Sure enough a lieutenant came up behind us; then came to one side asking for our papers. After looking at our ID's he asked, "What are you doing in these parts?"

"I'm a missionary and we have visited some Christians and churches near Carare and Puerto Parra," I responded.

"Where are you from?"

"He's from England, and I'm originally from Australia."

"Australia, that's interesting, I was in Sydney last year. I sailed on the Colombian navy sailing ship GLORIA to Australia and I really enjoyed it there."

That was the beginning of a conversation that went on for an hour talking about what I was doing in Colombia and about Australia. Thankfully this fellow thought Australia was a fun place but it was also God's protection of a situation that could have been difficult.

Eventually the train arrived and Alan and I boarded for the trip back to Barrancabermeja. We were again on the platform outside the last carriage enjoying the cooler air. That was when Alan asked the really significant question, "I can't understand why these poor people in the jungle - who have nothing, hardly enough food, no real commodities - seem to be so happy. Why is that?"

That was like a barn door wide open for me to talk about God's love for them! "They have the Lord Jesus as Savior and know that their sins are forgiven and they have the security of going to heaven one day," I answered. This conversation continued all the way home in the train and the two-hour car ride home. What he may not have understood in Spanish, he certainly understood in English. As we parted, back home in Bucaramanga, he said, "You have given me a lot to think about. Can we talk again some time?"

"You are always welcome to come to our home any time," I responded.

"Thanks mate; I'll take you up on that." Then before he left for his house I handed him a Bible from our bookshelf and told him he needed to read God's Word; which was important to know who God is.

Now I also had a lot to think about. I had tried my hardest to not take Alan with me, but it was obvious the Lord was working in this pagan's heart and I, the missionary, had almost rejected one of the Lord's opportunities. I felt both bad about what I had almost done, but truly excited about what God was doing in Alan's life. On a following visit he asked, "How can I know there really is a God?"

"God is really there and He wants you to know Him. You need to pray and I suggest you ask Him for something that you really need and then wait to see how He answers that prayer. Is there something that you really need?" I asked.

"Well, since my wife left me, the apartment I am renting is too expensive on just my wage, so I'd like something smaller and cheaper."

"OK, we won't tell anyone else about this, but you and I will pray that the Lord will get you something cheaper, deal?"

"How do you pray? I don't know how."

"Think about it like talking on the phone. You can't see the person you are talking to, but you are able to express your thoughts to that

136

person. Praying to God is just like that."

He went off and the next day came back when I asked him "Did you pray?"

"Well, I got on my knees and started, 'God, are you there? This is Al calling. I don't know if you can hear me or if you are listening, but I want to know if you were really there or not. You know that I need a smaller apartment. Can you arrange something?'"

It was hard not to laugh, but I congratulated him on starting a prayer life.

Two days later Alan came to the door and very excited began, "You won't believe this! I was helping some Peace Corps people move into their apartment last night and when we had finished moving all their stuff upstairs to their apartment, they said, 'You know there is a maid's room on the roof that we won't be using. It has a small bedroom, bath and a small cooking area; you can have it for $10 a month if you like.' I hadn't said anything to them about praying for something smaller, what a coincidence!"

I quickly replied, "There are no coincidences with God. Didn't we agree to ask God to reveal Himself by answering your prayer? Well, God is real and He has answered our prayer."

Alan, with tears in his eyes said, "How can I fight against a God like that?" That afternoon Alan received the Lord Jesus as his Savior and Lord and we became "brothers" in the family of God.

"By the way, how is the Bible reading coming along?" I asked.

"Well I was reading in Genesis and it became a bit boring, so I started reading in Revelation to see how the story would end! There's a lot I don't understand and maybe you can explain it to me." That was the beginning of several months of Bible study in Revelation, prophecy, and all sorts of basic doctrinal matters, which was really a very intense discipleship.

Alan grew rapidly and it wasn't long before he wanted to be baptized. He did not want to be baptized in the new chapel in Bucaramanga, but rather in the jungle where he had come to know the Lord. By that time we had been in several country and jungle areas visiting believers, and so on a visit in a country area just North of Cúcuta, there were a couple of young people in a family we had been visiting who wanted to be baptized. That same day Alan was baptized in a small creek, taking yet another important step in his

Christian growth.

Very soon Alan wanted to teach Sunday School but as I felt he wasn't ready for that just yet, he and I started a children's outreach work in a suburb of Bucaramanga, called Ciudad Valencia. We drove around the suburb with loud speakers inviting children to the local park. Then with about 50 children sitting on the grass behind the Jeep, Alan gave his first class, telling the gospel story to

Baptism La Silla, Alan Tonkin was next

the children. As he continued to grow in his faith and knowledge of the Bible he helped me with this outreach as well as participating in the local church.

Because of Alan, I learned valuable lessons about using every opportunity God puts in front of me (and all of us) to present the gospel and teach the Word of God. Alan was educated and a thinker, he asked many, many questions about what the Bible means, how Christians should live, and why. Also, he would not take the often-used answer, "Well it's just the way we do things." Oh no, I had to produce chapter and verse, which was a tremendous exercise for me to have a scriptural reason for everything I believe. This is the way God would expect us to defend our faith. I thank the Lord for sending Alan to my door.

A couple of years

Alan Tonkin, back row after his baptism

later, Alan returned to England, married an Australian girl and moved to the city of Melbourne, Australia. He became involved in the local church there along with other activities, and even directed a youth camp on several occasions. He continues to follow the Lord to this day.

Missionary Work Continues During Construction

While the plans for building were going on I made several visits to the jungle area of Carare, as well as El Cerro. This was an area where several Christian families were living with whom we had come in contact, and who needed Bible teaching. On a couple

Alan teaching Sunday School - La Silla

of occasions Alan Tonkin, by then a true believer, accompanied me to El Cerro. The trip began with driving over the eastern range of the Andes and over Picacho, which is the highest mountain near Bucaramanga. It is 35 miles from Bucaramanga, reaching a height of 11,155 feet. Starting at Bucaramanga the drive is dramatic as the 35-mile climb begins immediately with continuous curves, winding to the top and then actually crossing the top of Picacho. The drive continues across a tabletop area for about 40 miles at about 10,000 ft. This is a great farming area for growing onions and potatoes because of the cold climate. There are also many sheep grazing in that area. Continuing on, the road begins to descend down the other side of the Andes eventually to the large frontier city of Cúcuta. We took with us the Bell and Howell 16 mm projector and several gospel films that we would show in the El Cerro area, another hour's travel from Cúcuta. The believers had built a chapel out in the country area with a thatch roof and mud walls. We had some meetings there and screened the gospel films in the nearby village.

On one trip, in February 1973, we had a very interesting time at El Cerro. One lady professed faith at the evening meeting. She was a "granny" and since she was getting her life straightened out she was thinking about finally getting married! The following day we walked a long way to the river to baptize five people. On the way there and back, I drank a lot of water as the heat and the long walk aggravated my thirst. Well, you can imagine the result. I had a very bad time and had run out of toilet paper. Thankfully I had some pills to stop the trots, which eventually helped. Such are the rigors of missionary life.

That night there were not any mosquitoes and since I was alone in the mud walled chapel, I decided not to use my mosquito net. At 3:00 AM I was awakened by something flapping near my neck. I whacked it away only to find it was pretty heavy, too heavy for a moth. Grabbing my flashlight I swung it around until I spotted the creature. It was a vampire bat about as big as a dove! They often go for the jugular vein which can be life-threatening; and are dangerous, not only because of the bite, but because they can carry rabies. I immediately put up my mosquito net. The next day I was told there were many of these bats around that area. They often drink the blood of the cows and sometimes bite the toes of sleeping people. Their teeth are so sharp, most people don't even wake when they bite. The next night one that must have feasted on a cow, hung in the rafters of the chapel and vomited blood all over the mosquito net. I subsequently read an article that stated that vampire bats had killed over 7,000 head of cattle in the previous 5 years. Yes, I was thankful for God's protection of me while sleeping and I remained vigilant on future trips in such regions. We inaugurated the new chapel building in Bucaramanga in February 1974

A Man Called Julio

In 1975 Gilberto was among some of the first believers baptized in the new chapel in Bucaramanga. With him were David and Barbara Carreño who were also baptized that same day. Gilberto was excited about his new life in Christ having been an alcoholic and without much hope in life. His wife soon became a believer and his children began attending the Sunday School.

Julio with his family

One morning, not long after his baptism, Gilberto was on the bus heading off to work in the city. A man was already on the window seat beside him. Gilberto greeted him,

"Hola, ¿Cómo está? ¿Muy buen día, ¿No?" (Hi, how are you, Nice day, right?).

"Qué hay de bueno? ("What's so good about it?) was the response.

"You sound as though you're having a bad day."

"Bad day? Bad year, bad life, nothing's good."

"Sorry to hear that," replied Gilberto, "you got some problems?"

"Life is a problem. I work at the liquor factory and I'm an alcoholic. I've got problems at home, not enough money, and I've been on the run for years."

141

"I'm Gilberto and I was an alcoholic and also had my fill of problems too. But I found out about God, got saved and that changed my whole life."

"Well, I'm Julio, why don't you tell me how you got saved?"

"Well I can't really explain it, but tell you what, I'll meet you this evening and take you to the meeting at the church and the brothers there will be able to explain it better than I can."

That evening Gilberto brought Julio to the prayer meeting after which he and I had a long conversation and I explained the steps to salvation. There was no need to talk much about the fact of sin, but the really great news was that, "Even while we were still sinners Christ died for us." (Romans 5:8). I went on to explain that no one could perform sufficient good works to get into heaven; there was not enough money to buy forgiveness for sin because salvation depends entirely on the work of Jesus on the cross. Because of His sacrifice in giving His life, and because He suffered our punishment for sin, we can be saved. He was the only person who could save us because he was God's own Son who is perfect and never sinned. God showed his acceptance of that sacrifice by raising Jesus from the dead. What do we have to do to receive His forgiveness and a new life? We need to open our lives, invite Christ into our lives and so receive Him as our Lord and Savior.

As I said these things, along with reading the corresponding Scriptures, Julio asked, "Well then how do I receive Him?"

I explained, "Well first of all, knowing that you are a sinner, you need to repent of all sin. (Romans 3:23) In other words, turn right around from the life you have been living. Revelation 3:20 says that Christ is at the door asking permission to come in. What do you do when a friend knocks at your door? Of course, you invite them in. In the same way you need to ask the Lord Jesus to come into your life and when you do as John 1:12 says, 'Yet to all who received him, to those who believed in His name, he gave the right to become children of God.'"

"Would you like to invite Jesus into your life today?"

"Yes, I really would. I need that new life and I want to be saved."

Right there, the very first night Julio came to the church, he accepted the Lord Jesus as his Savior. We read together 1 John 5:12,

"He who has the Son, has life; he who does not have the Son of God does not have life," and from this I was able to show him that having received the Son into his life, he had also received eternal life and that was something secure.

I made arrangements to have further conversations with Julio to be able to disciple him and encourage him in his new life. When I met him a couple of days later, Abigail, his wife, told me that he had told people at the liquor factory that he was now Christian and a follower of the Lord Jesus. He made this announcement the first day on the job after his conversion. The following day a number of men were lined up at the entrance of the factory waiting for him. They were chanting, "Evangelical, evangelical," and continued scoffing. Julio said, "I had to keep my hands in my pockets as I would have normally punched them out."

As Julio's faith grew, he would hand out gospel tracts at work and witness about his new found faith. After one of our Bible studies he asked, "Hermano Juan, do you think I should leave the liquor factory now that I'm a Christian?" I thought about a suitable answer for a few minutes before answering, asking the Lord to help me. "Julio, having a job is important as you have a wife and children to support. It's not easy to get a job right now. I don't think you should do anything suddenly. Let's wait on the Lord and if you were to leave there, you need to be sure you have another job lined up. It also may be that the Lord has you where you are for a purpose."

"Gracias Hermano."

Julio then went on to explain a little about his life. When he was a small boy growing up in the town of Silos in the mountains northeast of Bucaramanga during the time of the violence, people from the conservative political party came into the town and began killing their political rivals. Some men came into his home and he saw one of the men shoot and kill his father. That man then violated his mother while Julio hid behind the couch. At that moment, Julio vowed he would one day kill that man. Later as a teen he became a tough street fighter, had trouble with the law and because of other problems finally had to leave that area for safety's sake.

Several months after Julio's conversion he asked me to accompany him to his hometown as he still had family there and there was someone he particularly wanted to see. I readily agreed and

143

we drove over the mountains to the town of Silos. It was a pretty town on the side of the mountain very steep on one side of the town and rising suddenly straight up on the other. In that town there are the remains of a track that the Incas used for their travel before the Spanish arrived in Colombia. We were walking along the main street when suddenly Julio said, "That's the man I want to see," and began walking quickly to where the man had gone into a coffee shop two blocks away.

Now, I had heard the story of the vow he made to kill the man who had killed his father and abused his mother. Following Julio down the street I was feeling rather nervous not knowing exactly what might happen. We finally entered the coffee shop and the man's eyes opened wide when he saw Julio coming toward him. He also knew of Julio's vow. I was two steps behind Julio as he approached the table where this man was sitting. Julio walked boldly up to the table, put his Bible on the table in front of the man and said, "I vowed to kill you one day. But because of this book on the table in front of you I can forgive you and tell you that you need to be saved because hell is waiting for you. Because of the message of salvation and the work of Jesus Christ, I now have a new life and want to remove any hate from my heart. God loves you and wants you to be saved. I will leave this Bible with you and you need to read it."

With that said, Julio turned and we both walked out of the coffee shop together. I breathed a sigh of relief and we went to visit Julio's mother. Another person we visited was Julio's grandfather. When we arrived Julio presented the gospel to him and told of the great change in his own life. After some time of explaining these things to this older gentleman Julio left another Bible with his grandfather and told him he really needed to read it.

We made another trip to that town two months later and when speaking to Julio's grandfather Julio asked him, "Were you able to read some of the Bible?"

"Oh yes, I have been reading it every day."

"How much did you read?"

"I read all of it," Julio's grandfather replied.

Julio went on to talk more about the Lord Jesus and the need for salvation, and his grandfather came to know the Lord Jesus as Savior.

One evening after a meeting back home, Julio seemed a little distracted and I asked him is something was bothering him.

"I'm having trouble sleeping. Just about every night I wake with a terrible pressure on my chest."

"Do you think it is a heart problem?"

"No, I don't think so," he replied.

I continued to ask health questions until eventually he told me a little more about his past. He began by telling me that before he was married he became involved with witchcraft and had received a spiritual gift from Satan or a demon enabling him to read tarot cards. People would consult him. As the cards were turned, "Ideas and words would come into my head, and when I expressed those thoughts, the people would respond, 'That's exactly right.'"

I began to think that his problem was not a health matter, but rather a demonic attack. Using scripture I explained that when he received Jesus as his Lord and Savior, the demon involved in the tarot card-reading gift could no longer come into him. The Holy Spirit had indwelt Julio at his conversion; he had become a temple of the Holy Spirit, who would not share that with any demon. Obviously the demon was seeking to control Julio again, but "the one who is in you is greater than the one who is in the world," (I John 4:4). "We need to pray about this, Julio," I said after showing him that verse.

We both made a pact to pray for victory over this demonic oppression. Happily, in a few weeks Julio told me he was at last free of the oppression. It wasn't long before Julio told me that even though most of his fellow workers openly made fun of him, some of the men came to him secretly to ask for his help. As time went by Julio began a lunch-hour Bible study for any of his coworkers, and several began attending. A Bible study in the liquor company! Unbelievable!

Because of the tremendous change in Julio's life the management transferred him to security. One occasion, during that time, this government-sponsored liquor factory was placed on alert, as word had come that the revolutionary guerrillas planned to place a bomb on the property. As Julio was working that night, he prayed, asking the Lord to either help them to find the explosive, or not let it happen on his watch. He sent his men to look around the extensive property but nothing was found. As he continued to pray about it, an idea came into his mind about a dead-end deserted area beside one of the main production areas where an accumulation of old machines, pipes and general debris was left to rust. He went to look at that area and there behind some of the garbage was a large pipe bomb. He raced back to the office and called the bomb squad. The bomb disposal unit arrived in time to defuse the bomb before it detonated.

The following day management called Julio to their office. Several of the top management personnel were present. "Tell us Julio, whatever made you decide to look in that particular area? All the steel and old engine parts would've caused considerable damage and loss of life had the bomb gone off. Flying metal would have been like shrapnel."

"Well sir, I was praying that the Lord would show me, and I believe that the Lord answered my prayer. There's no other reason to explain it." Respect for Julio grew and more latitude was given for his witnessing.

There was one section of the liquor factory away from the main building where it was deserted and unlit. A small one-room guardhouse equipped with only a small table, one chair and a phone was at this location. At night the guards were always afraid of that section as there had been attacks on the guards by bandits or urban guerrillas. They would kill the guards to get their guns. Because of this problem the company changed guards every two hours as the men, sometimes overcome with nerves, would shoot at shadows in the scrub surrounding the guardhouse.

A co-worker shared with Julio that he was having domestic problems and asked Julio to pray for him. About midnight one day, when on duty at the guardhouse, he decided that he would use these two hours to pray for the co-worker and his problems. Half way through his two hours, on his knees beside the little table, he heard a whistle. He lifted his head and looked out the window but saw nothing so he continued praying. His relief person came along and it was the same man for whom he had been praying. They greeted and then Julio went back to the main security office.

Ten minutes after Julio arrived back, he suddenly remembered hearing the whistle and thought, "You'd better call and let the other guard know." He dialed the other extension and on the third ring the guard answered. Julio was in the middle of telling him about the whistle when the sound of gunfire was heard on the phone and also by others in the main guardroom. All five of the guards grabbed their shotguns and with their pistols already on their belts ran toward the isolated guardhouse. They shot into the dark area around the guardhouse. Upon arrival they found Julio's friend on the floor, blood streaming down his face. Two of the guards quickly picked him up and ran back to the main guardhouse. The in-house nurse came and swabbed out the wound on the man's head. The bullet had literally parted his hair with a shallow head wound.

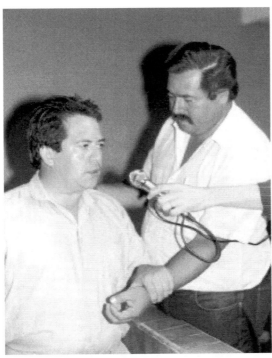

Luis who was shot, later at his baptism

The guard said to Julio, "What made you call just at that moment? I was sitting on a chair just outside the guardhouse when the phone rang and I ran inside to answer it. Had I been outside I would have been killed." Julio responded, "I believe the Lord is in control and he had me call you just at that precise moment."

Needless to say, that guard was at the prayer meeting at the Lagos Dos Chapel the following Wednesday, and gave his heart to the Lord Jesus. Eventually, with his wife, he was baptized and continued following the Lord. Talk about a message from God!

Julio had a gift as an evangelist and Bible teacher. When preaching, his eloquence was obvious, and the Lord used him to lead many people to salvation. One of those converts was the company psychologist. His interest in salvation began as he worked with the many alcoholics at the company. There were times when he went to Julio and said, "I've done all that I can with this person, but he needs what you have, can you please counsel with him?"

Julio's family has gone on serving the Lord to this day. His eldest son, Julio Cesar, has a call-in program in the city of Pereira where he counsels and helps many people as he preaches the gospel and answers Bible questions. At the time of this writing, it is a testimony to God's mercy and love to see Julio's family faithfully living out what they learned; all because a simple new believer, named Gilberto, shared what little he had come to know of the love of Jesus with a sad man on the bus. He brought that sad man to our church where we were entrusted with teaching and discipling him in his new faith. To God be the Glory!

The night Gilberto was baptized along with four others. Last on

Silos, Julio's home town

11

AN EVENTFUL VACATION

San Andrés - August 27, 1973

We had been extremely busy after arriving back in Colombia from our furlough in 1972 and decided to make a booking for a one-week vacation on the island of San Andrés in the Caribbean. In the Avianca office I checked out the air bookings and found that there were two possibilities for our flights from Bogotá. One was flying on an Avianca 727 jet that would get there faster and with more comfort than the other airline that used Lockheed Electra planes. The Electras were four engine, turbo prop planes and would take an extra hour to get to San Andrés. Ann had not been well over the past few months and was three months pregnant, so I opted for the more comfortable and faster jet, even though it cost a few dollars more. So on the 26th of August, we left Bucaramanga on the short national flight to Bogotá. Coming over the mountains about 15 minutes out of Bogotá we hit a huge air pocket and dropped seemingly several thousand feet. People flew off their seats and plenty of screams and curses were heard. This was not a fun way to begin the journey.

It was enjoyable to have an evening with Hedi Reimer, our missionary friend whom we had met in Language School in Costa Rica, and to spend the night there. The following morning as we were driving to the airport, we heard on the radio that a plane had crashed on take-off from the Bogotá airport. It had failed to get over the mountain ranges east of the airport and all were killed. We looked toward the mountain and could see the smoke from the fire of the crashed plane. Arriving at the airport we discovered that the plane was an Electra headed for San Andrés, the one we would have been on had I chosen the cheaper fare. I thanked the Lord for prompting me to consider Ann's health over the cheaper fare.

149

Thankfully, we had an uneventful flight to San Andrés. The Colombian archipelago is approximately 140 miles east of Nicaragua and about 470 miles north east of the Colombian mainland. It is an island with coral reefs, geysers, groves, and cays. Legend has it that Captain Morgan, the pirate, hid his treasure in one of the caves around the coast.

After being taken to our hotel and getting settled in, we put on our swimsuits and headed to the beach just 100 yards from the front door. The beach was really beautiful with golden sands like those of the Sydney beaches. 200 yards off the beach was a small island covered with palm trees and the sandy beach there was really inviting. We decided to get a three-man paddle boat and paddle

San Andrés

to the island the following day.

The next few days were wonderful just enjoying the relaxation on the beach. We were swimming, eating typical food at the restaurants, building sand castles with Diane and David, and just enjoying a time of physical and spiritual refreshment. That third day, a Thursday, I was

150

with Diane and David on a paddle boat just 30 yards off the shore when I noticed Ann waving excitedly. I paddled in as fast as I could and when I reached her she exclaimed, "I'm having a miscarriage!"

The baby was coming out and Ann was in her swimsuit. I grabbed a towel and pulled it with one end in front and the other behind, between her legs and half carried her back to the hotel just off the beach. Diane was bringing little David along behind us with the rest of the towels and beach things. I managed to get Ann and the kids up to our room, helped Ann out of her swimsuit and by then the little baby boy had arrived. I cleaned Ann up because she was covered in a lot of sand, got her into her nightgown, packed the little baby in a towel; and gave Diane, then nine years old, instructions to look after David (16 months old), to stay in the room and not leave for anything, and to order some food on the phone. I ordered a taxi and left for the hospital, as there were no ambulances.

Ann was taken to the operating theater and after two hours the doctor came to tell me that Ann was all right. While doing a D&C and cleaning her up, he discovered a very large ovarian cyst and a tumor on the uterus. He told me that if Ann had not had the miscarriage, the tumor would have burst at some stage and the hemorrhage would have taken her life. He felt that the baby would not have come to term because of the size of the tumor.

Ann came out shortly after, heartbroken, as we both had so badly wanted to have another child. How to spoil a holiday! And yet, God had overruled as otherwise Ann would have died because of the hemorrhage had the miscarriage not happened.

We flew back to Bucaramanga the following Monday. Ann decided to make contact with her friend Margaret in New Jersey, USA to discuss options for medical care as the doctor had explained she would need further surgical attention. Margaret had told her about a Christian gynecologist from one of the local churches who, when he knew about Ann's situation, offered to do the necessary surgery.

Arrangements were made for Ann to travel to New Jersey for the surgery and on Saturday September 22, Ann left for Bogotá, staying the night with Elsa Barolin and then the following day flying to New York. Margaret Glaser, whom we had met when coming through New Jersey returning from our furlough in Australia,

151

met her at the airport. On Sunday she was able to accompany the Glasers to the Sunday meetings at the Mahwah, NJ Chapel. Later, Margaret took Ann to meet Dr. George Mikhail the gynecologist, a believer from the New Hope Church, who had kindly offered to see Ann and perform any surgery necessary.

Ann wrote in a letter to family in New Zealand, *"We got to the Mikhail's at about 6:30 and I stayed the night there. They have a lovely home a two-storied homestead set well back from the road in 100 acres or so of farmland. They just rent the house and someone else cares for the farm, but it's a peaceful setting especially now with the leaves turning color in the woods at the back. I have a delightful room with my own bathroom and central heating if I find the night chilly. I'm looking forward to going back there to recuperate, but then my room here is lovely in the hospital and better than a Colombian hotel.*

The doctor is a busy man. He left at 6 AM Monday as he was scheduled for surgery at 8 AM, and he was still here in the evening at 8:30. Leona, his wife, drove me in after lunch – an hour on the freeway – and I saw Dr. George at 2 PM. For my examination I modeled a really fetching creation! First time ever worn and the last! It went from me to the rubbish bin. It was all paper, three ply, open at the front but when he wanted to sound my back he just ripped it straight down. But I kept my shoulders covered (a humorous reference to the earlier account from Ian's visit to Monte Loro in chapter 8). *Then he called in another doctor to examine me to see what his diagnosis was. Then till 3:30 I had to sweat on it wondering what was going on. He was too busy before and they were waiting for one test, so finally about 5:00 he got Leona (who is also a nurse) to help me get admitted.*

Next day, Tuesday, I was ready for the (operating) *theater at 11 AM, I didn't get called till 3 PM, which was quite a wait. Surgery took from 2 to 2 1/2 hours apparently. Later Ian called me and actually got through and I could talk to him within five minutes of calling. For some reason, the doctor's earlier call went to the Rothlisberger's home, and Lord must've sent Ian over there as he was with Andrew and able to take the call. Dr. Mikhail said he had told Ian I won't be home under four weeks so that looks like the end of October. Anyway, things could've been worse. I had what one doctor called* a very big "chocolate cyst" – and according to the doctor's indications, it was the size of a large bread and butter plate, or bigger. One ovary was almost completely destroyed by it and had to be removed, but they worked hard to save the other and the uterus. Several times Dr. George said he just didn't know what to do next and both he and the other doctor decided I would want the uterus saved if possible, although I had said we were prepared for it to go. Dr. George knew that we had hoped to have another child. When in doubt he said he stopped and prayed each time and he managed to save the uterus and one ovary, though they had a lot of trouble stopping the bleeding when the ovary was exposed after cutting away the cyst.

Dr. Mikhail slept here at the hospital Tuesday night on call, in case there were complications and had to open me up and remove the rest. The doctor doing my dressing today counted the external stitches for Diane. There are 16, but said that was nothing to the number of stitches inside. The cyst had apparently grown over one ovary right around behind the uterus and around the other ovary. The doctor said it is caused by the body absorbing some of the menstrual clear-out each month and sucking it up into the fallopian tubes instead of expelling it all, and that this increased each month so that it was about 80% loaded. Hence the "chocolate cyst," I suppose. He said it is usually associated with excruciating pain, so I suppose that is why I was in such agony after the miscarriage. Tuesday night and Wednesday night I was fed intravenously which they removed yesterday morning. Last night I had two solid meals and was up all night vomiting and had a terrible night. So today was back on fluid diet and tonight they put me on a bland diet, so I'm praying I'll have a better night. I have received four lovely lots of flowers from different folk from the church and four cards also, so I am not forgotten. I'm certainly feeling a lot better and not much pain when I'm up."

My letters home:

October 2, 1973

I called Ann a couple of times, but this really wasn't very satisfying as three minutes cost US $20. Ann still sounded tired and weak which would be natural after her ordeal. I asked Ann to ask the doctor about the lab work. Tests on the fibroma, or cyst, and the smear test they did prior to the surgery were positive, but the Dr. called and said he thought it was benign.

After the surgery Ann went to stay at the doctor's home. I hate to think what the hospital bill will be, probably in the vicinity of two or three thousand dollars. The hospitals are terribly expensive in the States. Gus Kaschel has opened a fund for the hospital bill and already many have contributed. The doctor is not going to charge and they are really spoiling Ann. From what she writes many of the believers are visiting her and that is a big help to her morale. Quite a few women have visited Ann several times, some having driven up to four hours to see her. It's good of them to come and see Ann. One sister gave Ann a Joy box, I think they call it, which had nine gifts all wrapped and you have to open one a day. A good idea especially for sick people as it gives them something to look forward to.

October 25, 1973

Ann is to have a final examination tomorrow, Friday 26, and I trust that this will give her the okay to travel. She should be coming in on the 30th. I hope so as I'm sick of dirty diapers each morning before the maid arrives. I bought Ann a General Electric washing machine as the old one has had it and won't agitate or pump out the water. You can't even control the rollers on the ringer. The General Electric is fully automatic, which will make washing easier. It was terribly costly, but you cannot buy them in Colombia as they are smuggled in from the states, so it should be a good one and not a Jerry made Colombian one. I bought it in a back street shop here in town and didn't ask any questions for conscience sake. It will be a surprise for her on her birthday the 30th.

154

November 12, 1973

Ann wrote, *I returned to Colombia at the end of October was met in Bogotá by Ian and Diane and was very pleased to see them. The plane was one and a half hours late as we stopped in Miami changing flights, and then it was after 10 PM when I finally got through customs. It was a long tiring day, but it was wonderful to see Ian and Diane again.*

A few days before I left for the states a Christian lass, Graciela Blandon, began helping in the house and she has been, and still is, a wonderful help. She begins about 8:30 each morning, Monday to Saturday included, and leaves when she has cleaned up after the evening meal. I have been particularly grateful for her help in these first few weeks home when I am supposed to take things quietly and only after four weeks gradually resume normal activities. She is cheerful and pleasant in the house and very good with David.

After a natural tiredness the first 10 days I now feel really well and able to cope with most things. Diane has just finished her end of year exams, and this week we attended the school break function after which the year's grades were handed out. She is now on vacation until February 5. She passed in all subjects so next week will be enrolling her for the coming year when she will be in fourth grade. To be enrolled each pupil has to have a current health certificate so last week Diane had to submit rather unwillingly, to a blood test, TB injection and medical examination.

David at 19 months is a very normal little boy. He likes plenty of action and protests loudly if daddy goes out and leaves him behind, especially if he goes in the car. He loves playing with the monkey, Paco, but gets very offended when Paco grabs something he is eating out of his hand and runs up to his box with it. He plays quite happily for an hour or so in his room after he wakes in the morning, but now that he can get out of his cot, the mess at times has to be seen to be believed. Several months ago he would strip his cot regularly each morning. Now he has graduated to emptying all the drawers in his room and tossing the contents on the floor after taking off his pajamas and singlet. We have finally tried to curtail his morning activities by removing the drawers from the closet.

Ian has been showing Moody science films in the two suburbs where we have children's groups weekly, and visits also with adults. Thursday evening they were forced to postpone the film showing, as a young man from the same street had been stabbed to death in the nearby town, and only a very short time before they arrived the body had been brought home. Last night they showed the gospel film to a good-sized group in another suburb of Provenza.

There is always the unexpected happening. Like two nights ago when a little girl knocked at the door after supper and said she had no mother or father. Could I give her some clothes or some toys? Maybe it wasn't true, but her dress was very torn and she was very appealing even though so dirty. I thought of all Diane's clothes in the cupboards and thought, "Inasmuch as you've done it unto one of the least of these," (Matthew 25:40) so I found her some clothes. We do need so much wisdom to know how many of these constant requests for material help are genuine. Then yesterday morning Ian and Diane were driving along one of the main streets in town where they were hanging up a huge Christmas decoration ready for December. As they drew near, one of these fell from its mounting on top of the light pole hitting a passerby on the head and knocking him unconscious. As Ian was right beside the man when it fell he was able to rush the man to the nearest hospital for emergency treatment. (there are no ambulances here) And so we could go on, suffice it to say that we need and value your prayers for all aspects of our lives as well as for the work here.

As you read in Ann's letters, missionary life goes on no matter the circumstances or difficulties. We knew that God was in control and that whatever the outcome, we would continue to serve Him as long a He gave us strength. I was thankful to have Ann back home and soon feeling well enough to take on the responsibilities God gave to her also.

First Chapel Bucaramanga - Centro Bíblico
1st Bookshop to the right of entrance

12

INITIATING VARIOUS MINISTRIES

Providing Good Literature

During our language training in San Jose Costa Rica, Ann and I had several orientation classes, one of which was how to teach the illiterate to read. We were taught about a program called ALFALIT, a method of teaching the illiterate to read and write as a means through which the gospel could be preached. When we arrived in Colombia and lived in Puerto Boyacá, the principal of the school, Juan Ayala, was interested in the program and went to Medellin to do a further ALFALIT study. At that time illiteracy was 75% in Colombia. Together with Juan we began by training eight teachers, and then with 12 students the literature program began. This arrow was once again being shot into a service.

There were many books available, many of which had been translated from English by some of the larger publishing companies in the United States, but there were not many that were simple reading for new readers. Another problem was that many of the books that had been translated carried teachings and doctrines that were not necessarily biblical. Because of this problem I decided to open a bookshop to make literature available to those in our church and also believers from other denominations. For our local congregation I decided to make copious notes of my messages and Bible studies which could then be duplicated and handed to the believers, written in simple language, and above all with solid Bible doctrine.

When Ann and I moved to Bucaramanga, I continued with a desire to get good literature into the hands of believers. Beginning with a stand inside the front window of our home, I soon had many people coming to the door to purchase Bibles and books. Obviously there was a great need for a good bookshop in Bucaramanga. For this reason, when Andrew Rothlisberger and I spoke with the architect about the plans for the first chapel, we included a large area at the front of the building for a bookshop. I already had contact with Timothy Anderson who lived in Cúcuta, who was a supplier of good Christian books and from whom I could purchase doctrinally trustworthy books to use in the new bookshop. The new Chapel, Centro Bíblico (Bible Center), opened in February 1974 and with the shelves fully stocked, Ann and I, helped by Alan Tonkin, served in the bookshop daily. It soon became very busy with believers coming from the city as well as from outlying country areas.

Eventually Esau Parra, who had been managing the bookshop in Puerto Boyacá handed over the literature work there to Juan Ayala, and then came to Bucaramanga to manage the new bookshop. This relieved Ann and me of the daily responsibility, freeing us for other areas of ministry. He soon had a new helper, Marina Delgado, a teenager at the time.

With the two churches in Bucaramanga becoming more established and growing in number there was also a need for a better printer to produce notes for messages as well as other tracts and Bible studies. For a short time I was using a mimeograph machine, and then moved on to using a small desktop letter-sized offset printer. With this equipment in our home I was then able to publish notes for the Intensive Bible Study Retreat and other teaching meetings. Using the offset printer, I also prepared and published a monthly newsletter for our local churches. The next requirement was for a folding machine, as manually folding took a lot of time and energy.

Mobile Bookshop - Taking Books To The Country

As our bookshop became better known among other churches in the city as well as surrounding areas, many of them invited us to bring supplies of books and Bibles to sell at their conferences. Edmundo Arenas, who was partially retired, offered to attend these conferences. We were able to obtain some collapsible tables, along with shelving for the books, and set up a canopy over the tables with our display. This became very popular and a great means of getting good literature into the hands of believers.

After a couple of years, Edmundo was unable to continue this work. In 1978, I spoke with Gonzalo Pinzón, who had been driving a delivery truck for a soft drink company, Hipinto, and we discussed the idea of a mobile bookshop. This would help to not only serve at conferences, but to go to some of the country areas and towns scattered in the mountains surrounding Bucaramanga. I had a Ford F100 pick-up with a canopy over the back, which would serve our purpose well. We fitted it out with shelving and the literature became another means of taking the gospel out into some of the remote mountain areas. Gonzalo began driving into the mountains east of Bucaramanga visiting a number of villages on market days, setting up the vehicle at the market and not only selling books and Bibles, but also giving out tracts, preaching, and having good conversations as he shared the gospel.

Each of the villages had an open market-day on a different week day. People from around the countryside could travel from one place to another to sell their produce or other wares. The market is usually held in the town's main square. We did the same with the mobile bookshop.

First we surveyed the area by visiting some eight towns of various sizes to note which days were the market days. The mornings are merry as the people sell their wares and stock up on necessities. The afternoons can be quite different. They drink the hours away swapping stories, which sometimes end up in deadly fights with knives and pistols.

I decided to make one of the trips with Gonzalo and we traveled into what was a new area for us. It was a fanatical Roman Catholic region situated in the mountains to the southeast of Bucaramanga. After traveling over one section of the ranges we came to a major city called Málaga, which we used as a base for further visits into the surrounding villages. One of those villages is called San Miguel, which nestles in a mountain valley. Getting there was quite an experience. We drove along roads, some of which had sections that were more like goat tracks. Landslides of small stones had to be driven over and in several places our wheels were just 6 inches from a 500-foot drop into the valley below. We set out from Málaga at 5:30 AM and two hours later we arrived in San Miguel to be greeted by the stares of the people. We were strangers in their town.

Not many years before, a stranger would have more than average risk of being assaulted and killed. During the years of the violence the usual treatment for a stranger, and this included members of the liberal political party and even evangelicals, was for a couple of men to greet him with the words, "For Christ and the King." They would flash knives from under their ponchos and simply eliminate the subject. Gonzalo could tell some chilling stories of bigotry and intolerance. Fortunately, there was a little more law and order when we were there, but the priest was still the overlord and controlled

the town.
When we arrived in that town we went to see the Alcalde (mayor) to get permission to sell Bibles in the plaza. He told us to wait a while and then went off to talk with the

Typical village Market

priest who was in the town square where the market was being set up for the day. While waiting for him we went back to the truck to get some Bibles out. The mayor and the priest came over to us and the priest said sarcastically, "What are these Bibles you want to sell? Are they these false translations which are incomplete?"

Gonzalo handed him a Bible. "This is a Nacar-Calunga and here is a Paulina edition." Both these editions are put out by the Roman Catholic Church and include the apocryphal books. "Well I suppose these are all right," he grudgingly admitted, somewhat deflated, "but how much are they?" We told him the price and he started calling us thieves and liars and said that he was selling them much cheaper. But this was doubtful, as he probably did not have any Bibles let alone sell any. It was obvious that he was just nitpicking.

"Of course we have cheaper editions," Gonzalo went on, "here is a paperback which only cost 80 pesos (about two US dollars), and here is one with some good notes in it – we call it a Scofield Bible." The priest complained about the "incomplete" Bibles – but since we had some Catholic editions he could not very well refuse us permission to sell. He said to me "While I can't stop you from selling your Bibles, I can't guarantee your safety if you stay." This was a very thinly veiled threat, which harkened back to the days of the

160

violence. These priests did not like to lose control in their own town and could easily get men to do their dirty work. In spite of what the priest had said we continued to set up in the town square opposite his imposing Spanish-style church.

Some of the locals overheard the interchange between us and came over to look at the display. We played hymns on a cassette recorder over our loudspeakers and handed out Bible Society tracts, which are non-controversial as they are all portions of Scripture.

We did not sell much at first because the people were plainly frightened by the priest. He ranted over the church tower loud-

Gonzalo with the mobile bookshop market day

speakers that the evangelicals, "Have some approved Bible editions," but that they also, "have some false Bibles that were incomplete." So he said, "Be careful what you buy and make sure you don't get any of their literature as it is contaminated." But as he was speaking, the village clown began doing an act with a flute over the loudspeaker from one of the stalls. People everywhere started rocking with laughter. By 11 AM we were still in town. Things were beginning to flow and we began selling more and more Bibles. One

161

onlooker, who had been watching us for over an hour, finally came over and told us that he was a believer, but that he had lived in fear because of the fanaticism in the area. He invited us out to his farm on our next visit.

Two ladies, a mother and daughter, bought a Bible and told me they had long wished to own one. They had been listening to the gospel broadcasts on Trans World Radio, a missionary station broadcasting from Bonaire in the Netherlands Antilles. They still went to mass they said, but each Saturday a number of people got together on a farm outside of town to listen to the Word of God and to encourage one another. I asked how many were in the group and was amazed when they told me that it numbered from six to 30. While we were talking the daughter pointed to a fellow who was buying a Bible from Gonzalo. "I'm surprised," she said. "He is one of the fanatics." It turned out that he invited Gonzalo to visit his father and said he would get about 20 workers together who were also listening to Trans World Radio. That man told us that they were interested to hear more about the Lord Jesus Christ.

Praise the Lord for Trans World Radio! It is a wonderful work! Way off in the mountains of Colombia, cut off by the fanatical attitudes pervading in that region, we discovered people listening to God's message of love beamed to them twice a day by means of radio. We found evidence of dozens of people seeking the Lord.

After that visit to San Miguel, I did not like the idea of Gonzalo being alone in those mountain areas because of the fanaticism and possible dangers, so I hired Jaime Batero to accompany and work with Gonzalo. Jaime had an interesting background prior to his conversion, which is told in a separate chapter, but I knew he would be a good co-worker for Gonzalo.

On the second trip to Malaga and San Miguel, Gonzalo and Jaime had a letter from the governor of the state asking all the mayors to collaborate with us. When he arrived in San Miguel he was not quite sure what sort of reception he would get as it could have been with stones being thrown at them. When he did arrive he had to wait a few minutes for the mayor to come to him. Meanwhile he got into a conversation with a fellow he had seen in Malaga carrying a camera. After talking with this man it turned out that he was a reporter from Bucaramanga with the *Vanguardia*, the primary newspaper in

162

our state of Santander. Gonzalo had a good talk with this reporter explaining our work and also the way of salvation, including saying that to be saved you don't need to confess to a priest or get involved in religious rituals. He used the thief on the cross as an example of someone who did not do anything like that, even baptism, but was assured of a place in heaven. The reporter left a few moments later and Jaime came to Gonzalo, who at that moment saw the priest and pointed him out to Jaime. Jaime was surprised and told Gonzalo that the whole time he was talking to the reporter, the priest was standing behind him listening.

The mayor's secretary finally came out of the office where Gonzalo was waiting. Gonzalo walked right past and, without talking to him, went straight into the front office. The secretary followed Gonzalo into the office and Gonzalo said, "Thank you very much," continuing into the mayor's office as though he had been told to go in. He then took out the letter from the State Governor in Bucaramanga, who is over all the mayors in the state, and said, "I got this from my friend (naming him) the governor to save you all the trouble you have had with the priest in giving us permission to sell and work in this town." Well the mayor went three different shades of red and then became very friendly telling Gonzalo to sell just as much as he liked. He no doubt took off right away to tell the priest that we have friends in high places and to take it easy, as the priest didn't make a murmur all morning. Gonzalo gave away more than 600 booklets to the adults entitled *The Way of Salvation,* and made some good contacts with the local people. Several of those who spoke to us the first time came along and again asked that we visit them. The priest probably thought we had arranged for a reporter from the newspaper to be there to get a story of the rebellious priest and mayor. Whatever the reason we could see that the Lord had overruled in a wonderful way and that there were real openings in that area for the gospel.

We were thankful that the mobile bookshop was working very well. On one of Gonzalo's trips he visited 45 towns and villages. A lot of literature was sold and distributed and good contacts were made.

The City Bookstore Is Opened

In 1981 we were able to purchase a location in the center of Bucaramanga at a new mall, called Omnicentro. When we moved the merchandise to our new shop, the old shop at the chapel became available for other printing possibilities. For some time I had wanted to purchase a larger printing press to be able to handle not only the needs for our churches, but also the needs of many of the churches that were requesting printing. By this time I had hired a couple of workers to help with the printing on the old table-top offset printer but we needed to have a press that could handle all the work that was growing.

Bookshop - Librería Luz - Omnicentro Bucaramanga

On one trip to the capital, Bogotá, I visited a good friend, David Peacock, with W.E.C. (World Evangelization Crusade) who had a very large printing and publishing outfit. While talking to him about my needs he said, "I am buying a brand-new press and need to sell my old Harris press." The Harris press could handle large sheets of paper and print thousands of copies a day.

"How much do you want for your Harris press?" I asked.

"Seeing it's for you, you can have it for $3000," he replied.

Well I did not have $3000 so I said to him, "I am leaving for Bucaramanga this afternoon, and I will be asking the Lord to provide, if this is His will for us."

164

It was a five-hour drive from Bogotá to Bucaramanga, plenty of time for prayer. When I arrived home, Ann had collected the mail and there was a letter from Belgium. The believers there had a fund, which churches in that country could use to support missionary workers. I opened the letter. Along with the news from that country was a check for $3,000! Some people ask, "How do you know God's will?" Obviously He shows his will very clearly when we are walking with Him and allowing Him to guide our lives. He has promised to meet our needs and to care for us in all circumstances. He proved Himself to us, many times over and over again. I called David Peacock the next morning telling him that the Lord had provided and I would send my printer, Jhon Garcia, to Bogotá to get some lessons on how to use the Harris press.

Jhon (this is not a typo, many Colombians have their name spelled that way, trying out English names!) and Juan Serrano began working full time in the new locale. With the purchase of the large Harris press, I arranged for Garcia to go to Bogota to get some training on our new, (but really old) second-hand press. Previously we had been buying tracts from a Christian printing company in Medellin. Now with this equipment we could begin printing our own tracts for our own use and also for selling in the downtown bookshop. Sales in our new bookshop increased rapidly with the easier access for believers. It was not long before we were selling more than US $5,000 a month, worth a lot more in 1981 than it is now.

Along with the new press the amount of work also increased and the need for more staff became necessary. I bought an industrial sewing machine and one lady began making leather Bible covers and Bible bags. I am still using one of the Bible cases today, which shows the quality of workmanship. We sometimes purchased hard-cover Bibles from the Bible Society, cut the cardboard covers off, and then covered the Bibles with leather. This was cheaper than buying original leather-covered Bibles, and we not only could cover the costs of the work in making the covers, but also made a profit selling them in the bookshop. The next step was to purchase a gold lettering machine to stamp names on the Bibles.

Two years later I felt the need of a much better press so that we could do better color work. To print in color we had to run the paper through the press four times, once for each primary color.

Often the register of the four ink colors was not exact and the job was not as professional as I felt it should be. I thought of buying a Heidelberg GTO press, a top-of-the-line German press. A fund for the new press was started as I had mentioned this in one of my prayer letters. About a year later, the fund had reached US $25,000 and a brother in Switzerland, a businessman, wrote to me suggesting that I go ahead with the purchase, as the dollar value at that moment was strong against the Deutschmark. Working through the Heidelberg Company in Bogotá, I made the purchase with the cost being $25,000. Usually it would have cost many thousands more with the higher exchange rate. It was imported from Germany taking several months before we actually took delivery.

Bookshop and Print shop staff

Later on, Jhon Garcia moved to Bogotá so Miguel Arenas took on the printing, using the new press. Miguel eventually married Marina Delgado who was managing the downtown bookshop. With the beautiful new press there was now a need for other equipment such as a graphic arts camera, a computerized paper cutter, a professional plate burner, a bookbinder and a large laminator. Obviously, this equipment was worth many thousands of dollars. When we first started using the Harris press, Jhon and Juan invented a plate burner. We built a box with two sheets of glass on the top. Then we had a vacuum pump to seal the two sheets of glass with
166

the aluminum plates holding the negatives in place together. We then took the box out into the street in front of our workshop, placing it in the sun for 20 minutes to burn the images onto the plates ready for printing. This was certainly primitive printing.

God's Provision For Printing Work

"And my God will meet all your needs according to his glorious riches in Christ Jesus." Philippians 4:19

Miguel our printer with the Heidlberg printing press

In the early 1980's Ann and I, along with fellow missionaries Andrew and Anne Rothlisberger had been able to plant three new churches and were heavily involved in other ministries. Andrew was burdened with the need to open a school in a very poor and crime-filled area in Bucaramanga, which was neglected by the government due to the dangerous conditions. I was continuing to build a publishing work for printing gospel tracts, books, posters and printing for other churches. I had also started to publish a monthly magazine called *Sendas de Vida,* (Pathways of Life) writing some of the articles, translating articles from English, editing the magazine, as well as doing the layouts and art work. Bill Van Ryn also translated and wrote many articles for me over the years. My purpose was to bring good Bible teaching, encourage believers to grow, read more than they usually read, and to be able to effectively reach out with the gospel.

Both Andrew and I were in need of significant funds to support these two ministry projects.

While the local authorities had given Andrew a building for the school, it needed much repair. Also he would need to provide all

Anne and Andrew Rothlisberger our missionary co-workers

Miguel with the new computerized paper cutter.

the school supplies, desks, and uniforms as well as food each day for the students, most of whom had very little to eat at home. I was in need of the expensive equipment for the printing operation. All these items were very expensive and both Andrew and I, along with our wives, were praying for the Lord to send a large amount of money so that we could move forward with these projects. We committed these needs to the Lord in prayer often, and particularly when we met weekly to pray and discuss the work in this area.

One day I received a letter from a lawyer in New Zealand stating that Mrs. Watson, whom we all knew well, and who had supported and prayed for our missionary work, had passed away and willed her entire estate to both Andrew and me for our work. Her estate amounted to $76,000, a very large sum in those days, and I was more than thankful and excited. I immediately called Andrew and said, "What would you think if I said we have come into an inheritance?"

He replied, "I wouldn't be surprised at all."

"What! Why would you say that?"

"I knew time was running out and in order to be able to do the work to open the school in January, I was on my knees in my office praying, and I had just prayed, 'Lord, the only way I can think it possible to get such an amount is if there was an inheritance.' At that

169

moment the phone rang and you asked what I would think of receiving an inheritance for our work." Excitedly, Ann and I drove over to Andrew's home where the four of us had a time of giving thanks and were really "high" with excitement.

Two weeks later another letter came from the lawyers in which they stated that the brother of the deceased was contesting the will, which could lead to long proceedings in the probate court. He suggested that Andrew and I offer him a third of the money to see if we could buy him off and therefore avoid a lengthy court case and possibly not get anything. Once again Andrew and I, with our wives, got together; a little more somber than the last time. We prayed again about the whole matter, asking the Lord for guidance as to what we should do. We knew the brother of the lady was not a believer, that he had a car sales yard and did not need the money, and he just did not want the money to go to the missionaries. His sister, from our churches in New Zealand was well known to us and together with her husband, who had passed away several year before, had prayed for us and supported us over the years. In fact, her husband officiated at my wedding to Ann in Timaru, New Zealand. Andrew's wife, Anne, was a New Zealander and also well known to that lady and her family.

Six weeks later another letter came from the lawyer enclosing a check for US$76,000! Thank you Lord! We divided the money and Andrew arranged to have the school renovated and made ready for students, purchasing all the equipment needed. It was a rush, but the school opened and proved to be a tremendous blessing, eventually having a positive effect on this whole suburb of Esperanza. That is a story in itself. Eventually the fourth church in our area was established there.

I purchased all the equipment I needed for the print shop, and the literature work progressed by leaps and bounds. Along with Bible study notes, and books, the monthly magazine, Sendas De Vida, (Pathways of Life), was eventually being sent out to at least five countries in Latin America.

About one year later Andrew returned to Australia and New Zealand for a short furlough. Before leaving, Andrew took photos of the children in their school uniforms, sitting at their desks with their schoolbooks and papers. He also took photos of the new printing equipment and the 13 full time workers at the print shop. While in
170

New Zealand, Andrew visited people and churches that supported our work. One day he went to the home of the man who had contested the will with photos of the work to confirm that we had not used the money for ourselves, personally. He knocked on the door and was greeted by Mr. C's wife and said, "Good morning, I'm Andrew and wonder if I could speak to Mr. C."

"Oh, I'm sorry, my husband was crossing the road in front of the courthouse as he had to be there for a court case about a year ago and a car hit him and killed him."

The judges and lawyers were no doubt wondering why he was so late, little knowing that the Lord had intervened and judged the case Himself.

Andrew, stood there for a few moments really shocked, then gathered his thoughts and expressed his condolences to the wife of Mr. C, shared the photos with her, and then bid her farewell. We had wondered what had happened when the money came through so quickly, and were surprised that the Lord had over-ruled in such a way.

Seeing how the Lord dealt with this matter confirmed to us that He would certainly look after his own in whatever way he sees fit. If God wanted us to have these funds for our work then neither Mr. C, nor anyone else could hinder Him. Sadly, Mr. C met a terrible end as he was going to court to contest the use of those funds. But we learned a valuable lesson about relying only on God to supply ALL of our needs, and we were grateful as well as awed by His answer to our prayers.

"It is a dreadful thing to fall into the hands of the living God." Hebrews 10:31

When I left Colombia in 1988, rather than pay severance and bonuses to Marina who had been working for me for 13 years at that time, I was able to give her all the stock in the bookshop. Over the next few years she paid rent on the locale until she could eventually buy it. Together, with her husband Miguel, she continues to manage the bookshop to this day, some 40 years later to meet the literature needs in that area.

Good Tidings Publishers

In 1986, several men from our churches in the USA visited the missionaries in Colombia to be of encouragement and help. One of the men, Lee Baseler, approached me after a meeting in which we had discussed the Spanish literature work. As a business-man with Monsanto Chemical, he had many years of international experience. In retirement he sought to serve the Lord and visited many different mission fields where he was particularly helpful addressing business and personal problems of the missionaries. Lee told me he was very impressed with the publishing and literature work in Bucaramanga, which I had begun and was continuing to oversee. He went on to tell me about the Good Tidings Publishers ministry that had been going through some difficulties and was in need of new leadership.

Although not fluent in Spanish, he had taken over the directorship of Good Tidings Publishers (G.T.P.) and had been making sure the publication of their flagship paper, "Buenas Nuevas" *(Good News)*, continued to be edited and published on a bimonthly basis. Along with the *Buenas Nuevas* paper, there was a similar bimonthly paper in Portuguese, a line of 70 tract titles, a yearly Calendar, and a series of Bible teaching books. This Spanish literature was being sent out to about 27 different countries where Spanish is understood. The tracts were being continually updated and new tracts written from time to time. He mentioned that the printing of the two papers was being handled in Mexico City, and the books and tracts were being stored and distributed by Grace and Truth Publications in Danville, Illinois. I would only need to write, edit and prepare the layouts for printing, but the distribution would continue to be handled in México and the USA. After explaining what was involved in the publication work he said, "I think you are the person who could take over this Spanish Literature Ministry and would like for you to pray about it. I'll be leaving Colombia in three days and it would be wonderful if I could return to the USA with a positive answer."

That evening I told Ann what we had discussed. I explained that the GTP publishing work had been established 110 years before. First in 1876, by Robert Grant, a missionary in México, then William Crabtree for a time, being continued for some years by Will Missen who had traveled with me on my first trip to Colombia; as well as others who had also been involved with GTP. In some ways I felt tremendously honored by the thought of taking over a publishing work begun so many years ago, but in other ways I knew this meant more responsibilities for me writing and editing in addition to what I was preparing for our printing work in Bucaramanga. We prayed about it and decided that this work fit in with what I was already doing and I should go ahead and accept the offer. The next day I was able to meet with Lee Baseler and confirm my acceptance. He later sent the legal documents with all the necessary information I would need to take on this responsibility. At that time I began writing and editing the bimonthly magazines which I have continued to do to this day.

Thinking back to my family heritage I am reminded that my grandfather Corson was involved in printing work. Also the many years in my Sydney church when I helped to edit and publish the monthly magazine, which included the letter from a Colombian missionary seeking help, the Lord had used to prepare me when I did not know what lay ahead. Even today I am thankful to be involved in spreading the Word of God through literature while serving on the Board of Trustees for Emmaus Correspondence School, which yearly provides Bible study materials for millions of people. In this world, with many forms of media, the printed word is still valuable and I am thankful to be a part of this service for the Lord.

Helping The Blind To See

I had developed the habit of praying each morning after my daily Bible readings and asking God, "Please give me an opportunity today." One morning in January 1974, I had to change some U.S. dollars into Colombian currency and went to Citibank at Cabecera in Bucaramanga. Having been there many times before, taking care of my banking needs, I had gotten to know the bank manager well. On that particular occasion, after we had made the transaction, she asked me, "Would you be able to help a client of ours who needs to purchase some books in the United States? The books will only cost around US $10, but to purchase the dollars at the bank, with the commissions for such a small amount, makes it an expensive way to handle the transaction. If you would be able to write her a check for the $10, she will give you the equivalent in pesos."

"Of course," I replied, "Give me her name and address and I will go there right away."

With the address in my hand but not really knowing much about the person, I set off to find her building in downtown Bucaramanga. I went into the office and asked for the lady involved, telling her that I had been asked by the bank to help her with some dollars. She was very happy that I was able to help. After she gave me the pesos for my US dollar check, she began to ask me questions.

"You're obviously not from around here. Where are you from, and what brings you to Bucaramanga?"

"I'm a missionary from Australia and I am here to preach the gospel and teach people about the Bible. We have already started a church here in Bucaramanga, and we are having Bible studies with some folk in Ciudad Valencia, where we hope to eventually start another church."

"That's interesting!"

She then went on to tell me, "As you can see, this is an institute for the blind. We work with many children who go to normal schools during the week and come here every Saturday for extra tutoring. We teach them braille so that they can take notes at school, but often they miss some concepts and we are thus able to help. I don't know if you are someone who might be able to help, but part of the school curriculum is religion. I have asked the priest to come and teach religion, but he didn't seem to be too interested in helping. I also asked an evangelical pastor if he could help but he was too busy. Is this the sort of thing that you might do? Could you come and give religion classes?"

Now remember, I had prayed that morning for the Lord to give me an opportunity and this opportunity was so big it was like a barn door wide open. I prayed about it (a one second prayer of thanks!) and said, "Would you like me to start on Saturday?"

"That would be wonderful I am so glad that we have met."

Leaving the Blind Institute building I went to the Post Office to collect our mail, made a quick visit to the bookshop to check that all was going well, and then hurried home with the news.

"Ann, you won't believe what happened this morning!"

I told Ann about the conversation with the bank manager and

with the director of the Blind Institute, and the unexpected invitation to begin working with the children on Saturdays. Immediately I began to prepare lessons for the next Saturday and to work out how to teach the children choruses for their religion class. I could not use flash cards or song sheets as we do with our own children's classes. The class was organized so that I would have one hour with the children each Saturday morning. In that time I would play my guitar, teach them some choruses, and then teach them from the Bible. Now and again Ann would also come to tell a Bible story and help with the singing.

Arriving that first Saturday morning the children were ready for my class. The first chorus was one they probably already knew, "If you're happy and you know it clap your hands!" We sang that a few times then moved on to a couple of other easy choruses. I repeated the choruses a number of times to help the students memorize them. Then for about 20 minutes I taught them something about the life of the Lord Jesus, after which we had a time for questions.

All the children had come from a Catholic background and so they had some basic understanding about who Jesus is, along with many of the Catholic traditions. This made it easier for me to explain not only who Jesus is, but also the reason why He came. I followed a similar format each Saturday, but realized most of them had never read a Bible. My desire was for them to be able to read the Scriptures themselves. I made contact with the Bible Society in Bogotá and bought New Testament books in braille, with 10 copies of the gospel of John. I also bought a supply of large print gospels of John for those who were partially blind. Eventually I was able to purchase enough copies of the gospels of John, in braille, to give a copy to all who could read braille.

One of the older students, Cristobal Covelli, a blind man about 22 years of age, was already studying at the University of Bucaramanga. He taught the younger students how to read braille. Cristobal asked many questions and was showing a great interest in the gospel message. He decided to use the Gospels of John as his textbook for teaching braille to the younger students. This was fantastic as the students were not only learning braille, but were reading the Word of God.

The work at the Blind Institute continued on for many months, and Cristobal eventually decided to ask the Lord Jesus into his life. He was the first of many of the students who would come to know the Savior. This was a cause for great joy, not only for Ann and me, but also for the folk in the first church we were a part of establishing in Bucaramanga. Over the next three years, when I was not on the road, I picked him up from his home and took him to all the meetings. He was baptized in June that year and became a lively member of the church. Prior to his conversion he had been reading many books in braille on the occult. At his baptism he wanted to do what the Ephesians had done when they burned their books on the occult. After the baptismal service we placed his braille occult books in a pile on the patio just outside the chapel and set them on fire. Unfortunately, some of the books were plastic which gave off a toxic smoke that caused us all to leave while the fire burned out. Toxic teachings were giving off toxic smoke!

Cristobal also wanted to be able to sing the hymns in the church

Cristóbal Covelli typing hymns on his Braille machine

meetings and asked me if I would dictate hymns to him so that he could type them out on his braille machine. He eventually had 180 hymns. He continued teaching the blind children from the Gospels of John and a number of these students came to know the Lord Jesus as Savior. Two young men began attending services at the

176

chapel, and another older, totally blind man got saved. His wife was clinically blind and, together with several of their children, became a part of the local church. Felix Amado Mendoza and his wife learned the art of broom-making at the Blind Institute; and also other professions, such as making aluminum plates, spoons and other articles from melted down soda cans. With these crafts he was able to support his family along with some help we were able to give them. Eventually the family lived in an old house next to the Bucaramanga chapel, which was owned by the church. We are thankful to the Lord that Feliz and his wife and children had gone on living for the Lord. He went to be with the Lord December 22, 2008.

As the months went by, I continued to get more and more involved with the activities at the Blind Institute, sometimes using my vehicle to transport students to recreational activities. The director had more and more confidence in me and on one occasion asked if I would be able to take her, and the state representative of the health organization, to a town in the mountains called Contratación. This was a town about five hours drive into the mountains south of Bucaramanga, and was a leper colony. Many of the lepers had not only lost fingers, toes and other extrematies, but many had lost their eyesight as well.

That trip was a very interesting experience, being in a town with around 900 people suffering from leprosy. There was a hospital for treating the lepers with qualified doctors and nurses. The town had their own radio station run by lepers, with an announcer who also suffered from the same disease. Many of the lepers were there with their families and their children, bringing the total number of inhabitants to about 2000.

Knowing about how the lepers were treated in the Bible times made me feel a little uncomfortable when meeting some of these people. I had been told that the disease was not contagious when under treatment, unless there was an open sore and contact was made that way. Nevertheless, when I was invited with the director and a representative into one of the homes I felt a little "strange," especially when in typical Colombian style, we were welcomed with a hug by a blind leper. Then they offered us a drink and brought glasses of lemonade from the kitchen. I managed to drink the lemonade, but not without feelings of reserve!

Blind lepers at Contratación

Sadly, the work among blind lepers is difficult as these unfortunate people have lost their sense of touch and cannot learn braille, plus the difficulties of the emotional complexes they form as a result of the disease. The only way they can be helped is by utilizing their hearing. So the Blind Institute rented a couple of rooms for a library of tape recordings. I was able to include a large number of tapes with Bible readings of the Gospels and Psalms, plus some stirring gospel messages and Bible teaching. Being there as a helper of the Blind Institute, there was no difficulty in being able to leave those evangelical messages for the blind people. The Catholic Church generally ran the town, and normally it would be virtually impossible for me, as an evangelical missionary, to set up something like that. But, praise the Lord, nothing is impossible with Him!

Latin American Congress For The Blind, November 1975

In early October 1975 I was speaking with the Director of the Blind Institute, who asked if I would be available to help with an upcoming international Congress for the services to the blind. I agreed to help, thinking that I would have opportunity to at least find out what the Congress was all about and get some insights into ways to help blind people. At the first general meeting, I accepted the position of public relations where I would be in a position to help some of the foreigners who were coming, and to translate for them. However, as it turned out, I was also placed on the reception committee, which was really the central committee for the organization of the entire Congress.

There were four of us on that committee including the director of the institute. We had to work out the full program, bringing together the other five committees, so that they would know what was expected of them. Of course if they fell down on their part, then those of us who were on the central committee had to take over. In other words we were running the whole show. They even put my name in the local newspaper a couple of times, as it was a rather big affair with 14 countries represented, plus 20 observers from the United Nations. I had to be involved in meeting the 80 who were coming from outside Colombia, plus 100 more delegates from Colombia itself. There was a welcome at the state governor's office, followed by a cocktail evening so that people would be able to get to know one another.

The second day, a Saturday, there was an outing to the country club with a full-blown fiesta that included a roasted calf over an open spit. They actually had two calves as there were more than 300 people attending. We had to arrange simultaneous translations for the English speakers and I had a part in that. I must admit I did have difficulties with some of the technical medical language, but fortunately, many of the words in English and Spanish, had Latin roots that made it possible for the doctors to understand my sometimes poor translations.

We had to organize transport to and from the hotel and meals for all those people. Fortunately, the other committees did work well and that was a tremendous help. I was hoping to get some good contacts from these people from different countries, which did come about. During that time I became friends with the Secretary for Education in our state, plus a few other important people. One of those contacts was with Dr. Richard Hoover, the man who invented the system for the use of the cane. I also met the director of the Braille

179

With Dr. Richard Hoover and his wife.

Publishing House in the USA who promised to supply, on demand, Bibles and books in braille for us. Another doctor invited me to go to the United States for six weeks to do a specialized course in working with the blind.

However, this was not possible, much to Ann's relief. At one point Ann said to me, "I have hardly seen you all week. While you are going out to restaurants to eat fancy meals, we sit at home eating bread and jam." The life of a missionary wife is not always easy! But this time was beneficial because it made possible the many good contacts and specialized training in working with the blind. On a visit to New York some months later, I met with the doctor who promised Braille books and Bibles, and was also able to purchase a number of folding canes as well as the small portable apparatuses the students could carry in their bags for writing in braille. I was able to explain what I had learned and Ann also came to understand and appreciate working with the blind believers that became part of the local churches in Bucaramanga.

The work with the Blind Institute continued for almost three years. But, eventually the children who had been accepting the Lord as Savior were talking about their faith at home. This caused these Catholic parents to complain to the Blind Institute about the evangelicals teaching their children. Very sadly the director told me that the complaints had come to her from higher up and that I could no longer continue with the Saturday religion classes.

During the time I was able to serve at the Blind Institute, many had come to know the Lord as Savior. Several years later, one of those blind young men went to the bookshop in the Omnicentro. While conversing with Marina, he asked her to tell me that he was pastoring a small church in a country area. Praise the Lord! He had produced much fruit for His glory.

In all of these things we see how the Lord opens doors of opportunity for those who are seeking them (or He shoots the sharpened arrow). He has a time for a special work that he blesses and then the time comes for the door to be shut. For me it wasn't a time to be discouraged as the Lord was opening a new door, a new work. The planting of the Lagos Dos church was beginning.

Revelation 3:7 *"What he opens no one can shut and what he shuts no one can open."*

Intensive Bible Study Retreats

At one of our regular missionary meetings in 1978, I proposed having a time of intensive Bible teaching with the view to training and preparing our younger believers to be more effective in their work in the local churches. The idea was approved and we decided to hold these "Intensivos" at the church camp, Campamento Betania, near the village of Felidia, in the mountains just west of Cali.

My vision was to help these students of the Word to be leaders with a strong biblical foundation. The first year we had seven one-hour teaching periods each of the days except on Sundays. At the end of the 15 days we had exams with prizes for those who excelled. These were mostly expensive reference and study books from my bookshop. These studies were very exhausting for the students and teachers so we later dropped the daily lessons to five each day. During the planning of the retreat, I asked each of the

Intensive Bible Study Retreat students and teachers early 1980's

Intensive Bible Study Group another year

presenters to make detailed notes of each lecture so that the students could take them home for use in their home churches. This would also help the students remember what had been taught.

At the first retreat the teachers were made up of three missionaries, a national believer and an overseas visitor. Alden Poehner lived in Cali and had studies on the tabernacle and the offerings, while his wife Inge gave insights into children's work, including the preparation of Sunday School lessons. Julio Palacio, a national brother and wonderful teacher, had lessons on angels, demons and created beings, including mankind. He later had some courses on Systematic Theology. Bill Van Ryn was a missionary in Puerto Rico for many years, but by the time the retreats started he was back in the USA and so attended the Intensivos each year. His topics at those early retreats were on the book of Hebrews and many of the Epistles.

We had some very practical studies such as open air preaching, door-to-door visitation and street evangelization, as well as hermeneutics (the art of interpretation) and homiletics (the art of preaching,) to help with message preparation for Bible teachers. Each Saturday we went to the village of Felidia where open-air meetings were held, while others went door-to-door.

I also had teaching sessions and began a series, which I originally called, *A Bird's Eye View of the Bible.* I gave a one-hour outline on one book of the Bible each day, starting in Genesis and completing to 2 Chronicles that first year. I also had a study on paganism. In other years I taught the New Testament, Matthew to Ephesians and continued the next four years alternating between the Old and New Testaments until I had covered each book of the Bible. I also had more in-depth studies on the Pastoral Epistles. As a result of these and other studies over the next ten years, I had many notes, which I was eventually able to edit, expand and publish as study books. The Bible survey of 371 pages, I called *A Panoramic View of the Bible;* the Pastoral Epistles were a collection of three much shorter books.

There was, and still is, a lot of superstition and witchcraft in Colombia and after giving a series of 16 studies in the local church on Satan, demons and the angels, I again edited the notes to publish the book entitled, *Satan and the Heavenly Hosts.* Another series, which I used as a basis for discipleship, was the *Gates of Jerusalem*, in Nehemiah 3. Using the names of the Gates, which have interesting meanings, and the order of those names gives a basis for teaching progressive growth in the Christian life. I eventually wrote *Jerusalem's Gates* in English, which was published by Emmaus Correspondence School Ministries, and is available for purchase today.

The retreats were a real blessing for the remaining years I was in Colombia. Many of the original students went on to help in their local churches and some became commended full time workers. After circumstances caused me to leave Colombia, other missionaries carried on the studies expanding the number of days to months, and now it is a full year of intensive Bible study.

13

LAGOS DOS CHURCH PLANTING

The first church in Bucaramanga was growing in 1976 and there were a number of families living in the suburb of Lagos Dos south of the city. In our discussions together with the Rothlisbergers, we decided to begin a children's work on Saturdays in that area with the view to starting a new church. This was the same area where Alan Tonkin and I had begun a children's outreach about three years earlier in the nearby suburb of Cindad Valencia. Several members of our church in Bucaramanga, including Mario Puentes and Gonzalo Pinzón lived in this suburb. They lived in row houses side by side so we decided to use the front parlors of each house and their small backyards for the Sunday School type classes. The front rooms were very small, about eight-by-ten feet, and when packed with 30 children there was no room to move. We started each session with singing, using guitars for accompaniment, and then the children, according to their ages, moved to different areas of the house and backyards for their classes.

Once a month we projected a gospel film from the open area in front of the houses. By running an extension cord to the Ford van, for power, and setting up the projector in the back of the vehicle with the doors open, and loud speakers on the roof, we projected the film onto a bed sheet hung on the front wall of the house. There was no color TV at that time so a movie was a great attraction and we often had more than 200 people standing in the open area around the Ford. At these open-air screenings we usually stopped the film at a strategic point. Then we gave a short gospel message with an invitation for any who were interested to talk with us after the movie, or to talk with one of the family members who lived there. Had we not stopped the movie midway to give the message, the people

The house we purchased to turn into a chapel

would have left to go home. Stopping projection was a bit like having a "commercial" and the folk usually stayed to see the end.

We had a weeknight prayer and Bible study meeting, and the little original group of about five families began to grow. It reached the point where we really needed more space and a corner row house a few blocks away from the Puentes' and Pinzóns' homes became available for purchase. Renovation was needed and because homes there are built of concrete block this is more possible than with other construction. Some of the interior walls of the ground floor were pulled down and eventually the entrance area was extended to give as much room as possible for the meetings. The second floor was also changed to provide a couple of Sunday School rooms and a small apartment for a caretaker. The inside stairs were taken down and an outside staircase built making the upstairs apartment independent and also giving more room for the meetings on the lower level to hold about 80 people.

The work was finally done and we planned the "inauguration meetings" for a couple of weekends hence. Meanwhile we told the children about our plans, arranging for some literature and handouts to be printed as well as driving the Jeep-style Toyota around the suburb with the loud speakers on the roof announcing the planned meetings.

However, one issue caused some consideration, and matter for prayer. There had been many blackouts during that time because the revolutionary guerrillas had blown up several high-tension power towers. We were discussing our concern that there might be a blackout during the inauguration. The older children's teacher had told them about the upcoming meetings and had "hoped" we would not have a blackout during that time. The following week a couple of the children in that class told their teacher, "You have taught us

186

that God answers prayer and so we have all decided to pray that we won't have a blackout, so you don't have to worry." When that teacher told us what her class had decided, we were really concerned, as we didn't want these children to doubt the Lord's promises for answered prayer. So we told all the believers to really pray diligently so that these children's faith would be strengthened. What a lesson for us "mature" believers this was that challenged our faith and prayer lives.

Each of the three nights we had special presentations with singing and testimonies. Then one of us would preach the Gospel, after which we screened a gospel film. With the projector inside the chapel and a sheet hanging at the entrance, which was the original garage opening, the film could be seen from both sides. Every night the chapel was completely full, not even with standing room. There was also a crowd of more than 100 on the lawn in front of the chapel. At the end of each meeting we made an appeal to receive the Lord Jesus as Savior and Lord, and many made professions of faith.

The first meeting was Friday evening at 7:00 PM and the lights stayed on, for which we all breathed a sigh of relief. It was the same on Saturday night. Sunday night went really well, we had the largest crowd of all three nights. The first part of the meeting went well

A house becomes a chapel at Lagos Dos

while Andrew Rothlisberger was giving a 40-minute Gospel message before the film, and the lights remained shining. While Andrew was in the middle of his message, every light in the suburb went off…. Except…in the chapel! The upstairs lights went off and even the illuminated sign at the front of the chapel, CENTRO BÍBLICO went out.

I was standing out in front among those who could not get inside that night. Some commented to me, "Great that you have your own generator."

I said, "We don't have a generator, what you are seeing is a miracle, God is answering prayer." One of the young brothers came out to me and asked, "Hermano Juan, should I go home and get a couple of flashlights?"

I replied, "No, if you go home, stay there. We don't need that sort of faith."

Now a major test came. Do we turn off the lights downstairs, and turn on the projector for the movie? If the Lord has given us light, then we need to trust Him. So we turned off the overhead lights, screened a 45 minute film, then switched off the projector (a 16mm Bell and Howell, reel-to-reel movie projector which requires a powerful light). At the end of the film, we turned the overhead lights back on to make the appeal for people to receive the Lord Jesus for salvation.

After the film, there were some who came and were counseled; others stood around talking yet, and still, the ground floor lights were like a beacon in a dark night. Gradually people began to leave and one by one the chapel emptied so that only Julio Villamizar, who was the caretaker at the time, and I were left standing at the front door marveling at the wonderful answer to prayer. We finally said "Buenas Noches!" Julio began to shut the door to the chapel and then the ground floor lights went off to join in the darkness of the blackout. We could not help just laughing and rejoicing at God's timing and in seeing just a small part of the awesomeness of God in answering children's prayers.

14

EL PLAYÓN

Lagos Dos Church Reaching Out

The local church in the Bucaramanga suburb of Lagos Dos had been established and growing for three years. One Sunday evening the church elders were together, as usual, before the gospel meeting to pray for the speaker and seek direction about speakers for the subsequent weeks. After our prayers, Mario made the comment, "Hermano Juan, you missionaries have been here now for many years and have helped us establish these two churches. We think it is time for us to reach out and try to start a new church ourselves."

I was really encouraged hearing this, as the Lagos Dos church was a hive-off from the first church we planted in Bucaramanga that had begun in 1972. I was thrilled to hear that there was a desire for the on-going work to be done by the nationals rather than the missionaries always heading up new endeavors. We prayed together asking the Lord to give us guidance as to where a new church could be established and on several weekends visited towns and villages in the mountains around our area. In one small town we set up the amplifiers on our vehicle, started to sing and then stones were thrown at us, so we packed up and decided that perhaps this was not the place to start a new work.

Then, on November 25, 1979, another Sunday evening a few weeks later, the men were again together for the usual prayer before the evening meeting. Esau arrived late and with excitement announced, "Did you hear about El Playón? The town was being inaugurated as a municipality yesterday with all sorts of celebrations. Then this morning at 6:00 a flash flood crashed through the town killing hundreds of people." We had heard of this small town of about 2000 people, but had not visited there before.

We all discussed this calamity and had some prayer for the survivors. One of the men suggested we contact the Civil Defense people to see if we could help. Another one of the men, who lived close to the chapel, went home to make contact with the Civil Defense. They informed him that they would be making arrangements to take in doctors, medical supplies, and some engineers to see what could be done at 6:00 AM the following day. He then offered my 15-seat Ford Club Wagon, and the Civil Defense people told him they would send the doctors and their equipment in my vehicle.

Together with Gonzalo Pinzón I drove to the Civil Defense pickup area early Monday morning and collected five doctors and a couple of nurses, loaded their equipment, then headed north out of Bucaramanga for El Playón some 50 miles away. We made pretty good time over the mountains through Rio Negro and back up more mountains to about 10 miles from the town. This was the rainy season so there were numerous landslides, which we were able to drive around. But 10 miles south of El Playón, where the valley was narrower, there had been a very large landslide during the night, which had totally blocked the road. This landslide left most of the road collapsed down into the valley so it was impossible to drive around it.

I left Gonzalo with the vehicle and, together with the doctors, walked around the landslide carrying all the equipment. Traffic coming from the opposite direction was also backed up, including several dump trucks. These dump trucks had turned to drive back to El Playón, charging a fare for any who did not want to walk. Many climbed on board including the medical people and we continued to the edge of town where we were able to climb down with the medical gear and walk into the devastated town. It was a horrific sight; most of the center of the town had disappeared. It left sand and dirt up to four feet deep covering the road and over the ruins of houses and shops. According to the newspapers, some 2,000 tons of tree trunks and timber was scattered where the town used to be. Here and there were a few buildings that were damaged but still standing. We headed toward higher ground on one side of the town. The Catholic Church was up on the hill overlooking the town along with some residences that had not been affected.

190

The main road entering El Playón the day after the flash flood

The Civil Defense men set up a few tables in an open area close to the Catholic Church from which they directed the workers and helpers. Because I had come with the medical team I think they thought I was also a doctor. I was asked to set up a clinic in the Catholic Church and, without correcting their thinking that I was a doctor, just went up to the church and decided one corner of the church would make a good place for the clinic. I called on a couple of men standing around to move the benches and clear an area where we could set up tables for the medicines and vaccinations against cholera and typhoid, as well as the first aid materials. At first they said they would have to ask the priest, but I said, "Listen, I am in charge here; the priest is out of town, and the Civil Defense has ordered this place to be used for a clinic." Someone had just told me that the priest had left for Bogotá, as he did not want to be there and be called on to use all of his supplies, which he had locked up somewhere in the church.

I told the men what I wanted and finally had everything set up, then went looking for the doctors who were working at the Civil Defense tables treating folk for injuries and cuts. After telling them that the church was ready for their use one of the doctors said to me, "Why don't you just go ahead?"

I replied, "I am sorry but I am not a doctor." He was surprised at this information, and sent one of the nurses to the church to start treating patients there.

A "chopper" takes the most seriously injured to Bucaramanga

Watching, as a helicopter picked up some of the more seriously injured and took off for Bucaramanga, I was overwhelmed by the chaotic and sad scene. While looking for any way to be helpful, I listened to some of the stories of the survivors and their close encounters with death. Soon we learned exactly what had caused this disastrous flash flood and about those who heroically tried to help. This is the account they described:

At 6:00 AM that Sunday a natural dam, made of debris from landslides further up river, burst; and a 30-foot wave crashed down the valley, bringing with it trees, rocks, mud and sand which battered the town when it finally reached there. During the early hours a pharmacist, whose pharmacy was right on the north side of the town and situated on the road not far from the bridge over the river leading into the town, soon realized that the level of the river, which was usually high during the rainy season, had dropped to a trickle. Just before 6:00 AM he began to use the microphone and the loud speakers on the roof of his building to warn the people that there might be a flash flood. Some people listened and went to higher ground; others did not take any notice, not really believing what he was saying.

Suddenly they heard a rumbling, which soon became a roaring sound, getting louder every second. The pharmacist looked out from his building and saw a dump truck passing with people climbing into the back as it was moving down the flooding street. He continued calling out, warning the people to run, and many managed to get onto the truck. The driver accelerated as fast as possible, south toward higher ground on the other side of town. The wave was now roaring down through the town, the water as high as the rooftops and rapidly catching up with the truck. Fortunately, the truck began to climb to higher ground as the riverbed turned away from the road, but even so, the waters at that moment were rushing over the rear wheels. The pharmacist continued warning the people until the wave crashed through his home and business. He disappeared in those crashing waters and was never seen again. Another truck did not make it to higher ground and was left on its side half buried in the sand. All on board that second truck were among the more than 1,000 people who disappeared that day, whose bodies were never found. The pharmacist was the real hero of the day.

Many houses and also the police station had disappeared. The town then resembled a huge beach with a few buildings jutting up here and there. Any buildings that remained intact were full of sand up to the lintel of the doors. The majority of the homes had completely disappeared.

One lady, holding her eight-month-old baby son was about to be washed off the roof, when she slipped and the baby was thrown

Distributing food and clothing the 2nd day after the flash flood

193

from her arms as she was caught up in the rushing waters and swept miles downstream. Miraculously, even though battered by branches and household appliances that were by then being washed along with the tree trunks and other debris, she found herself at the edge of the rushing waters at a turn of the riverbed, and managed to pull herself to safety. Heartbroken that the baby was gone, she was able to find her way back to town. She was a terrible mess, looking like she had been mashed in some sort of grinder. As she came up to the Civil Defense tables for treatment, a neighbor came up to her and said, "You won't believe this, I had just gotten to higher ground when I turned around and a little baby was floating at the edge of the waters. I picked the baby up and he cried." Yes! It was the injured lady's baby; both had survived the tragedy of the flash flood and were reunited!

We had several displaced people sleeping at the chapel in Lagos Dos for a couple weeks after the flood, including that young lady who had been washed off the roof and carried down the river. We had presented the gospel to her and her husband who were, as you can imagine, very receptive.

Arriving back in Bucaramanga Monday evening, we had a meeting with as many as possible from the church and decided to use the chapel as a center-point for the collection of food and clothing. We moved the benches to the back of the chapel and set up some tables where we could organize and pack food bags to take to El Playón. Two of the men took my Toyota Land Cruiser with the amplifier and loud speakers on the roof to advertise around the suburb that we were collecting food and clothing. They announced that any who wished to help could leave their donations at the chapel. We made up a roster of people from our church who could help with the packing and organization of the food and clothes. We were happy to see that everyone in the local church was cooperating in one way or another.

Tuesday morning I went to the local Cajasan supermarket to speak with the manager about what we were doing. He was sympathetic and told me that he would give us as much as possible at his cost price. We purchased bulk quantities of basic dry goods and canned foods. I arranged to get a load of large paper and plastic bags from him, which was a great help in organizing individual
194

packets for distribution to families.

By this time the work in the Lagos Dos chapel was up and running. Together, with Andrew Rothlisberger's Toyota Landcruiser and my van, we loaded up the bags of supplies along with a good quantity of clothing and set off for El Playón later that day. Bulldozers had cut a road around the largest landslide so we were able to drive around it and on to the town. We set up distribution not far from the Civil Defense people and began to hand out the food and clothing.

El Refugio - The Refuge

By Wednesday, three days after the flood, we realized that there were people from areas outside of the town who were taking advantage of the emergency relief, claiming they had lost everything, in order to get free food. By the end of the week we also discovered that many of the disaster refugees were moving to a farmer's land just south of the town to build shacks from whatever materials they could find to use, and began squatting there.

I spoke to Julio Villamizar, who had come along every day to help, and said, "Why don't we build something on the land with the refugees and work from there? We might be better able to control the relief work." Julio agreed, and Friday afternoon I went to a local lumberyard in Bucaramanga to speak with the foreman.

"Our church people are helping the damnificados (refugees) in El Playón and we would like to put up a small building from which we could distribute the food and clothing. It would be helpful to have a distribution center for better organization. People are coming from everywhere to try to get free food and clothing and some of the truly needy may be missing out." This man agreed to get some timber for us with which to build a small building and told me to come back the following Monday to collect it.

The next Sunday, after our usual meetings, we discussed the help needed and everyone wanted to become involved in whatever way they could. There were several men skilled in construction who were willing to come with us to build the distribution shack. Others offered other help and the ladies each took responsibility for the time they could be at the chapel to receive and process the donations coming from citizens of the city.

Monday morning, after taking all the seats out of the Ford Club wagon, Esau and I went to the lumberyard to see what the foreman had collected for us. We loaded the van to the ceiling with rough timber. Most of the wood was offcuts with very few perfect boards, but he told me he would not charge me anything for it, so I had no reason to complain. After taking two loads of supplies that day we began the construction of our little building. Several men with construction expertise rode in the Land Cruiser. With a few pounds of nails, hammers and saws, and a number of sheets of corrugated steel for the roof, the building project began. In two days we had the walls up and the roof was going on. By late Tuesday we had a room about 25 feet long by 20 feet wide. We had a six foot wooden shutter on hinges that we could open by lifting into the room, which was held up with a piece of rope hooked to a nail in the ceiling. The main room was divided with a small area at the back that was used to store bags of rice and other dry goods. The next job was to make benches, with no backs, and with their bases dug into the earthen floor. This room was to be our meeting room, or church. I took a small can of paint and painted the words *"EL REFUGIO"*, The Refuge, to the right of the front door of our small building. Together with Julio, I went around to every one of the 125 shacks now built on the farmer's land, to take a census of every family. I had a book with the family names, how many people lived in their shack, as well as the

Construction of the "Refuge" El Playón

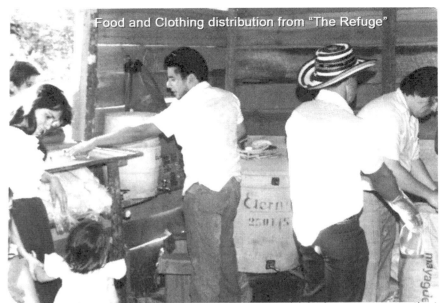
Food and Clothing distribution from "The Refuge"

names and ages of the children. This would help us ensure that those needing help were the only ones receiving it.

The police inspector visited us and was impressed that we were more organized than the authorities. He used the lists from my census to add to his lists of all the displaced persons. He encouraged us to continue on there and the authorities were pleased with what we were doing.

There was also need for fresh water, as the river water close by was contaminated and not good to drink. A Baptist minister in Bucaramanga had wanted to do something to help and since we were already heavily involved there, he asked me what we needed. I told him about the fresh water situation and that we knew of a fresh spring about a half mile away. His congregation paid for a half mile of two inch heavy plastic tubing, which we ran from the spring down into the "settlement." Our builders came the following Saturday and built a water tank six feet high and four feet square. The tank had a one-half inch pipe for a spout out each of the four sides near the top. That provided a continuous flow of clear, fresh water. The people quickly brought their buckets for good water; and most also, half-dressed, had a sort of shower under one of the spouts.

Hygiene was also becoming a problem as people were just using the field near their shacks as a toilet. I asked a couple of the men from the settlement to see if they could find a drainage pipe somewhere on the property. A few hours later they came back and took me to an old 5-inch sewer pipe where a house had once stood. We still had some materials from the water tank project, which could be used for this also. After they had opened a hole in the top of the pipe they built a brick donut shaped stool and seat over it. I still had four sheets of corrugated steel from our building so we stood them on end around the new toilet. One could be used as a door giving a little privacy and as we finished it, the locals stood there "oohing and ah-ing" over this new addition to the community. Oddly, over the next few weeks the tin sides began to disappear each night, only to be seen on the roof of someone's shack. We continued to bring tin to place around the toilet as well as extra for their roofs.

Ten days went by and it was becoming apparent we had need for some electricity. I had a small Honda generator that we some-times used in the country areas to screen one of our 16mm gospel films. I sent the word around the refugee community for everyone to go look for a good stout pole for their shack to which we would run some electric wiring. The following day, along with supplies for The Refuge I brought a large roll of electric wiring suitable for the job. I had the men run a couple of wires to each shack and put a light fitting inside their shack, together with a 25-watt light bulb. Of course we included several light fixtures for The Refuge as well, which would be needed when we had the nightly meetings there. The work was very primitive and I'm sure would not be up to the American standards of approval, but it got the job done. That night we had the "Light Inauguration." Everyone was excited and as soon as it was dark I started up the Honda generator, and then came the big moment when I hit the switch to send out the power to 125 shacks. For a moment, I thought some great soccer team had just scored; there was a loud cheering from all over the area. Yes, the light worked!

We had a town hall meeting in The Refuge with at least one member of each family attending. I laid down the rules for the use of the electricity, telling them that since we only had a small gen-erator, they could use just one 25-watt light bulb. One of the main reasons for the electricity was so that they could have some light for the evening meal and the children could do their homework. Nothing else could be connected as it would damage the generator and everyone would lose. If anyone broke the rule, they would lose their connection.

All went well for two evenings and then suddenly, on the third night, the generator slowed down and the lights dimmed. I turned off the generator and went around to each shack to find the culprit. It wasn't long before one lady confessed to hooking up her electric iron to press some shirts. She apologized profusely, so I used that as an example of "grace" and forgave her, but told her that if it happened again she would be cut off. It was a good example for the whole settlement and we had no more trouble.

One of the regular gospel meetings in the "Refuge"

In early January, with our Bucaramanga churches fully involved, Julio offered to take a month off from his regular work and live in The Refuge to protect the food and materials, as well as to conduct gospel meetings every night. We hung a hammock between two supporting poles at one end of The Refuge for his bed and this became his home for the month. He did a magnificent job caring for our goods, and handling the distribution of food and clothing each day. Also he was helping the different families with the "improvements" to their shacks, keeping a record of tools that were lent for construction and preaching the gospel every evening. After Julio

199

had to return to his regular employment other men from the Bucaramanga churches would volunteer to stay for a few days or weeks at a time to continue the oversight and help at the Refuge. Jesús Trejos, a full time worker, joined us February 20, and continued at El Playón for several years.

Every Saturday, for a couple of months, the young people came down from our two churches in Bucaramanga to El Playón and held a mini-VBS with the children from the settlement. During the afternoon they had games, competitions and Bible stories. In the evening we set up the 16mm Bell and Howell projector to screen a gospel film. Of course we needed all the power from our small generator for the outside lights and the projector, so I cut off all the house lights. It was wonderful to see just about everyone come out to the meeting in the open air just outside The Refuge! There were too many adults and children to fit inside. Along with some rousing singing, a gospel film, followed by the preaching of the gospel, many came to know the Lord as Savior.

It wasn't long, however, before some opposition began. A communist activist built a shack beside our Refuge and began to tell everyone what they should do and started trouble by trying to get the people to rebel against the order established by the local police inspector. That year was an election year and the people would be going to the booths to elect a new president. Unfortunately, some political maneuvering had already been underway in El Playón. Some politicians were giving things to the flood victims two months after it happened, in order to get votes. About that time the mayor of a nearby town arrived to get everyone who didn't have property deeds in the old town off the land where they were squatting. This was really unfair, as many who had lost all they owned had been renting their houses and, therefore, were not owners with a deed. He also made reference to the religious groups saying they would have to go. He stated that in 15 days after his visit he would send in the Army to move everyone by force if we were still there. It wasn't difficult to see what he was getting at, as we were the only religious group working in the area. He obviously could not claim to have helped the victims of the flash flood while we were there, as everyone knew exactly who had been helping continuously.

Because of this harassment, Jorge Ocampo and I made arrangements through a local politician that Jorge knew in Bucaramanga, to have an audience with Doña Nidia de Turbay, wife of the president of Colombia who was overseeing that particular project. A letter of introduction got us as far as her secretary, but unfortunately the First Lady wasn't in Bogota that day. We had a good talk with the secretary who asked us to put our requests and complaints in writing, and she promised to deliver a letter outlining the situation for us when the president's wife returned.

One of our requests was that the government quickly settle the matter of the purchase of the land where the flood victims were squatting so that proper homes could be built. Our visit was on Wednesday and by Friday that week we read in the newspaper that the property had been purchased by the government with a view to allocating plots to the flood victims. I don't know if our visit and letter were directly responsible for this rapid arrangement, but at least it was good news for the folk in El Playón. We gradually stopped giving out the same quantities of food as before, as many were then working again and there wasn't the same need for the majority of the people. We did continue giving out milk and vitamins to the families with children.

A Church Is Planted

As more people accepted the Lord as Savior we began classes with candidates for baptism, which not only included teaching about the Christian life, but also about the meaning of the Church and fundamental doctrines regarding the believer's part in the Church. After the tragedy in November the first fruits of our labors were seen on May 10, 1980, when Jesús Trejos baptized six new believers, four women and two men. I spoke on the meaning of baptism while standing on a rock at the edge of the river. After the baptism we walked back to the Refuge and had the first worship service with breaking of bread (communion) in El Playón. There were three carloads of believers from the two churches in Bucaramanga who had come to share in that joyful event.

The Sunday following the baptism, we had many from the Bucaramanga church come again to join with us for the meetings. Together with these newly baptized believers we had a wonderful worship service, partaking of the symbols of the bread and wine, as the Lord

Jesus Trejos baptizes the first Believers El Playón

Jesus desired, and a local church was formed in El Playón. The Lord had answered the prayers of the believers at Lagos Dos and used them, along with folk from the Bucaramanga church, to establish this new church in El Playón. As the work continued over the following months, others were saved, baptized and added to the local church. We were able to bring in medical doctors, dentists, and other workers to teach and help these people who had lost everything they possessed. The Lord had done a magnificent work!

By the river for the first baptisms

Finally, in mid-September, word came that the government had finally decided to do something to help the *damnificados*, (refugees) and the town was to be rebuilt on higher ground not far from where the people were squatting. Together with Jorge Ocampo, a good friend from the Lagos Dos church, we went to Bogotá again to speak with the president's wife. We were told that all the *damnifica-dos* who had lost their homes in the flash flood would get a block of land free and an interest-free loan to rebuild. Jorge and I were given a copy of the architectural plans for the new community, showing the streets and blocks of land that would be available.

We were happy to report all this good news to the refugees and committed to continue working with them in their eventual reloca-tion. As with any government project, this did not happen quickly, but

Believers outside the new Chapel - El Playón

we continued as usual working out of The Refuge. Julio and I went around to all the shacks in the settlement showing the plans to each family and telling them about the future plans for the town. A short time later when the engineer who would be overseeing the project arrived, I recognized him right away. We had held Bible studies in his home in Bucaramanga and knew the family well. He suggested that since we had been squatting and helping these folks for many months we could have three blocks of land to build a chapel.

"Which blocks of land would you like?" he asked. We opened up the plans and after checking for a good central location I said, "Those three blocks right in the middle of the settlement would suit us really well!" This was an ideal spot, a place that usually the Cath-olic Church would take in any town. It is always wonderful to see how the Lord prepares and works out His purposes. The land was being cleared, the streets were being marked out and the area was getting to the point where everyone would soon be able to move to the land they were allocated.

Approximately nine months after the flood, with life for these displaced people being more settled, they could look forward to rebuilding on land provided by the government. I continued taking food and supplies to El Playón on Wednesdays, not needing to go every day with Jesús Trejos being there to carry on the daily work. I continued to visit regularly to stay aware of needs, bringing supplies and encouraging the new believers.

Newspaper article on the day of the inauguration. The President stated that the new suburb was to be called "El Refugio." Unfortunately politicians later changed the name.

Revolutionary Guerrillas, Death Threats And High Speed Chases

At the end of the Tuesday evening meeting in The Refuge on September 16, 1980, a man from the settlement called me over and told me that the revolutionary guerrillas were telling the squatters that the plan to give them land and an interest-free loan was just a government trick to get them off the farmer's land. These guerrillas said they had a plan to bring in guns and would stand and fight alongside the people when the army came to move them. They would fight to help them keep what they had struggled to re-establish for themselves after the flood. When I heard that, I took

Julio and together we again visited all the shacks on the farmer's property and I personally guaranteed that they would get what had been promised. Because we had been the only ones to help them over the past months they believed us and told the guerrillas they would not fight.

By this time we had people not only from the settlement but also from the old town now in the church, as well as some from the farms in the surrounding mountain area. A week or so later, on a Wednesday evening before the meeting, a believer from outside of town came up to me and called me away from the people standing around in The Refuge.

"Hermano Juan, I'm sorry to have to tell you this, but you should not come back here to El Playón any more."

"Why, Luis?" I asked

"The guerrillas are marching around in the mountains near here and telling everyone that you are an American spy with the CIA, that you have an emerald mine in the mountains, are exploiting the country's wealth, and that all the people you have in the settlement will be forced into slavery to work your mines. They have you on a hit list and are going to kill you!"

I didn't know what to think about that, and said, "I am not with the CIA; I am not even American!" I wondered if this wasn't just some story to stop me from helping in the town. However, at the meeting that evening, two very uncouth, dirty, sullen, and tough-looking men were standing at the back of the Refuge and just stared at me all through the meeting. "Maybe there's some truth in what Luis said!" I thought.

A couple of days later after Luis told me that, as I was walking back from the post office in Bucaramanga, 50 miles away from El Playón, a decently dressed man called me over and asked, "Why are you here? Who pays you? What are you doing here in Colombia? I want to come to your house tonight and talk with you."

Then I was really worried! With many disconcerting thoughts running in my mind I went to the hardware store and bought a couple of heavy padlocks and headed for my bookshop in the Omnicentro (a local mall) where the car was parked. While there I checked in with Esau and Marina who were working in my bookshop, warning them to be aware of any possible dangerous situation. Then I drove home to Cañaveral, the suburb where we lived. I told Ann and Diane, who at the age of 16, needed to know about the accusations that had been made saying I had an emerald mine in the mountains and the M-19, as the guerrillas were called, were threatening to kill me. It was then that Ann told me about a strange woman taking a survey that afternoon. Ann was home because the time of the ladies' meeting had been changed that afternoon. The woman came to the door claiming to be a neighbor from a nearby street. She said she was doing a survey about Toyota vehicles and all sorts of questions like, "Where do you use this vehicle: in the mountains, rocky areas, or just on paved roads?" Then she wanted to know about our finances: did we have a farm, how many cars did we have, the age of the cars and the vehicles our friends might have. She even asked about Andrew Rothlisberger's car. At that moment, Diane who was listening to the inquiry, demurred and said, "We shouldn't be talking about other people." Ann agreed and at this point the lady left.

I warned them that we now really needed to be careful and always aware of what was going on around us. We had a steel front door with a good deadbolt lock as well as a sliding bolt door latch that could be secured with a padlock. I put the padlock on and told the family that the door needed to be securely locked at all times.

Next, in a very un-missionary-like way, I oiled my pistol and shotgun, and then gave Diane instructions about how to load the weapons in case there was an assault on the house. At that moment, thinking of protecting my family, I thought, "Well, I'm not going to be taken without a fight." Again, most un-missionary-like! You have to understand that this was Colombia in 1980 and people were being shot all the time, homes broken into and many being kidnapped by either bandits or guerrillas. But in spite of all of this preparation, prayer was our strongest weapon and we used it often!

The next day Ann and I went to the suburb Pan de Azucar to collect Diane from a friend's house and then we all went to a fair where my bookshop had a literature stand. From there we went to a fast-food shop for supper. As I pulled out to drive home I became aware of car lights that turned on in a car up the street and then it followed us across town. Driving like crazy by squeezing between a tanker truck and another car I lost him at the lights at the Puerta del Sol exit. I then flew down the highway to the suburb Provenza turning off before the car following could see me. After a short time I went back to the main highway to get to our suburb Cañaveral but at the entrance ramp a red car was parked in the middle of the main road slowing down all traffic. Avoiding that ramp I turned off at another exit and drove to a nearby suburb circling back to where the car had been stopping traffic as that was the route to our house. However there was another car parked near that exit. Obviously there were several cars involved in following us and trying to block every road we might take. We did manage to get home safely, parking the car inside our locked garage.

The following Saturday at 1:00 PM Ann took Eloisa, who lived with us, to the chapel for a planned young people's activity. On the way home a red car pulled out in front of her so she slowed and allowed the car to go on ahead. This car turned into our suburb so Ann continued on to the home of our friend Barbara Carreño. Later Ann drove to Provenza to buy bread and as she left the store two motorbikes pulled out and followed her.

Next, the strange phone calls began to come frequently, totally irrelevant to anything we were doing as missionaries in Bucaramanga, and in a short time I noticed that every time I drove away from our home, I had someone tailing me. With this turn of events I decided to go to the F-2, (Secret Police) to let them know that threats had been made against me. I asked to see the man in charge and was taken into the office of a teniente (lieutenant) who asked me, "What seems to be the problem?"

I told him about the work we had been doing in El Playón and how we had been helping the people over the past ten months. Then I shared what the people there had told me about the guerrillas wanting them to fight, along with the subsequent threats against my life. I mentioned that I thought I was being followed and that I decided I should let the authorities know.

The teniente at that point broke in and said, "We know all about it. The M-19 has a loose connection with the FARC and is planning a revolution starting in El Playón. They would have started the fight and then left in the middle of it so that the authorities would kill the refugees. Then the guerrillas would use that as a means of recruiting more followers and march on the old Simon Bolivar route to take

Bogotá. So you spoiled what they were planning, and that's why they want to kill you."

"I had no idea," I replied. The thought suddenly occurred to me, "I stopped a revolution? Unbelievable!"

"Do you know of anyone in El Playón who might have ties to the M-19?" the teniente asked.

"The only one I can think of might be the man who is called Saturnino, a communist activist, who is using the north side of The Refuge as one of the walls of his shack. I don't really know of anyone else," I replied. Saturnino's mother faithfully attended our meetings and had become a believer in Jesus Christ. We would hand out the church bulletin from our Bucaramanga church, which would tell about our activities and need for help in El Playón along with Bible stories and verses. Because she could not read she would have her son read it to her. Therefore, he was also reading about all of our plans. When we realized that he was connected with the guerillas, we started reading the news to her at church and not sending the newsletter home.

I heard a few days after that conversation with the teniente that the communist neighbor had left and we did not ever see him again. One of the other neighbors in the settlement told me that a few men had come to Saturnino's shack and told him that if he was still in El Playón in 24 hours after their visit he would be killed. Colombian justice, I guess!

The teniente went on, "This is what I want you to do; I want you to get the car registration numbers when you are being followed and call them in to me. Here's my card. You can call this number and if I'm not here someone else will take the information for me. Try to act naturally, but be aware of all that is going on around you."

I did not feel too much like acting naturally, knowing that these guys carry automatic weapons and do not have any compunction about blowing people away. I had read some of the James Bond books and learned some ways to drop a tail. "This would be a good time to start doing some of this around the city of Bucaramanga," I thought. The men following me were sometimes a couple of cars back so whenever I had the opportunity, coming up to changing traffic lights, I would slow down on yellow, then fly through just as the lights turned red. This left the "tails" sitting behind cars at the lights. I stopped using turn blinkers so that they had no idea when I was going to turn to fly up a side street. One time after speeding down a side street and up another, I saw a home garage open, drove in and switched the motor off. Then I sat there and watched the chase car fly past in my rear view mirror. It was all very exciting, even though I was really scared. The cars and motorbikes following me continued over the next three months until January 1981.

The following Sunday, after my conversation with the teniente, an officer from the F-2 arrived at the chapel and sat through our two meetings with his gun in the usual carrying bag, which looked like a Bible case. The F-2 followed us the next few days looking out for the ones who had been following us.

Soon after my visit with the F-2 teniente in September, Ann and I had a very long and serious discussion. I had told Andrew and Anne Rothlisberger what was going on and we continued our Thursday times for prayer and discussion. They, along with other missionaries in different parts of Colombia, suggested that we leave Colombia for a while until things cooled off. Ann and I prayed much about this, but did not really have the liberty or direction from the Lord to leave.

"Darling, what are we going to do?" Ann asked.

"I don't know, but I don't feel free to just leave. I am afraid. But if we begin running from fear, we will be running the rest of our lives. I have been thinking that maybe the Lord might want me to die for some reason, possibly to stir up the believers to be more faithful and true to the Lord. Remember how He used the deaths of the five missionaries in Ecuador. BUT, if the Lord doesn't want me to die, then there is nothing they can do to me. Philippians 1:21 came to mind. *'For to me, to live is Christ and to die is gain.'*" The following day the devotional in the *Our Daily Bread* was titled, "Facing Death Fearlessly" with the main thought, *"Those who truly fear God need not fear death."* Here was another timely reminder.

That evening I began our time of reading and prayer with several passages from scripture, reading: Psalm 34:1-10, 46:1-3; Mathew 10:26-31; John 16:33; 2 Kings 7:15-17. With this encouragement we decided that if the Lord wanted to use us to stir up the believers we were willing to pay the price and that this was all worth the anguish.

We made our decision to stay and then let the other missionaries know our decision so they would know how to pray for us. This news went to many churches around the world; so there was much prayer going up on our behalf.

Life Takes On A New Normal And With God's Protection

During one of my regular visits to take supplies, Esau Parra and Noé Valbuena accompanied me. They wanted to come along for encouragement and to be of help in case of an unsafe situation. Coming down the mountain toward the settlement, on the now clear main road, a car began to follow with three men in it. When we arrived in the town 15 minutes later, we stopped in front of The Refuge and the car following stopped 50 yards behind us. We unloaded the supplies and I said, "I don't like the look of this; let's go on down to the police station and let the policeman know."

There was only one policeman in El Playón and I had gotten to know him and had shared the gospel with him. The two-room police station was about three blocks and two streets away in the undestroyed part of the area. But when we arrived the police station was locked up. I said, "Let's get out of here." We jumped back into the Ford Econoline Club Wagon and I swung the vehicle in a sharp U-turn in the open area in front of the station and, spinning the wheels, sped off back toward the main road. Just as we were in the middle of the turn, the car with the three guys came into view past the last building on the street ahead. They must have thought we had collected the policeman, so they accelerated, taking off in the opposite direction going north out of the town. Seeing them run, I decided to chase them and cranked up the speed following in their dust. They were flying to get away and after a mile I pulled a U-turn and headed back South at top speed to Bucaramanga.

Wednesday the 24th, instead of picking up food supplies as I usually did at the Lagos Cajasan (the local grocery store) I decided to purchase more building materials for the people in El Playón. That day my wife Ann decided to go shopping at the Cajasan for our

210

family groceries. When she was driving toward the parking lot, she saw that there were men at different intervals around the parking lot with pouch bags over their shoulders (for holding weapons) and a car close to the entrance pointing out. She made a mental note of the number plate, but drove past, deciding to go to another market. She parked the Toyota Land Cruiser and went into the market. After she had a couple of items in her shopping cart she noticed a man following just two steps behind her. He had nothing in his basket, just carrying it on his arm. She described him as the "ugliest and most brutal looking man," she had ever seen. Leaving her cart behind she hurried out to the car, which by now had cars completely blocking her with one directly in front, behind, and on the street side next to her car. Ann had seen me do some strange things when driving, so she just drove up over the sidewalk, down the path, back onto the road and then hurried home.

When Ann arrived home she called the F-2 teniente and told him what she had seen and what had happened at the market. He replied, "Don't worry ma'am, it's your husband they are going to kill, not you!" That really did not cheer her up! She then told him the car's number plate at the supermarket, at which point he suddenly hung up.

Within a short time the army had surrounded the Cajasan area and picked up six urban guerrillas with their guns and propaganda leaflets. This was news the following day in the local newspaper.

One evening Ann wanted to visit the Rothlisberger family, but before she left I told her, "Don't drive too fast, I will stay back a bit and follow you in the Club Wagon. I want to visit Edmundo and his family in Provenza." She left and a few minutes later I followed her about a hundred yards back. I saw right away as I came out onto the dual road from Cañaveral to the city, that she had a tail. I sped up and drove beside the car. The driver was speaking on a radio of some sort and I just looked down on him as he was in a smaller vehicle. He suddenly looked up and saw me, put the radio down and sped up. I stuck close beside him and then he slowed down again. This went on for a while until Ann had disappeared over the hill. I then turned off into Provenza suburb where Edmundo lived, and drove to his home. There was a blackout that evening in their suburb when I arrived. I drove the Ford onto the short driveway right up

211

to the front door. Ringing the bell, Edmundo's wife came to the door.

"Hola Berta! ¿Como Está? (How are you?) Cómo están las muchachas? (How are the girls)? Está Edmundo? (Is Edmundo home?)"

"Hola, hermano Juan, Edmundo hasn't come home yet."

"Don't worry, I won't come in, I'll just chat for a couple of minutes."

We had only conversed for about 5 minutes when a maroon Dodge pickup flew up the street past where I was standing, then turned around facing back toward where I was with his headlights still on. A minute later a smaller car came into the street facing toward me from the other end. There were at least four men sitting in it with the headlights still on.

"Well, I think I better go now, it's not convenient with the blackout. Give Edmundo my regards." (Obviously I would not go into the house where a woman was alone, especially in the dark, as the impression to anyone watching would be that I was there for immoral activity.)

With that I jumped back into the car and backed it out of the drive, then took off toward the small car now facing toward me. I got out to the dual road leading back to the main road home. A few blocks away a semi-trailer pulled out in front of me blocking my side of the road. I had to slow down and at the same time made it look as though I was going to drive behind the semi. The driver put it into reverse giving me just enough space to squeeze in front of him, and while he was again changing gears, I flew through the narrow space. Continuing out onto the main highway, then at 80 miles-per-hour I drove on to Cañaveral, right into my garage and shut the gate just as the Dodge flew down the street. I ran inside, called Ann, and said, "You had better hurry home there are *gente* (guerillas) on the streets." When she arrived home we thanked the Lord again for His care and protection.

During these three months of fear and the daily expectation of my being killed, we continued to read from *Our Daily Bread* each morning. It was really amazing how often the daily verses and thoughts were exactly what we needed for that precise moment. An article in November, titled "He Died Climbing", was about a guide climbing in the Alps to try to rescue a stranded tourist, but died in the attempt. On his memorial stone were inscribed the words used in the *Daily Bread* title. The thought in the article, using Philippians 3:14, was that we should press on toward the mark for the prize of His calling. *"Spiritual progress requires consecration without any reservation."*

Another article that was a tremendous encouragement was based on 1 Peter 5:10. "And the God of all grace... after you have suffered a little while, will himself restore you and make you strong, firm and steadfast." A paragraph in that article stated: "At this very moment you may be wondering why you are undergoing pain. The Heavenly Father's purpose is to "establish, strengthen, settle you." Your present distress is part of His divine plan. You may be sure it will work for your ultimate growth and fruitfulness." These articles, along with the Scripture readings, were a real help in our time of stress.

Ann and I left for the weekly prayer meeting one evening and upon arriving at the chapel in Lagos Dos, I parked the car. We were walking across the lawn to the chapel entrance when I noticed three men standing at the shop next-door drinking aguardiente: "high oc-tane" liquor, which could be purchased there. This shop, which was right next door to the chapel, sold a mixture of food, some hardware, and also liquor. They were dressed in dirty clothes, and were really evil-looking men. One of them turned, looked at me, pointed his finger at his neck as though it was a gun, and then pointed to me.

I looked at Ann as we continued on into the chapel and said, "It looks like I'm going home tonight!" While fearful, I was ready to go "home."

Ann squeezed my arm as we went inside.

We sang a few hymns and then all the believers in the cha-pel kneeled at the benches for prayer. About ten minutes into the prayer time, I heard footsteps on the concrete floor coming into the chapel. Looking up I saw that the three men were now standing around where I was kneeling at the end of the bench and looking down at me. I thought, "This is it!" Then I looked up at the three men and said, "As you can see we are praying. I'm sure you have a lot to tell the Lord about, why don't you kneel down and pray with us?"

Then I did the most difficult thing I have ever done in my life; I bowed my head to pray not knowing if they would shoot me in the back of the head or just kidnap me. By this time all the ladies were crying openly as everyone knew about the threats that had been made against me. They knew that if the threatened person does not leave the country, they would surely be killed. Everyone in the chapel was urgently praying. A few minutes later, which seemed like a very long time to me, I looked up and the men had gone.

Several months later I called my sister, Anne, in Australia to tell her what had happened. She asked me, "What day and what time did that happen?" I told her and she did the calculation for the time difference, then told me, "It must have been at just about that time I had a strong feeling that I should pray for you. I didn't know why, so I just knelt down and prayed for you. Obviously, the Lord had put this on my heart and He surely answered that prayer!"

I often wonder why those men left in a hurry. Did they see an angel? I have heard stories like that, but nobody in the chapel saw anything. I just like to believe that the Lord shut the lion's mouth! To this day I do not know what happened to them as I did not even hear them walking out. Perhaps it was another example of what the Apostle Paul relates in 2 Corinthians 1:9, *"Indeed, in our hearts we felt the sentence of death. But this happened that we might not rely on ourselves but on God, who raises the dead."* We were certainly learning to rely on God and take comfort only in Him.

Shortly after that incident, I was visiting the teniente at the F-2 office and told him about the vehicle that had followed me into El Playón.

He then asked me, "What were you driving?"

"I was using the 15-seat Ford Club wagon," I replied.

Now, in those days, the "A-Team" show was really popular on Colombian TV, and was a favorite of everyone. I think the teniente had this in mind, as he went on to tell me of a plan to get some of these guys. "I'll tell you what we can do. I can have a couple of armed men in the back of your vehicle and when we are in a suitable place, they can throw open the back doors and take these guys out."

Immediately, in my mind, I could imagine us driving down some lonely mountain road in my Club Wagon, with the words printed along each side, "Jesus said, 'I am the way, and the truth and the life;'" then seeing the back door flying open and hot lead from automatic fire killing the men in the vehicle behind. A couple of days before this conversation I had been reading in Ezra 8:21-23 where the king had offered to send troops to protect Ezra and the Jews returning to Jerusalem with the priceless articles of the temple. But Ezra said, *"I was ashamed to ask the king for soldiers and horsemen to protect us from enemies on the road, because we had told the king, 'The gracious hand of our God is on everyone who looks to him.'"*

"I can't really do that," I replied. "I am just going to trust the Lord for protection on the road."

I told the teniente about Ezra and the king, how he had refused the king's troops, because he wanted to just trust the Lord to protect him, and I explained to the teniente that this was what I needed to do. We shook hands and Ann and I had no further contact with the F-2; we had to practice what we preached. This was a hard lesson, but with that decision we also had a measure of peace in our hearts.

God Is In Control

Also during those very tense months I was sleeping very lightly and if there was any sound I woke immediately. Regularly, there were many sudden sounds like a motorcycle going down our street, or the night watchman blowing his whistle to let all the neighbors know that he was walking his beat. The night watchman was a strange man; he had a uniform of sorts and carried some kind of gun. At one time our dog ran out barking at him and he aimed the gun at the dog. I spoke to his boss about that, but he said, "Don't worry; we don't allow him to have any ammunition!"

However one night in December, about 2:00 AM, I was awakened, by deep breathing. With my eyes half open I listened, it was not Ann as I could hear her breathing beside me. I slowly turned my head toward the window facing the street and saw the most evil face I have ever seen, just inside the window. I thought the guerrillas were coming in through the window. My heart stopped for a few seconds, then my brain caught up with what I was seeing. We had the customary iron bars on the windows because of so many burglaries in Colombia, and I had not heard anyone sawing through the bars, or any noise of them being broken down. It was then I realized that this was only a head. I quickly switched on the bed-light and the head disappeared.

I took a deep breath and thought, "It was only a demon!" Obviously, Satan had inspired all that had been happening over the past months. Ann had awakened with the light going on. Of course I told her what I had seen, then I prayed and thanked the Lord for His protection, rolled over and slept the best and deepest sleep in months.

You see, just prior to the threats and the fearful time through which we had been living, I had done a comprehensive 16-message study with the Lagos Dos church on "Satan and the Heavenly Host." In the early studies I had spoken on Job chapters 1-2, which clearly shows that even though Satan has tremendous power and wisdom far beyond anything human, he is still subject to God and cannot touch any of God's people unless God specifically allows it. He had to get God's permission to bring trials into Job's life. God gave Satan permission to touch Job's possessions, including his children, and then in a second attempt to make Job curse God he had permission to bring horrible sickness into his body. But even in that situation, God specifically told him, "You can touch his body, but you must spare his life." We don't need to fear Satan or the demons as they are heavily restricted and were not only defeated at the cross, but were also condemned. Their sentence is soon to be carried out. Colossians 2:15 *"And having disarmed the powers and authorities, he made a public spectacle of them, triumphing over them by the cross."*

This was an epiphany! GOD IS IN CONTROL. This is why I must trust God completely! He knows what is best for me, my family and every believer down through the ages. He has everything in His hands and I can have confidence that even in the worst circumstances, *"And we know that in all things God works for the good of those who love him, who have been called according to his purpose"* Romans 8:28. That is what this verse really means! From that moment on, after sharing these thoughts with Ann, we both had complete peace, knowing that whatever happened, if I was to die or live, God had total control of this arrow and His purposes and will are always perfect.

Ann and I learned many important lessons during that very difficult time. We need to walk closely with the Lord every moment of our lives. We need to understand that He is in control and there will be blessings when we submit to His control and guidance. While we may have natural fear, we can have an inner peace and find ourselves being drawn closer to Him. We will mature spiritually as James 1:2-4 tells us. *"Consider it pure joy, my brothers, whenever you face trials of many kinds, because you know that the testing of your faith develops perseverance. Perseverance must finish its work so that you may be mature and complete, not lacking anything."*

Ann and I usually read from the Scripture every day at suppertime with the children, along with the *Our Daily Bread* devotional. Our minds were in turmoil, not knowing what we should do or how we should react to all that was suddenly turning our world into a time of fear. We were amazed just how often the *Our Daily Bread* devotions were relevant to our situation and had a message exactly for the moment. Even though the articles had been written more than a year previously, the Lord used them to encourage and give us strength, hope and direction. The October 13th devotion had the title, "Pulled in Two Directions." The verse was Philippians 1:21; *"For to me to live is Christ and to die is gain." Along with the article was the Thot For The Day: "The more of Heaven we cherish, the less of earth we covet."* This started a conversation that brought Ann and me to the conclusion that even though we knew that the threat was real, we should not be afraid of dying. Of course this was easier said than done! A couple of days later the devotional was about H.G. Spafford whose daughters were all killed when the ship on which they were sailing collided with another vessel and sank. His wife was saved but his daughters all died. Later he wrote the hymn "It Is Well With My Soul." The Thot: summed it all up with, *"To rest in the care of God is to realize peace with God."* We were reminded in other Bible readings how the Apostle Paul addressed adversity in 2 Corinthians 4:6-10, *"For God, who said, 'let light shine out of darkness,' made His light shine in our hearts to give us the light of the knowledge of the glory of God in the face of Christ. But we have this treasure* [the glory of God] *in jars of clay to show that this all-surpassing power is from God and not from us. We are hard pressed on every side, but not crushed; perplexed, but not* in despair; persecuted, but not abandoned; struck down, but not destroyed. We always carry around in our body the death of Jesus, so that the life of Jesus may also be revealed in our body." These thoughts and verses were a real help as we made this journey, which would be a great trial of our faith.

January 19,1981, at 6:30 AM, seven M-19 guerrillas entered the Summer Institute of Linguistics' housing facility in Bogotá, where the Chester Bitterman family was staying at the time. Not finding Al Wheeler, the director of SIL's Colombian Branch, they kidnapped Bitterman instead. The M-19 guerrillas demanded that SIL leave the country. Finally, 48 days after his abduction, on March 7, Bitterman's body was found sitting dead in a bus near Bogotá, having been shot in the chest. Why Bitterman and not me? This question has been something I have thought of many times since. Of course the answer is that God is in control; He has His plans and purposes for each one. We can trust Him to do what is right and what is best for us all.

I had no idea, at the time this was all happening, that unknowingly, simply by convincing the refugees in El Playón not to fight with the guerrillas, I had interfered with and completely blown one of their planned attacks to begin the revolution. This was why they had accused me of working with the CIA. Early March 1981, the M-19 began their revolution attempt, coming into the south of Colombia via Ecuador, but because of the difficult conditions of the rainy season, and the tenacity of the Colombian army, the guerrillas were driven back into Ecuador where they surrendered to the authorities, seeking asylum. The Ecuadorians, however, loaded the guerrillas onto trucks and drove them back into Colombia where they were jailed, including one of their best-known leaders, Dr. Carlos Toledo Plata. Three years later some of the M-19 guerrillas were given amnesty and returned to civilian life. However, on August 10, 1984, Carlos Toledo Plata was gunned down in the suburb of Provenza in Bucaramanga.

The end of the M-19's revolution can be seen on pages 283 - 285 of the book written by René De La Pedraga, "Wars In Latin America, 1948 - 1982. The Rise of the Guerrillas." http://books.google.com/books?id=kChyVw5MYB4C&pg=PA285&lpg=PA285

PART THREE

MISSIONARY LIFE ROUTINES

Psalm 84:5-7a

"Blessed are those whose strength is in you, whose hearts are set on pilgrimage. As they pass through the Valley of Baka, they make it a place of springs; the autumn rains also cover it with pools. They go from strength to strength…"

Engaging in gospel ministry is exciting and rewarding, knowing that the work is being done to reach lost souls for salvation and to build up the Body of Christ in the church. However, there are ordinary daily activities that all everyone must face no matter where he or she lives or what their occupation may be.

In Part Three you will read about the day-to-day life of a missionary.

David, Ian, Ann and Diane - Front Adriana and Philip

15

FAMILY LIFE

While a missionary may be called by God to serve a particular geographic or cultural region he, or she, also has a personal family needing attention. There are day-to-day routines, which must be maintained, education and medical needs of the children provided for, along with upholding a healthy relationship with their spouse. Also, there are the routine maintenance of living quarters, purchase of goods for the family, communication with supporters and any number of other daily living chores people must address no matter where they live.

This chapter highlights some of the situations, with which we dealt as God directed us. I was very happy that my wife Ann was an integral partner with me in raising the children and attending to the needs of the family as well as her responsibilities in serving those in the church. As you will see, we did have a maid to help but Ann kept a close eye on all the domestic details and, in discussion with me, made wise decisions for our family.

Help In The Home

Often missionary families will hire local women to help in the home. There are several reasons that this is effective. It provides employment for someone in need and gives help to the missionary family in babysitting, cooking, cleaning, etc. so that the wife has time to attend to ministry responsibilities. In Colombia these women are called "maids" and we hired several during our time there. Some were very helpful and others not so much.

Following is an excerpt from a letter written home (to our families) by Ann, concerning our situation:

"Having a maid can be helpful as long as they are doing the work

the way you would like them to do it. However many of them have minds of their own and just want to do things opposite to what you want them to do. We are having trouble with Gladys L, our maid at the moment; she walks around in a dream, takes one hour to do the dishes after each meal, and does about half of what any normal maid would do in the same time. She doesn't even have to do the ironing as we have a little widow lady come in to do that as a means of helping her.

The widow gets the equivalent of a dollar a day, which doesn't seem very much, but she would get much less in a Colombian home for a 12 hour day. This widow has four kids under the age of 10 and we thought we could help her by giving her some work. She comes in for a bit more than half a day and sweeps the street in front, and washes the floors in the garage as well as the lounge, and does the ironing twice a week.

Additions To The Family

Early in 1979 Ann and I began to talk about the possibility of adopting a little Colombian boy. David was seven by that time and we thought the addition of another little boy to the family would be good for him and for all of us.

I began to make enquiries at the Bienestar Familiar, an organization that handled, among other family issues, adoptions. I spoke with the lawyers of that organization who told me about the legal requirements and the paperwork needed. I wrote to my parents in Australia asking to send my original birth certificate; Ann also needed to get the same from New Zealand. Then with bank records, a home inspection, and other detailed requirements, we began the process.

I had been speaking to the matron of the orphanage about the possibility of an adoption. She was a neighbor whom I had come to know when working with the Blind Institute. She did part of her internship at that institute while getting her degree in sociology. The matron told me she would help in getting a suitable child once the paperwork was approved.

A week before the adoption, I was parking my car in front of Citibank at Cabecera. As I closed the car door, a woman was walking by screaming at a pretty little girl who was walking about 10 feet behind her saying, "Adriana, muevase, (move)! If you don't hurry and catch up, I will leave you behind," along with other similar rants. I told Ann about this incident and said, "She was such a pretty little thing. If we would ever want a little girl, I would love one like her."

By early June the paperwork was complete and talking with our neighbor she told us there were a number of boys available. We asked about a good time to visit. The following day Ann and I went to the orphanage, papers in hand, and with a lot of impatience and excitement. We did the right cultural thing by chatting with the Matron about her family, the weather, and finally asked about adopting our boy.

"Wait here while I go and see what we can do," she said as she left her office.

After what seemed like a very long wait (it probably was no more than five minutes) she asked us to follow her. She took us to a large room and, to our surprise, there were a couple of blankets on the carpeted floor with no less than 10 babies lying on their backs in all sorts of positions and baby clothes. Some were crying, a couple were asleep and the majority just looking around, no doubt wondering what was going on. The oldest would have been no more than five months, and some just a few weeks.

"Which one would you like to have?" she asked.

Ann and I just looked at each other, dumfounded. How on earth were we supposed to make a choice from all those little babies? We both closed our eyes and said a short Peter prayer, "Lord, save me!" At least we asked the Lord, "Please show us!" in silent prayer. I opened my eyes and turned to look at this "carpet" of little boys and just at that moment, one of them in the middle of the "crowd" looked up at me and smiled. It was love at first sight. Now I don't know if it was an attack of gas that caused the smile, but I would rather think the Lord had done one of His Moses tricks. You remember how the Lord caused Moses to cry at the moment the princess opened the little ark in which Moses had been floating? I strongly believe it was one of those God things.

"I think we will take that one," I said as I pointed to that cute little three-month-old boy.

"Yes, he is a fine little boy and I think he will fit into your family really well," the Matron replied. "He has had a bit of a cold, but it's nothing serious." Why she thought this particular baby boy would suit our family I will never understand, but I had come to believe that in all things God is in control. She took the baby to his crib and Ann and I stood there gazing at this little life that had been brought into our lives. Well he did have a bit of a cold. He sneezed and a large gob of snot came out of his nose onto his top lip. My very first interaction with our new little boy was to get out my handkerchief and clean his nose. We bonded for life!

We went to the office to sign all the necessary papers; there was no charge for the adoption, just the formalities. Just before the signing, the Matron asked us to stop for a moment. "Before we finalize all this I have a question for you. Is there any possibility that you would rather take a little girl? We have this little three-year-old girl who was left on our doorstep as a newborn baby. She was adopted by a couple, but when the mother became pregnant with twins she totally rejected this little girl and was treating her so badly that the husband thought his wife might kill her, and he brought the girl back. She has been physically abused and traumatized; what she needs is a lot of love and care. I know you have a loving family and you would be an ideal home for her to get the love she needs. Would you consider doing this for us and her?"

Ann and I just sat there wondering what had just happened. The matron left to give us time to talk about it.

"I really wanted a boy," I said to Ann after we had talked about it. We asked the Lord to help us and then I asked Ann, "Do you think they would let us have both?"

Ann nodded, but then said, "It would be a lot of extra work and take a lot of our time, but if you think we can manage it, let's do it."

Just then the Matron returned and had with her this beautiful little girl whom I recognized immediately as Adriana, the girl I had seen following her mother in front of the bank.

I said to Ann, "That's the little girl I told you about the other day." It seemed that God was setting things up as now I had been given what I thought were two "signs."

Ann nodded and also fell in love with this pretty little three-year-old.

I looked at the Matron and said, "We really wanted a little boy and if we have to make the choice we will take the little boy. However, if we can have both we will take Adriana as well."

"That's not a problem," the Matron said, "You have the papers approved for one and I will sign off on the second one. You will just need to get everything legalized with name changes made and notarized downtown. We don't have the exact birth date for the little boy and you will have to go to the Bienestar Doctor who will calculate his birthday."

Ann and I returned from the orphanage where we saw our little boy, whom we named Philip and found out about Adriana. When Diane and David got home from school we asked them what they thought about having another sibling. They both thought it would be great, and then we told them about another little girl who needed a family and was in a sad state physically and emotionally.-

We all went to the orphanage to meet both children. First we went upstairs to the baby room. There were so many cribs in the room. Philip's was against one wall and we all went over to see him. He was all smiles when he saw us but cried when we had to leave. Back downstairs we went to the office of the director. Adriana was brought in. Diane said she liked her and felt sorry for such a scrawny little girl. We took her home with us.

It was another week or two before Philip came to live with us. He had to have been abandoned two months before he could be considered for adoption, and he had not been there that long. After a week or so, the director, suggested that the likelihood of his mother coming back was low, and he might as well be living with us instead of at the orphanage where so many were needing help. Unofficially, she said we could have him, ahead of time. It was a Wednesday when she dropped him off at our house, in the afternoon. Due to Ann being at the ladies' meeting, and I was out running errands, Diane was the only one at home to receive him.

Diane still remembers her excitement, as well as nervousness, at being "in charge" of his arrival. She held him, cuddled him, fed him, and changed him. He became her "baby" at that time. He was only three months old when he came to live with us. Adriana became Diane's little shadow, and was often in her room. She lost many things during this time due to Adriana's squirreling things. We figured this was her way of making sure she had things, as she had lost so much in her previous home.

We decided to call our little boy, Philip Ian and leave Adriana Maria's name the same, which she had been given, to avoid confusing her more. After registering Philip Ian and Adriana Maria with their new family name as Taylor, we went to the doctor who decided that Phil was born on April 1. I argued with him that April 1 was a bad day, couldn't he make it a day earlier or later as April Fool's Day wasn't a good idea. He insisted that his calculations were right and sent us off to get new birth certificates for both our new children. When we arrived home Ann whipped out the sewing machine and began making a dress for Adriana. We then had four children at home with us.

Family Letter August, 1979

Dearest family,

As you see from the photo the latest bit of news is that you are all grandparents, aunts, uncles and cousins again. Adriana Maria arrived in a rather large bundle which no doubt the stork found heavy, it seems that the stork got lost on the way and it took nearly 2 years and nine months to get here; late as this may be we are still very excited about it all and are very happy with who arrived. She's a little pet who was being neglected and so is rather undernourished and still manages to fit into one of Diane's dresses which she had when she was eighteen months old. It is obvious that the people who had her hadn't taken any time with her to teach her words or play with her. She is as bright as a button and after two days is saying, "thank you," in English, "night, night daddy," to me when she goes to bed and Ann is "mommy," right off from the start.

She is precocious and terribly independent, no doubt because if she didn't do it herself, with the previous family, she would be left with nothing. This morning when we got up she was dressed with her shoes and socks on and playing in her room. She is on the bottom bunk in David's room. Is he happy that he has a sister to play with! You better believe it. Diane is as happy as a lark also and Adriana won't let her out of her sight.

That's the good news, now here's how we came to have two. We went to the adoption office on Tuesday to get the papers and to ask how long things would take. The matron at the orphanage, when we presented the papers for a boy, asked if we would like to have this little girl who'd been abused. We asked if we could have both and was told that it was possible. The little boy we named Philip Ian Taylor. That shouldn't be hard for you to remember, as it rhymes very closely with the Philipp'ian jailer. David is just so excited about having both of them here. Before he knew anything about the adoption, he was praying for a little brother, and after reading a Jack and Jill magazine for children, he decided he wanted a sister. When I asked him why, he said, "Because Dr. David will have his sister for his nurse." Fortunately I remembered the story otherwise I would've thought him crazy. I didn't know how he was praying, but he got his request with a sister old enough to play with, and a baby brother who would one day also be able to play with him. Diane, now 15, always wanted a little sister and this one is like a little doll for her. All of us are extremely happy.

Schooling Of Children

Deciding which school the children should attend had to be addressed. This is often a challenge for missionaries serving away from their home country. The public schools did not have the same academic standards as our home Australian schools. Also the behavior of the students, discipline and all the cultural differences made the decision more difficult. Keep in mind that the abundance of curriculum for home schooling was not available at that time and with Ann being as involved in ministry as I was she may not have had time to oversee that activity. In Bucaramanga there were no evangelical Christian schools then and also we did not want to give the impression of being "above" others by not interacting with the schools available. The obvious alternative was to send them to the Catholic schools as the level of instruction and moral standard was much higher than that of the local government school and therefore closer to our way of thinking and liking.

Diane began in our school in Puerto Boyacá, and when we moved to Bucaramanga she was enrolled in a Catholic school where she did very well. She also had lessons to play the guitar and was able to play it in some of the activities at that school. She was pretty excited about being in a larger girls' school. But it was interesting for her to hear comments about subjects that were new to her. She related one conversation to us, "One of the girls forgot to do her homework and on the bus she was crossing herself (making the sign of the cross.) I don't think that will help her very much, will it?" Another time the girls were asked by their teacher, a nun who taught a religion class twice a week, to draw a religious picture on the front of their religion book. Many of the girls drew a "virgin" or a nun. Diane drew a church building with a big bell. I thought that was good thinking!

By the time Diane had finished primary school we had moved to the suburb of Cañerveral where there was an English school, run by an American director, for Colombians who wanted their children to learn English. She also did very well there and by the time Diane graduated high school we were thinking about college and her tertiary studies. One reason that particular school was beneficial was the good preparation for her later application to Wheaton College in the USA.

David began his schooling at a Jesuit primary school in Bucaramanga and did well there. He also went to the American School for a few years then moved to the Augustine High School not far from where we lived.

Adriana was at the San Pedrito primary school and had many difficulties with her studies. No doubt this was due to her learning difficulty in processing information even if she could read it. Ann helped her in every way she could, as there was not much available in specialized education at that time.

Philip also attended San Pedrito primary school. As a seven-year-old he already had his theology learned from our Bible teaching at home, however. One time, when he passed the school chapel he did not genuflect; a nun saw this and told him he must bow before the Eucharist. He promptly told the nun, "I don't bow to anyone or any thing. I only kneel before the Lord Jesus." When we moved to Cañaveral he also attended the American School not far from our house.

Diane Goes To The USA For College

We did not really know too much about the United States American educational system, but one of our American missionary friends had mentioned that Wheaton College in Chicago, Illinois was a good Christian school. Correspondence began with the college to see what was required and what courses might be suitable
228

for Diane. Something they required, as a basis for acceptance, was for her to take the Scholastic Aptitude Test (SAT) exams. We made inquiries about these tests, and discovered that they could only be taken at a private school in Bogotá. Once we knew the dates for testing we flew to Bogotá, staying with my cousin Bill Corson and family while there. Diane sat for the exams and the results were sent to Wheaton College. Not too long after, we received a letter stating that her grades were acceptable and they would be happy to have her as a student.

Due to the cost of travel, I was the only one going with Diane, and made arrangements to fly to the United States in August 1982, visiting my friend Bill Van Ryn in Florida on the way. From there we flew on to New Jersey to visit the Glaser family whom we had met on our furlough trip in 1972. They had offered to drive us to an international Bible conference to be held at a college campus in Grove City, Pennsylvania. We enjoyed the conference and made many new friends. Diane was in a dormitory with many girls her age that was supervised by a lady called Barbara Martin, who was a kindergarten teacher. We did not realize at that time that this lady would one day play an important part in our lives. After the conference the Fred Rau family from Kenosha, Wisconsin, who also attended the conference, offered to take Diane and me by road to Chicago (which is near Kenosha.) They dropped us off at Paul Hadley's home. He was another person I had met several times at conferences, and he, with his wife Beth, lived close to the Wheaton College campus.

As you can imagine this was difficult for us sending our daughter, who was just turning 18, to another country and leaving her there for studies. Fortunately, there were many people from our churches who were prepared to keep an eye on her and help her when necessary. Diane had ideas of studying medicine, but during her first year became involved with the local Wheaton College radio station. She really enjoyed announcing the news and setting up the selection of classical music during her time on the air. Her experience at the radio station influenced Diane to declare Communications as her major when she began her second year at college. During her final year, Diane was working on the air, January 28,

1986 when the shocking news of the Challenger Space Shuttle's explosion and destruction came on the news wire. She had the difficult task of announcing that heart-breaking news. Paul Hadley, a Wheaton graduate himself, told me that in all the years he had been listening to Wheaton Radio, Diane was the best announcer they ever had. Something of which the parents could be proud!

Diane Graduates And The Family Meets New Friends

We decided, as a family, to travel to Chicago for Diane's graduation in June 1986, and were all very proud of her accomplishments. After graduation we drove to Mountain View Bible Camp in Pennsylvania for a family camp, again meeting many new friends.

Among those friends was Sue Vorberg a Special Education teacher for the hearing impaired. She was Adriana and Phil's teacher at that camp. Ann and Sue became very close friends and they both kept in touch, writing to each other almost every week after that visit. This was another of those threads that the Master Weaver used to bring harmony into the pattern of His production and from which we would benefit as a family later.

Diane was unable to get a work visa to stay in the USA at that time so she came home. That meant she was able to spend the next year with us, as a family, as well as enjoy a time of close intimacy and friendship as an adult with Ann. She has always been thankful to the Lord for that year at home in Bucaramanga with her mother.

She eventually sent an application to the missionary radio station, Trans World Radio, on Bonaire in the Netherlands Antilles. They asked her to send tape recordings, reading in English and Spanish, and since she was totally fluent with no accent in either language, was accepted and worked there for ten years. Since she had grown up in Colombia, speaking both languages from her early years, and because TWR only allowed announcers to broadcast in their native language, Diane was able to use both languages on the air. I would sometimes listen on short wave radio to the 10:00 PM news just to hear her voice and get world news that wasn't usually broadcast in Colombia. This was a special treat for me because a missionary often misses having regular contact with family and friends.

230

16

INTERACTION WITH LOCAL CULTURE

Becoming part of, or immersed in, the local culture where a missionary has been called to serve is of greatest importance for success in reaching people with the gospel and godly living. It is imperative that the missionary and the entire family assimilate as much as possible with customs, clothing, food and life-style. This ensures the avoidance of looking better than, or superior to, the local people. Following are several accounts of interactions we had with people while in Colombia. These show how we had to recognize, understand and adapt to their cultural way of thinking and dealing with life situations. By understanding the background of their lives we could more effectively minister to their spiritual needs.

Jaime (James) Batero "Behold, Now Is The Day Of Salvation"

Jaime was in our living room playing with our six-year-old son, David. It occurred to me that I never thought I would see the day when I would be happy about a "Hit Man" staying in my home and playing with my children. But here he was, enjoying fellowship with my family and serving the Lord whom he had come to know and love. This is how it happened:

Mauricio, a full time gospel worker, was walking toward home along a bush trail with tall trees and thick bushes on each side of the track. He was about halfway home when he heard the sound of someone running behind him. Mauricio turned and watched as a middle-aged man with a 2-day-old beard was running

Jaime

231

toward him. This man's shirt was soaking wet from perspiration and fear etched on his face.

"Hey, you seem to be in a hurry," Mauricio stated, "is everything alright?"

"Someone is going to kill me," the man replied, "My friends just warned me; I am hurrying home to get some things and then leaving this area for good."

"Sorry to hear that", responded Mauricio. "But if you might be killed, you had better be ready to meet your Maker. There's only one way to be ready, and that's to tell God you are sorry for your sin, tell Him you want to live a better life with His help, and accept God's provision for salvation. God sent His Son to take the punishment for our sins by dying on the cross to die in our place. The Bible says, 'The wages of sin is death but the gift of God is eternal life.' (Romans 6:23) However, to get the benefit of God's gift you have to receive it just as you would receive a birthday gift. Would you like to pray and ask the Lord Jesus to forgive you and receive from him the promise of a new life and heaven when you die?"

"Look, I'm sorry, but I just don't have time. I have to get home, pack some things and get out of here," was his reply.

As this man ran on his way, Mauricio called after him saying, "Now is the time; tomorrow may be too late." There was no answer and as Mauricio came to a fork in the track he walked on praying for the man to whom he had just spoken.

Suddenly Mauricio heard a gun shot. He ran back to the fork in the path he had just passed, and then turned and ran the way the man had run. Coming around a curve in the track he saw this man lying on the ground, and blood slowly making a crimson pool beside the dead body. "What a fool," thought Mauricio. "He had every opportunity to prepare for eternity, but just rejected God's call and now he is in eternity without salvation and without Christ." Some of the people who lived nearby had heard the shot and with much shouting ran out of their houses, soon surrounding the dead body.

Some months later, Mauricio was in the city of Pereira and decided to go into a "tienda", a small shop/cafeteria with tables where you could drink a "tinto", a small cup of sweetened coffee. There were several tables and a number of men at two of the tables. Mauricio, with his tinto, headed toward an empty table. While passing

232

one group of men who were talking and drinking from their bottles of cerveza (beer), one of the men called out to Mauricio and said, "I know you; come and sit with us."

Mauricio sat with the men and wondered if the Lord was going to give him the opportunity to share the gospel message. "My name's Jaime," said one of the men. He was wearing a typical Colombian straw hat, and a red shirt hanging outside his pants. This wasn't unusual, as many men did not tuck their shirts in because it covered their guns in holsters hung on their belts. "I almost killed you the other day," Jaime said with a crooked smile. He was one cool customer! "You remember when you ran up the track to the guy who was killed? I was just out of sight and reloading my 'chispoom' (a muzzle-loaded shotgun) and was going to shoot you as well. But I heard all the people coming and just took off. That must have been your lucky day!"

Mauricio looked into Jaime's eyes and said, "I don't believe in luck. You see, I am a Christian and servant of the Lord. My life is in His hands and I know it was the Lord that protected me. You know," he continued, "I spoke to that man about eternity, hell and heaven, before you killed him, but he was in too much of a hurry to prepare himself for death, and life after death. I don't think it is a coincidence that we met today because even though you are a sinner Jesus loves you and died on the cross to make it possible for you to be saved. Why did you do such a thing?"

Jaime, now rather somber, replied, "I did it for money. I was paid to kill him. I didn't know him, knew nothing about him, but I do this sort of thing for money." Jaime looking a little embarrassed said: "I'm sorry for the people I have killed and I know I'm headed for hell."

Mauricio went on to tell Jaime about the thief on the cross who found salvation after a life of crime. He spoke of God's love and the fact that the sacrifice of the Lord Jesus was sufficient to pay for even the most heinous of sins.

By this time the other men at the table had left one at a time, and Mauricio asked Jaime the same question he asked the man who had been killed. "Are you ready to meet your Maker? Do you want to confess your sin and ask God's forgiveness? Would you like to ask the Lord Jesus to come into your life and make you a new man and assure you of salvation?"

Jaime's face was in his hands and he simply said, "Yes, I do," Mauricio prayed with Jaime and that day he became a new man; his life was changed and he began to live that new life. "If anyone is in Christ, he is a new creation; the old has gone, the new has come!" 2 Corinthians 5:17.

A year later, Jaime began working for me. I had a truck fitted out as a mobile bookshop and Jaime accompanied another worker, Gonzalo. The two of them visited the open-air markets in the mountain villages on their market days. They would drive around to these villages sharing the gospel and selling Bibles and literature. Understanding the violent culture in which we were living, and seeing the changed life of someone who had come to know the Lord as Savior, I had no fear of hiring him. It was a privilege to have Jaime working in the literature ministry.

Learning How To Stand When Persecuted

For several years I'd been hearing many stories about what happened to people during the time of the Violencia (a time of national political turmoil, violence and anarchy in the 1950s that also included persecution of Evangelical Christians.) I often wondered how the Christians handled the persecution during that time. Jorge Ocampo and his wife Graciela were a great help to me both in Puerto Boyacá and in Bucaramanga with evangelization and Bible teaching. I knew that Graciela had come to know the Lord as her Savior as a young girl. When visiting in their home in 1975 I asked her to tell me about a man named Carlos Marulanda whom she had mentioned many times. The following is that account:

Carlos Marulanda   1895 – 1955

"Many thanks for the coffee, Graciela. It has been good talking to you both."

"No hay de que, hermano Juan. Glad you could visit."

"There is one thing I wanted to ask you, Graciela. You have mentioned on a number of occasions a believer by the name of Carlos Marulanda. Could you tell me a bit more about him?"

"Claro que si. Of course. He was a wonderful evangelist who

visited our homes when I was a small child growing up."

"I lived on a coffee farm about six hours walk, north of Líbano, Tolima, in the town of Santa Tereza. The farm was at about 6,500 feet in the Andes Mountains, and from the house we could see the Nevado del Ruiz, a sleeping volcano. It was pretty cold and the road actually continued from our farm and came to an end right under the shadow of Mount Ruiz. My parents were Camilo Antonio Gaviria and Aura Rosa Alvarez de Gaviria. I was the eldest with five siblings.

Carlos Marulanda was an evangelist who visited us a number of times and the work began with two families, ours and one that lived about an hour's walk from us, Cegismundo Mora and his wife Alicia. During that year the work grew with regular Bible studies and with many conversions. Eventually the group grew to about 30 who had been baptized and became a part of the fellowship with us, forming a local church. Every night we had meetings and many neighbors attended. Carlos Marulanda played the guitar and taught us many hymns."

Graciela went on to tell me about a priest by the name of Naranjo who started a mission in the nearby town, teaching the children and also visiting the homes in that area. He learned about the ministry of Carlos and the believers soon realized that the priest had come to hate Carlos. He began to speak openly to the children and their parents against Carlos, and he made schooling difficult for the children of the believers. He actually took delight in pinching the evangelical children, making them cry. He spoke so harshly against Carlos that many of the adults in the town began to cause problems for Carlos and all the new believers. A friend of the believers went to the town one Monday and some of the locals attacked him and cut off his head. The police in the town began to intimidate and persecute the Liberals (non-catholic political party) while getting support for what they were doing from the priest.

Carlos had a wooden leg and usually carried a bag with his belongings and Bible. He had nailed the heel of a shoe on the base of the wooden leg to make it the same length as his good leg, which was a help while walking. Because of his impediment the Gavirias loaned him one of their mules for his visits, as the roads were very steep in that mountainous region. He never complained and was always smiling. He was tall and thin, and at 60 years old his hair had already turned grey. Each of the families in the fellowship took turns bringing him food each day. He did not eat meat because he had an ulcer, so ate mainly fruit, vegetables and eggs.

While Carlos was living with the Gavirias he always worked during the day helping harvest the coffee, and since there were two harvesting times each year there was always plenty of work. But in the evenings he would lead Bible studies. The farm had three houses for their family and workers. Each house was made with board walls, board floors and a corrugated tin roof. The houses were about 200 feet apart. All the farmland was very steep on the sides of the valley where the houses were built. At the foot of the valley, the Gunilla River flowed and eventually emptied out in the Magdalena River. The water was very cold and that was where the new believers were baptized.

Carlos Marulanda was firm in the faith and at the baptism classes exhorted the new believers of the importance of standing firm, even to death if necessary. He stated, "If we are confronted by death, we need to remain firm in our faith. We should never deny our Savior. It is preferable to die rather than deny the Lord." He made these statements because of the extreme violence going on throughout the country. At that time the Catholic Church was working with the conservative party to convince them to use the opportunity to persecute evangelicals.

One day in the year 1955, Carlos Marulanda died at 8:30 in the morning. The night before, while he preached, everyone noticed his appearance as being really different. Some even said later, that his face must have been similar to that of Stephen in the Bible. His face reflected the hope of the glory of eternity that was coming. Waking at 5 AM the next day, he happily enjoyed his first mug of coffee. A half hour later he asked for water and sat down outside to read his Bible. He looked across the very wide, long valley and noticed a large group of people on the road to the river. They continued on down to the river and crossed over where he lost sight of them. It was unusual to see such a large group walking down the steep slope from the village high on the other side of the valley.

Carlos left the house and went down to the coffee plantation and began to work as usual. The large group, which turned out to

236

be only men, had obviously continued on toward the farm. Carlos heard their voices as they came closer. At this point he hid behind some of the coffee trees as he watched the men. Even though they passed by him several times they did not see him. Carlos made his way back to the house. Finally the men arrived at one of the houses where they found a number of women reading the Bible. They were reading and studying Psalm 91. Carlos stood in front of the house where he was living and greeted the men. At this time they went to him and demanded that he show his I.D. Carlos knew that his hour had come and entered the house, knelt by his bed to get his bag from under it and at the same time, while on his knees, was praying. The men entered the room and one of them swung his machete cutting off Carlos' right hand.

Graciela, age nine at the time, was in the next room which was the kitchen, not knowing what was happening as everyone else had fled. When she heard the sound of the machete taking off Carlos' hand, she thought someone was cutting up the meat for the lunch meal. That was when she heard Carlos's voice, "Father. forgive them for they don't know what they are doing!"

There was no further cry of fear or pain from the throat of Carlos, no begging for mercy. The second cut from the machete cut deeply into Carlos' neck almost severing his head completely. The men cut off his other hand, then took great delight in hacking his stomach and spilling his insides onto the floor of his room.

The men were excited and laughing as they attacked Carlos and continued laughing as they walked out into the passageway to the front of the house. There they wiped the blood off their machetes on the boards of the house and the stains remained for many years as silent accusations and witnesses of the horror of that atrocious crime that terrible day. Several of the men then raped a 12-year-old girl whom they had caught in one of the houses. This all happened during that time, known in Colombia as the time of the Violencia.

All the believers had run away along with a lady who was a political Conservative (the party with the Catholic Church). She had left the town where she lived the night before as the Liberals (the more secular political party) in that town had formed a guerrilla band and had taken up arms to protect themselves from the Conservatives.

When those men left the house, Graciela went into Carlos' room and saw the butchery. Carlos was on his back, mouth open; his dead eyes open staring into eternity, and his innards all over the floor. She couldn't react due to the fright of what was in front of her, and then began screaming. Her mother heard her and returned, also panicked and began screaming. She shouted to Graciela, "Grab all your clothes and the get the other children's clothes as well, put them into this sack and we have to run from here. They could return at any minute and kill us all."

There was a typical soup, sancocho, cooking on the stove for lunch in the kitchen, which they left, and the house was left deserted over the next 12 months.

Carlos Marulando's body lay for two weeks on the floor in his room, and was mutilated by dogs and other animals. Everyone in the area was too afraid to go near the farm. Finally sister Ordulia, one of the new converts, plucked up courage, went into the house and gathered up what was left of his body, wrapped it in sheets off the bed, dug a shallow grave and buried him near the Hortensia bush that Carlos had admired so much as he read his Bible every morning.

The Gaviria family all fled to La Dorada, a large river city on the Magdalena River. They went to the Jaramillos' home and told Misael, Domingo, Luiz and Herminia, all about what had happened. Rafael Rodriguez, who had a store in La Dorada, heard about their situation and brought a large basket of food. His store at that time was one of the most prosperous as he had the contract to provision the riverboats that plied the Magdalena River. The riverboats in that time carried passengers and cargo from Honda to Barranquilla on the north coast of Colombia. As the persecution increased, Rafael was eventually forced to leave La Dorada and worked for some time in Alto Bonito close to the small town of Puerto Boyacá.

Manuel Pareja and Jorge Ocampo lived in the same area and Jorge eventually married Graciela. A really strong work grew in Puerto Boyacá over the next few years during the time of the Violencia. Sometime later, Rafael's life was threatened by the enemies of the evangelicals and because his asthma was getting worse, went to live with Graciela and Jorge. Graciela couldn't do enough for him remembering the love and care he had shown the family in La Dorada when they had fled the violence in the state of Tolima.

238

More Visits With Rafael

Later, Rafael went deeper into the jungles and lived for some time in Carare. The next move was to Campo Capote where Alan Tonkin and I stayed the first time Alan made a visit to the jungle.

During 1975, a self-professed prophet arrived in the area. He had been in Puerto Boyacá and had gotten names and addresses of believers in the jungle areas of Carare, Campo Capote and Puerto Parra. He claimed that the day of grace had ended and that the Bible no longer had any authority as a new day had come. He ordered the believers to take down the Bible texts on their walls and painted an eagle on the wall that was to be the new sign. They would all rise as eagles when the Lord returned. When he arrived in Campo Capote, Rafael chased him off, being a mature Christian and well versed in Scripture. The prophet then went to a Pentecostal church in the town and, unfortunately, they received the "prophet" and were all baptized again, including their Pastor.

In 1976 my parents came from Australia to visit us and I decided to take my father to Carare and Capote so that he could see what the jungle was like. When we arrived at Rafael's home, he had just prepared some soup. He told me what it was, but I didn't translate that for my father. At about 4:00 PM that afternoon I asked my father, "What did you think of the soup we had for lunch?

"It was different, but OK I guess."

"Did you realize the soup made from Ox eyes?" Thinking about having eaten ox eye soup, he almost threw up.

In the late 1970's, Jorge Ocampo and Graciela bought a farm near Curití. After Rafael's wife had gone to be with the Lord, Jorge and Graciela invited Rafael to come and live with them again. They took good care of him at their farm. I received a phone call one afternoon from Jorge, telling me that Rafael had suffered an extremely bad asthma attack and had gone to be with the Lord.

"Could you buy a casket and bring it to the house to take Rafael back to Bucaramanga for a funeral?"

"Certainly, no trouble!" I replied.

After speaking with a funeral home director and arranging for a coffin, I loaded it into my vehicle. Together with Esau Parra and the funeral director we drove to the farm, which took about 95 minutes. The mortician checked out the body to make sure there had been no foul play, then we loaded Rafael into the casket, carried the casket out and loaded it into the back of my Ford pickup. The back was enclosed with seats along both sides, which we normally used to transport people to meetings and conferences.

On our return to Bucaramanga we had to go over one of the ranges, down the switchback road called Pescadero, and back to the chapel in Bucaramanga. We set up the casket in the chapel at about midnight on the trestles the funeral director had supplied. We opened the coffin to make sure Rafael would look all right for the open casket funeral. Unfortunately, Rafael had not handled the switchback road too well and had shifted around considerably inside the coffin. We lifted him and settled him in place, ready for the funeral the next day.

It was an honor to have known such a wonderful, faithful Christian.

A Sinner Becomes A Saint
Letter Home October 25, 1973

At the time of writing, Colombia and her neighboring country Venezuela, along with the general public and the Roman Catholic Church are in the process of making a saint out of a very kindhearted doctor of medicine, who died some 55 years ago. His name is José Gregorio who apparently lived his life doing good works and living in a very humanitarian way. He was also very religious and spent time when possible praying to the Virgin of Coromoto which was a statue in the town of that name. However, he died and since that time there have been numerous reports of how he had come to the bedside of the poor and written prescriptions when they didn't have any money to call a doctor. Many claim to have been healed by him including reports of those who have received their sight again; some cured of respiratory diseases and even had surgeries. So some claim!

Whatever it was, whenever many Colombians are sick they pray to "San Gregorio" as they call him and give him the benefit of their cures. The local priest of the town where Gregorio was born states from the pulpit that Gregorio is the guardian angel of that town. In many of the city's streets of Bucaramanga and other cities of Colombia, paintings of this doctor may be purchased for display on an altar in the home. He then becomes the patron saint of that family and all pray to the painting.

There are several witches and mediums in most cities that claim they can bring up the doctor when needed. People pay these mediums to "bring up the doctor" to their bedside. Some claim to have even seen the car seats depress as though someone was getting into the car to sit beside the medium.

This is all very spooky, and uneducated and superstitious Colombians fall into the trap very easily when they hear all this hocus-pocus, especially when the local priest encourages such baloney. Unfortunately for them, there have been no medical proofs of any real cures or operations. However, the people still call him St. Gregorio and want the Roman Catholic Church to recognize him as a saint.

What does the Bible say about all this? First Corinthians 1:2 says, "To the church of God in Corinth, to those sanctified in Christ Jesus and called to be holy, together with all those everywhere who call on the name of our Lord Jesus Christ—their Lord and ours:"

The Corinthians were called out of heathenism to a new way of life as followers of the Lord Jesus Christ, who were separated to Him, and that made them Saints, set apart for God. He also said, "With all that in every place call upon the name of Jesus." In other words all the believers in Corinth were Saints, and even those of us today who believe, come into the category of ALL who call on the name of the Lord. One thing important to note is that it wasn't necessary to perform miracles to become sainted as the Roman Catholic Church teaches, but simply to be a follower and disciple of the Lord Jesus Christ.

Another thing, we don't have to wait 50 years after we are dead to become a saint. In fact a dead saint cannot do anything for his Lord unless his death was as a martyr, or some other circumstance, drew the world's attention to the Lord. We are called upon to be saints, set apart for God while we have life and can show the world just where we stand.

What is happening in Colombia with the extinct Dr. Gregorio is a wonderful tool of Satan to turn the eyes of the people from God.

Instead of calling on God in sickness, most call on Dr. Gregorio. Satan will have triumphed again when God has been put in a category lower than a box of bones and dirt in some Cemetery in Venezuela. What a horrifying thought!

What do we learn from this? Do not wait until you are dead to be sainted. Give your life to the one who loves you and sent his only begotten son into the world to die for you and become a living saint right now, and then let your life be one set apart for God. The apostle Paul had the right idea and he put it very clearly when he summed up his life as a saint. "I have fought a good fight, I have finished my course, I have kept the faith." 2 Timothy 4:7 Wouldn't it be wonderful if we could say the same at the end of our lives?

Counseling In Family Matters
Letter Home December 4, 1973

Alan Tonkin and I visited a family on a farm surrounded by jungle north of Bucaramanga. We held several meetings to teach the Bible and encourage these believers and some Christian neighbors who came to meetings in their thatch roofed home. This family had moved from El Cerro and was doing much better as the land was more fertile at the new farm.

We had been stuck in Cúcuta because of mechanical car problems and had spent the morning looking for universal joints for the front wheel drive, which was one of the problems. During the afternoon we visited Susan, a nurse working with CUSO who was interested in visiting some of these areas to help. When Alan and I arrived at her flat, there were two others there, Hedi Reimer a Mennonite missionary friend we had studied with at the Language Institute in Costa Rica and with her was another Canadian nurse, a recruiting officer for the organization. They were interested in going to La Jarra to check out the possibility of getting some nurses to work in that area. We all went out for supper and happily CUSO footed the bill. We had a very nice evening and it was good to see Hedi again.

We left on Wednesday morning at 6 AM and arrived at the farm by 9 AM. We had some good talks with the believers and visited some of the nearby farms. The two Christian families living fairly close together are very enthusiastic about starting up a work there.

242

The daughter wanted to be baptized, when I say "the daughter" I mean the eldest, as it is a family of 11 children. The next day we talked a lot about baptism and what it meant, and Alan also had decided he wanted to be baptized. Later that day I baptized both the girl and Alan. That night Alan preached using a flannel graph and it was really good.

Alan has everyone in CUSO dumbfounded. His boss in Bogotá said to Hedi, "Those friends of yours have certainly changed Alan."

Hedi replied, "You know Alan as well as I do, and he isn't the sort of person to get talked into anything."

They were all saying that Alan had such bad language, and now they can't understand the change. At the dinner we all had together he bowed his head and gave thanks for the food in front of everyone. Then he started in on Susan to tell her how she needs the Lord in her life. Susan didn't believe him that he was going to be baptized, but after a while she admitted that she really would like to follow God. She said she was too worried about public opinion, and she might lose her Colombian boyfriend. Earlier on I had sent her a Bible and she said she reads it every now and again. It was interesting listening to Alan answering all her questions, the same ones he had been asking only a few months before himself. He was talking as though there had never been a similar problem in his own life.

After the baptism, Alan I went into the jungle nearby to let off some steam, clearing some jungle with our machetes. We started off trying to chop down a tree, but instead of falling sideways, the trunk just slid off the stump and stuck into the ground and it looked as though it had never been anywhere else. It was held up by vines and smaller trees around it; so then we decided that if we wanted to see the tree fall we had to clear away some of the nearby trees. After we had chopped down a dozen smaller trees, a whole lot went all at once and it seemed as though the whole jungle was falling down. Anyway we had a lot of fun and we were ready for the rice and yucca for supper.

After supper I was talking to the mother and her husband about having children and family planning and she agreed it would be better to not have any more children now that they had 11. Fortunately Ann and I had taken orientation classes regarding family planning at the language school in Costa Rica, and Dr. Cabezas, a Christian, gave some good advice as to how to handle some of the cultural problems and the ways to approach that subject with poor people in particular. One of the most difficult problems is that with the Catholic background, many think that any sort of family planning is sin. The result of our talk resulted in the lady wanting to come back to Cúcuta with us to speak to our nurse friend Sue, who was able to give good medical instruction.

When we arrived back in Bucaramanga late Friday night we found that a guy down the road took a good dose of poison and is in hospital. He is about 18 or so and his girlfriend gave him up. He has been coming to the [church] meetings for a long time, and the girlfriend also comes. There always seems to be tragedy with blessings in this work.

Interference From People In Home Countries

Sometimes well-meaning people in other countries see photos and read about the missionary work in which a missionary is involved. Then comparing what they see with their own culture, practices or traditions, they criticize and seek to impose their way of doing things on the missionary work. The following is a letter I wrote to help a representative of a missionary fund in Germany. This person had written to us severely criticizing the dress and hairstyles of visiting short-term missionaries, which he saw in a photo on a missionary newsletter. This letter was written to help them understand that traditions and practices can be different in other countries.

Dear brother in the Lord Jesus,

Thank you for your frankness in speaking on certain matters which worried you, and I likewise wish to answer you in that same spirit of love and frankness. You had seen a photo of some short-term missionaries in a newsletter and mentioned concern about the women cutting their hair and wearing trousers. I can only say that there is a divergence of opinion on these matters from country to country, which makes the subject difficult. When previously visiting in Germany, I saw a lady come into one of the church meetings in slacks, or trousers; however, I don't know if the person was a sister or an unbeliever. There may have even been some physical defect.

I also saw sisters from Germany in ski pants.

I don't think that Deuteronomy 22:5 refers to trousers as such, but that a man or woman should not look like one of the opposite sex. We should be able to clearly see the difference between a man and a woman. That portion in Deuteronomy 22 is dealing with showing a difference even to the extent we are told not to wear clothing with a mixture of woolen and linen. Today we obviously wear clothing with a mixture, such as woolen socks and linen shirts, but the teaching remains, and when spiritually applied means that we should not mix the worldly with what is of God.

So, for modesty and warmth, ski pants are worn in Europe while skiing. In Colombia women's slacks, (not men's clothes) are worn to save their legs from insect bites, scratches from thorns, etc., while traveling in the country or jungle, and for modesty while traveling by mule, or horse, etc.

With regard to the cutting of hair 1 Corinthians 11:26 is teaching that the head should be covered by a woman, and that she should show in this way her subjection to the Lord. In the early brethren writings J. N. Darby, in his synopsis, does not mention anything about cutting the hair, nor does W. Kelly in his writings on 1 Corinthians 11. In the Bible treasury volume 4 page 82 this can be noted. Also in volume N4 page 191 he says that this portion was written as a "reproof of the Christian females who were disorderly," (for not covering their heads) and again says nothing about cutting the hair. I realize that the translation in German gives the idea that it is a shame for the woman even if a tiny part of her hair is cut, but this idea is not conveyed in the Greek, nor in the English or Spanish translations, which clearly show that it means shaved, (with a razor) or shorn, (like a sheep, cropped close to the scalp.) This was actually done in many places to shame Street women, and after the war was also done to some women to shame them for fraternizing with the enemy. Mr. Darby also confirms this translation in his English translation (his first language) when he translated it, "cut off," which means cutting all off to the scalp.

I also noticed, while in Germany, that in a certain church many sisters covered their heads only when a brother prayed, which to me seemed very strange. While I am not making an issue of this, I would like to point out in love dear brother, that there are apparently differences within Germany itself on this matter. I also realize that there are many differences in other countries.

How wonderful it would be to have unanimity on these things.

Another time we had a visit from one of the European support fund managers. These folks would come to encourage us in our work and to see, first hand, what was going on. We were always grateful for the encouragement and happy to share the blessings God had given us in growth in the church and other outreach activities. These visitors would then report back to their home country so that those who were sending funds for our support would know that we were not misusing these funds for unnecessary activities.

However, after one such visit, we again received admonition given from the cultural standpoint of the visitor. This particular person suggested that he thought it would be better for us to simply stand at the front of the room of 80-100 Sunday School children and read directly from the Bible; in his opinion there was no need for flannel graph pictures, illustrated books or verse memory flashcards, etc.

Once again, I had to point out that these children came from a non-biblical background, and from a church setting emphasizing ritualistic religion and with no Bible teaching. The pictures, etc. helped them to "visualize" the various characters and settings in the accounts of Scripture. In that culture, at that time, this was the most effective way to meet the teaching needs.

Thankfully, the support continued so that we could develop a library of materials to be used by all the Sunday School teachers and Bible study leaders.

17

IS THIS THE END, OR
A NEW DIRECTION?

In November 1987, I was asked to share a devotional at the annual Thanksgiving celebration with other missionaries from the United States. Of course, this is a special holiday for them and we, being Australians but having many friends in the US, were happy to celebrate with them each year. For this message I prepared thoughts from Psalm 31, knowing that one missionary in particular was going through some difficulties and thinking they may have to leave the work in Colombia. Verses 14 and 15 say, *"But I trust in you, O Lord; I say, 'You are my God.' My times are in your hands; deliver me from my enemies and from those who pursue me."* Continuing, I made the statement, "Perhaps someone among us will not even be alive to finish out the year. Our times are in His hands and His time. God's plans are always the best." Then I went on to encourage us all that our strength only comes from trusting God to be with us and help us. Often I would find, after sharing a particular message, that what I said impacted my own life. It was almost as if I was preaching to myself.

While we were never prepared for a sudden or unexpected death, the Lord had been preparing both Ann and me for death through the experiences we had in Colombia. Some years earlier, when I was on a guerrilla hit list, we both had to face the possibility of me being killed. We came to the understanding that if the Lord wanted this to happen then it was His will and my death would be the best thing for us. If the Lord did not want me killed, then there was nothing that the revolutionary guerrillas, or anyone else, could do to me. We rested in that confidence and after several months the situation changed and the danger was no longer a fact. However we did discuss, at length, what we could or should do if one or the other of us should go to be with the Lord. Our concern would be to continue on with the work and do what was necessary for the good of the family. This included getting married again if the Lord provided the right person.

The Day Our Family's World Suddenly Changed

Sunday, December 20, 1987, I left for the chapel ahead of Ann to get things ready for the meetings and in preparation for that Christmas Sunday. Ann had some chest pain just prior to leaving home that morning, but did not tell me about it; instead she continued with her responsibilities. On the way to church with the three children, she stopped at the market to purchase flowers for decorating the chapel. As she returned to the car Ann told 14-year-old David that if anything happened while she was driving he was to apply the brakes and turn off the ignition. She sensed at that stage she was seriously ill. When they arrived at the chapel, Ann stayed in the car and David came to me and said, "Mum is feeling sick and you better go out to the car." I went straight to the car and saw that she was very grey, cold and clammy. She told me she had this terrible chest pain, so I jumped into the car, leaving the children at the chapel, and made a very fast trip to the clinic about ten minutes away. On the way Ann explained to me where she had hidden the children's Christmas gifts, ever thinking of others.

I helped her into the clinic where an EKG was immediately done and showed a definite heart attack. While the doctor was packing up the machine I noticed the pupils in her eyes suddenly change and I knew that her soul had just left her.

"She's gone," I said to the doctor and he immediately began CPR, but she was already with the Lord. The doctor called a nurse; they wheeled the bed up to the next floor and, with my mind in a whirl, I went out to the waiting room as they continued to work on her. I had to stand around in the clinic reception room wondering what was happening, and why the medical staff was not talking to me. I knew that she was now at Home with her Lord and Savior. After about a half hour I was finally taken into the surgery to see her. A priest dressed with his robes was standing in the surgery. Then I realized, no doubt the long wait was because they had sent for a priest who was now present and waiting for me so that he could give her the last rites. I told him she did not need this as she was already with the Lord. Then I proceeded to tell him why I was so sure, telling of the sufficiency of the Lord's work on Calvary. He was quite nonplussed and didn't know what to say. I suppose he had never had someone turn down his "benediction" at the end of a loved one's life. But I knew that God said in Philippians 1:21 "For to me to live is Christ, and to die is gain." And in Psalm 116:15 "Precious in the sight of the Lord is the death of His saints."

Leaving the hospital after settling the arrangements, I made a quick trip to the downtown chapel, about two miles away, to let the Rothlisbergers know. Andrew Rothlisberger was a real help with the funeral arrangements.

I then drove back to our chapel at Lagos Dos to tell the children and the believers there what had happened. I took the three children to a room at the back of the chapel to explain to them that Ann had gone to be with the Lord. Philip, age eight, with a trembling voice and tears in his eyes said, "Well, it is good for Mum, but it's really hard for us."

Ann's sudden death was a great shock and it really took several weeks before all the implications could be evaluated. The children, David (14) Adriana (11) and Philip (8), all needed extra love and care. Fortunately, they passed through the normal emotional stages of grieving without any major problems. David went through a rough time, but later settled down and since then has been walking with the Lord.

I was able to get a message to my eldest daughter, Diane, who was a missionary at Trans World Radio in Bonaire at that time. She was able to get a flight to Bucaramanga to be at the funeral on the following Tuesday. Knowing that Diane was coming we were able to delay the burial as usually, in the tropics, the burial is the day after death. She had mentioned in letters to us that she had met a special friend at TWR; and so along with this friend, Bob Tencate, Diane arrived for the funeral. Ann was laid to rest in Bucaramanga, Colombia, December 22, 1987.

Along with all the sadness, Diane told me that both she and Bob had been thinking of getting engaged and coming down to see us at a later time, but as they were in Bucaramanga, decided to announce their engagement as soon as I knew about their plans. I suggested Diane use her mother's engagement ring as her engagement ring, which she stills treasures as a memory of her mother.

I flew to Bonaire in June 28, 1988 and officiated at Diane and Bob's wedding. This, of course, was a time of joy after so much sadness six months previously. Diane and Bob continued on in Bonaire serving as missionaries for many years and became the parents of two fantastic boys, Alister and Malcolm, being the first of my grandchildren.

Ann Sides Taylor
October 30, 1933 — December 20, 1987

Ann with Ada Gresham Gown for outstanding studies, at her capping ceremony, Canterbury University, Christchurc N.Z.

While many of the events of our married life and missionary service are presented throughout this book and some accounts may be repeated here, their detail will be found in those chapters. However, this brief overview of Ann's life will give you a better understanding of the godly woman she was. She, too, was an arrow sharpened for service and spent for the Master's service.

Born to George and Ivy Sides in Timaru, New Zealand, Ann enjoyed family life as the youngest with six siblings. Her family attended the same group of churches with whom I was affiliated and she was brought to the church meetings all of her life. As a young child she, too, was taught the Scriptures and put her trust in the Lord Jesus as her Savior at and early age. As she grew she attended various camps and conferences, soon becoming a leader for girls' camps and other Bible study sessions. She loved the Lord and sought to serve Him with every aspect of her life.

Ann had received her Master of Arts degree in French and was awarded the Ada Gresham Gown for outstanding studies at her capping ceremony at the University of Christchurch, New Zealand. This award gave her the option of either a scholarship to study for a doctorate in Paris, or to teach in a French School for in-depth experience to enable her to immerse herself in the French culture and language. Ann chose the latter and taught for a year at a school in Grenoble, France. She very much enjoyed this experience as well as making many friends in our affiliated church in Grenoble. It was also a blessing to her when she could attend the church conferences in France and Switzerland.

After Ann and I married in Timaru, New Zealand, January 20, 1962 she moved to Sydney Australia where she taught French, English, and Mathematics at a local high school. Our first child Diane was born August 20, 1964. Ann became a full time homemaker the following year; then Alan was born March 1967. April 1968 we made our way to Costa Rica for Language School where she was such a great help to me. When two-year-old Alan was tragically killed just before leaving for Colombia, Ann bore the pain of being present when the accident occurred. But, along with me, she found peace in God's comfort. This was a most difficult time for her as a loving mother.

Ann's work in Colombia was varied, and as someone who took pride in excellence, she accomplished her tasks with zeal and verve. With a sincere care for the people with whom she was working, she in turn was deeply loved by the nationals. Some of her activities included training Sunday School teachers, playing the piano for church services, teaching ladies' Bible studies, teaching cooking, sewing, knitting, child care and a variety of other important areas of need, including family planning. Ann was a very good cook and it was quite normal to have many visitors for meals as well as preparing food for the whole church at times. When I began a monthly Christian family magazine in 1980, Ann wrote two sections of that magazine, one for children and another for ladies. While Ann had her MA in French, she also taught Latin and English, and had studied Greek. As a language perfectionist she became my chief consultant and proofreader.

When it became apparent that Ann was not able to bear more children herself we chose to adopt. First was son David, born in Australia in 1972. Then we adopted two Colombian children in 1979. Adriana, an abused child three years old, and Phil, a baby of three months. Along with all her other duties, Ann loved and cared for all four children and me with all her heart.

I can truly say that Ann was a companion and helper whom God provided for me. With her as my partner I could fulfill the mission God gave me to do with more energy and expertise. Why God chose to take her away so suddenly, and in the midst of serving Him, I do not know or pretend to understand. I only know that for one season of life, God allowed me to reap the benefit of His chosen person for me. I am so thankful that I had Ann with me those 26 years, loving me, the children, and serving her Lord and Savior.

Despair And Decisions

Ann's death was the beginning of a sequence of events that led me into a period of deep discouragement. Since Ann died December 20th, it made a very sad Christmas that year. We obviously had to cancel the planned programs in the church and for several years Christmas music had a negative effect on me. More challenges soon followed. In January I discovered that the man who had computerized my accounting for the print shop and bookshop, who was also managing the printing operation and its 13 employees, had been stealing from the literature ministry. After I fired him I had to resume again all the administration of both ministries. Ann had written and edited the ladies' and children's section of the monthly family magazine we published, "Sendas De Luz" (Pathways of Light), so now I had to also take over that responsibility along with the responsibilities I already had with the editorial work of the magazine and our other publications.

March 1988 news came that my father had a series of strokes, but I was unable to visit him because of the responsibilities of the work as well as caring for the children. He passed later that month, which brought a tremendous sadness that I could not go to see him before the Lord took him.

A short while later another employee was found stealing my computer programs in order to go into business for himself, and I had to fire him. Thankfully another brother could pick up that work. There were other discouraging incidents that took me to "the bottom of the barrel" and, in fact, I felt like I was falling through the bottom. I reached the point where I wondered if life was worth living. Sometimes I felt something like panic, because of the extent and scope of the ministry that was my responsibility, and also the enormity of the repercussions to the family and work. I tried to find my own solutions to many of the situations, which only resulted in failure and more frustration. I shed many a tear after Ann's death; I had not cried much before that time since I was a child. I sometimes felt my faith was failing and on occasions wondered if God was even there. These were times when I had to just keep going, relying on the promises of the Word and not relying on my feelings. God always brought me through these episodes, which, although varied in duration, were very real.

Even though I continued with my responsibilities of literature preparation and print shop oversight along with regular preaching and teaching it seemed that I was preaching without a real sense of purpose. Then I would find, as I preached, the Lord ministered to my own soul. So I continued on with the work, regardless of my own discouragement. As a single parent there were many extras to pick up in the home. I was unable to have female help in the house because of the testimony; so I was cooking, washing and ironing, mending clothes, and running the children to school. It was not unusual to be sitting up at midnight hemming a dress or repairing a boy's clothes for the next day at school. I was not getting more than four or five hours of sleep each night.

The children, naturally, required much more of my time, as they also were hurting with the loss of their mother. It would have been good to have church folk take the children for a day or so to give me time to get on with some of the urgent jobs that were lagging. The Rothlisbergers did, in fact, help in this way, as their schedule allowed, and I was grateful for this blessing. Companionship is also something that the single parent lacks. Having had someone for many years with whom I could confide my thoughts, hopes and daily activities, the nights would become long after the children were in bed. Loneliness is the constant affliction of the single parent who would like to have some adult conversation after the day of dealing with children.

As the months dragged on I reached the point where I was burning out, stressed, discouraged and crying out to the Lord, "What do you want me to do? I just can't keep going like this. If you want me to stay here you will have to bring me a companion, a wife, as I just can't continue like this." He very definitely closed that door, so I felt that the Lord was using these circumstances to change the direction of my ministry. By December 1988, a year after Ann died, I made plans to return to Australia for one year, to have time without all the pressures of the work in Colombia, and to seek the Lord's mind for my future. This was necessary for spiritual refreshment and renewal.

Assessing The Future

(As I mentioned in chapter 15,) when Diane had graduated from Wheaton College in 1986, we, as a family flew to the USA to attend the Graduation in that Chicago suburb. Following those festivities we had been invited to a family camp at Mountain View Bible Camp near Sunbury, Pennsylvania, a one-day drive from Chicago. At the camp Adriana and Philip were in a class of younger children with Sue Vorberg as their teacher. Sue had noticed that Adriana had some learning difficulties and, as a Special Education teacher for the hearing impaired, was able to give Ann good advice to help Adriana. Ann and Sue became close friends and after we returned to Colombia they wrote to each other every week.

Eighteen months later on December 20, 1987, news of Ann's death was told at the Mountain View Bible Camp where Sue was

254

again serving as a counselor during a winter camp session. Saddened by the news, she returned home thinking she would send cards to her two pupils, Adriana and Phil. Upon checking her mail, she found a letter from Ann, her last to Sue. Sue immediately prepared a card each for Adriana and Philip, which arrived a few days later in the New Year.

I had received many letters and cards but only responded to the letters, so nothing more was thought about Ann's American friend. A couple of months later, several cards arrived from Sue for the children, and this time I sent a copy of my latest newsletter as a response to her correspondence.

Meanwhile things were going up and down for me as I battled with my father's passing in March 1988, the extra work with the publishing and printing, other difficult things happening in my life, and I didn't think anything more about the cards from Sue Vorberg.

In September that year I received a letter from Sue addressed to me personally.

9/23/88

Dear Ian,

Just a quick note to encourage your heart. I read your letter in the Assembly Bulletin [a church newsletter sent all around the USA] and my heart was moved to prayer for you all. It must be difficult without Ann's love and support. But somehow I know the Lord will lift you up again - He always does. He cannot bear to see His loved ones sorrow and though we DO at times, that ultimate joy comes in "the morning" when He breaks through the clouds. (I meant that figuratively, but how true it will be when He does so LITERALLY, as well!!)

I'm sure you are no stranger to trials (for more perils and difficulties have been in your experience, than in mine!), but the one thing I have BEGUN to grasp is the preciousness of Jesus AS MY BELOVED. In Ann's absence I'm sure you have felt the Lord filling that empty place. When you find yourself feeling "alone", do seek the comforting refuge and love of YOUR BELOVED, Jesus. I have found Him ever ready to hold me up in those times. (His banner over me is love! Song of Solomon 2:4)

How precious it is that we have such a One to stand by us and undergird us in every heartache, trial and care. I know He will provide your every need - for your work, your children, and your own heart.

God above is aware of all that you are going through and He alone is able to do all these things - and HE WILL. Because He is God He can do nothing less than that which is right and perfect and because He is our loving Father He will never let us go. Such wisdom and love - all toward us! Amazing love indeed!

I hope you will be really encouraged soon. How painful life can be at times, but surely He has a purpose, which will be to His glory in the end - and YOU are a part of that purpose!! Praise God. May God richly bless and faithfully uphold you.
In Jesus name,
Sue Vorberg

P.S. He hears every prayer...."I have heard your prayer, I have seen your tears; behold, I will heal you." 2 Kings 20:5

That letter from Sue was a real encouragement and I wrote a long letter thanking her for her thoughts and prayers. I told her about some of my struggles with depression, how a close uncle had passed away late 1987, then my father went to be with the Lord in March 1988, as well as some of the difficulties with the printing and publishing staff. I also told her about a relationship that I thought had been working out, but had collapsed completely early that September. During the year before I left Colombia, I had thought that if the Lord hadn't brought a wife to me in Colombia, then I must leave there as I couldn't continue as a single parent in Colombia along with all the church responsibilities and domestic needs. I really wanted to stay in Colombia.

Two weeks after my letter to Sue, another letter arrived in which Sue again thanked me for my letter and confided in me some of the struggles she was having at the time. One was about a relationship in which she was involved but she wasn't sure about. She asked me for advice and to pray that she would know what the Lord wanted for her in that relationship. I, of course, had no idea who she was talking about, and really had little real knowledge about Sue herself. So I decided to write a very general letter with some thoughts about choosing a mate as a Christian and some of the basic things for a good solid marriage.

Dear Sue,

You mentioned that you had been praying for about a year and a half about a relationship...

Is your panic a natural fear for marriage and what is unknown in marriage? Or is it because deep down you know there isn't enough between you and him to make your marriage good and lasting? Many can get cold feet, and this is just a natural fear about the unknown and not a reason to back off, but if it is because you are unsure that there is enough real love and compatibility of personalities and thinking, then be very careful before committing yourself.

Are you seeing him as a possible husband because you want to get married and not be left on the shelf? Is he someone to marry just so that you can be married? (Sorry about that question - It's not meant to hurt you, but you should ask yourself that and be sure in your own mind.)

Of course I don't know anything about him so I will ask a couple of obvious questions.

Is he a Christian? If he is not a committed Christian - forget him. It isn't worth being married if you both are not walking with the Lord. Will he be able to set the spiritual tone for your marriage? Will he take leadership in the home and help you to grow spiritually?

Is he in the same church fellowship? Someone who is a Christian who isn't in the same church fellowship could cause grief later on because of struggles about where to go, doctrines etc. While I realize that all believers are part of the One Body, there can still be an unequal yoke if there are conflicting beliefs regarding the spiritual home (assembly/church).

If you are unsure about this being the Lord's will - don't make any commitment. Wait - take your time. The Lord will make it clearer later on if He wants you to go on with it. Once you make an official commitment it almost obliges you to follow though. You may just end up marrying because you are honorable and don't want to back down on a promise. Better not to promise in the first place.

Do you feel a spiritual attraction to him? Do you feel that you could both serve the Lord more fully as man and wife? Is there physical attraction? This is also necessary as if you don't feel really drawn physically to him then you should back off and go slowly. The physical side of marriage is very important and you should be prepared to give yourself wholly to him, without reservations. I know of some who have felt nothing physically but just wanted to get married. This results in a breakdown in the relationship very soon in the marriage. Without the physical attraction the sex life could become a terrible burden.

Try to analyze your real feelings for him to make sure you are both suited and on the same wavelength. These may seem like trivial things but in the long run are very important. Try to analyze the reason why you feel panic-stricken and "stand frozen" in your present situation. Search deep down to see if it is because you know or think that there isn't enough love for him to make a lifelong commitment. Is it because you don't think you could spend the rest of your life with him? Or is it just a natural fear that should be overcome? You may find that there is reason for stopping things now or, on the contrary, see that your fear isn't really anything serious and this will clear the way for you to go ahead with more confidence.

Do you need to wait some time without seeing each other to search out your feelings without the pressure of being often together?

Some of my questions are based on what happened to me a few months ago so don't feel I am being hard on you. Better to be sure now than marry and have the rest of your lives to repent of your decision.

Why I tell you this is so that you will take your time and be very sure before you make a lasting commitment. I know I can't really talk, as I was sure and I still ended up making a mistake. Thankfully the Lord stopped me from getting into a situation that could have hindered my ministry. It's good to know that He is controlling everything in spite of me and what I do! This of course confirms the need for patience and dependence on the Lord. I hope I can practice what I preach!!!

Sue, you are very right in your desire to not hurt anyone and hopefully you won't be hurt yourself. Talk to your friend. Tell him not to rush; tell him you need time; tell him you are not sure and not to get his hopes built up. By saying these things he will at least know to go slowly and if you decide not to continue the relationship, then there won't be as much hurt for either of you. Communication in the friendship is as important as in the marriage relationship. Many couples fall apart for lack of communication.

I will be praying for you Sue, that the Lord will give you special guidance and help, and above all that you won't make any mistake about whether you should go ahead with your friend or not.

Our letter writing went on for the next couple of months and we both seemed to feel a real confidence in each other, to be able to share our innermost thoughts and feelings. These letters, both from and to Sue, were a tremendous help in being able to keep going. They were like a lifeline of hope for a drowning man. Because of all the troubles I had been through that year, along with the extra work involved because I was single parenting, I felt I was burning out and did not have much left in reserve both physically or emotionally. I finally reached the point where I decided that I should return to Australia to have some time to get my life back together, to seek the Lord's mind as to my future and any ministry He might have for me.

I shared these thoughts with Sue. Finally in December we began our travel back to Australia. I decided to visit Diane and Bob in Bonaire, then Bill and Fayette Van Ryn in Florida, continuing on to New Jersey to visit Helm and Ruth Rink, and hopefully meet up with Sue while in that area.

During those last couple of months in Colombia, I received word from Sue that she had decided to break off the relationship in which she had been involved, and that she was very unsure of what her future might be. We did meet and had some long talks about the possibility of us getting together in a closer relationship. Sue was very nervous about starting another relationship after her past experience and was pretty negative about us becoming more than good friends.

Together with David, Adriana and Phil, I continued on to Canada to spend a few days with Sue and Albert Blok. This was the Sue I had met through Alan Tonkin. She had come to the Lord in Colombia during that time. On the plane from New Jersey, Adriana was sitting next to a woman who spoke Spanish and gave Adriana about US$40 because she "liked" her. This made me very nervous, especially when we landed because this lady stuck really close by us as we went through immigration then on to collect our baggage. I said to Adri, "If this woman wants you to carry that large stuffed bear she's carrying, don't accept it. She may be carrying drugs." My next thought was that she might try to walk through the customs beside us looking like a part of the family. However, we were among the last to get our bags and she was left standing there, which may have meant that something had been found in her bags and now they were being held. I breathed a sigh of relief, as I certainly didn't need any more troubles.

While writing a letter at the Bloks' home, I noticed a verse above the desk which read, *"For I know the plans I have for you, declares the LORD, plans to prosper you and not to harm you, plans to give you hope and a future,"* (Jeremiah 29:11). I had read this verse many times, but on that occasion, the verse was another real encouragement along the way.

PART FOUR

REDIRECTION — MOVING ON

When life is difficult we should run to our Heavenly Father. No one else can truly comfort, guide and lead us as we move forward following a tragedy. Various people may offer solace or suggestions but God alone is the One who knows our every need.

Part Four will show how God very definitely showed me the next step for being an arrow suited for the Master Archer.

Back to Sydney to Refresh

18

REFOCUSING

2 Samuel 22:31 *"As for God, his way is perfect: the Lord's word is flawless; he shields all who take refuge in him."*

Back in Sydney to Refresh

After my Dad passed away my Mother continued to live in the townhouse we had purchased for the two of them when they became too old to care for our house in Lane Cove West, where they lived when we left for Colombia. This townhouse was at Narrabeen, a lovely Sydney suburb on a stretch of land between the Pacific Ocean and the Narrabeen lakes, close to family and friends for visits or help.

I was able to rent another townhouse in the same complex very near Mum's unit. It was good to have Mum close by to "babysit" the children when I needed to get to meetings or be away for any reason. She was also a blessing in taking care of the domestic chores like cooking and washing; so we were often together, especially at mealtime. David actually stayed in her home, as there were not enough bedrooms for all the children at my place. The local churches were a great help as many of the believers loaned us furniture and household equipment for the apartment and Spencer Anderson, the man whom my father had led to the Lord back in the early 1950's and had lived with us then for several years, loaned me a car.

The school year in Australia begins late January through to December each year and so on arrival in Sydney I registered the children at the local schools in Narrabeen. David enrolled as a junior (grade 11) in the Narrabeen Lakes High School. Adriana and Philip both were in the Primary school and both excelled in school-sponsored swimming competitions. Philip managed to win all the swimming races for his age group at the school and the area championships. These activities helped the children to make friends and to become part of the community, easing the pain of their mother's sudden passing.

Each morning I would get the three children off to school. Then I would sit near a window overlooking the pathway to the lake, with an open Bible on my lap, just trying to read and make sense of everything that had happened. I prayed, but did not feel any connection with God. I wondered if God even cared, and had all sorts of doubts and inner conflicts. This went on for several months. I wondered, "Was my life, (my arrow) forever broken and of no further use for service?" Reading Job 30:11 he says, *"Now that God has unstrung my bow and afflicted me..."* I thought perhaps I was done being a useful arrow for God's service. But then I read in Job 29:20 where he encourages, *"My glory will not fade; the bow will be ever new in my hand."* Was this just another one of God's ways of sharpening me for something more? I just did not know.

In spite of the way everything was working out well, I was very depressed, feeling that my life and ministry were falling apart. One of the most depressing things was that I felt I had somehow missed the Lord's will and that my ministry for Him was over.

As I continued to try to read the Bible and pray, at the same time I was looking back over my life and seeing just how blessed I was as I remembered all that the Lord had done with and through me. Beginning with my childhood rheumatic fever, and how the Lord spared me; to the way He had guided me away from my headlong dash into the world as a teen; and to the decision to make the right choice to commit my life to Him and be baptized at the age of 15. I was reminded of my steering the ship back in 1956 and looking back at the wake, zig-zagging down the coast. I could see where I had been and eventually the wake would disappear in the constant movement of the waves. Could God wash away all the hurt and pain I had suffered over the past year? He had protected me through several years of secular work and decisions that had narrowed my focus to the point where I was challenged, by a hobo picking up a cigarette butt on the ground, to be really surrendered to His will. I remembered how God challenged me to be prepared to give up secular work, home and family to go where He wanted me to go; how he brought my wife Ann to the same decision, and how He had prepared me at the Language Institute in Costa Rica. I spent a lot of time thinking about my little son Alan and the peace that the Lord had given at Alan's funeral. I thought about the Lord's protection when I was on a hit list by the communist guerrillas, and then about all the blessings He had done through Ann and me in Colombia.

I believed that I should just stick it out and that God would somehow bring me through this time of stress and anxiety. I began to think about all the blessings the Lord had brought into my life and how He had protected me on so many occasions; remembering the hymn, *"Count Your Many Blessings See What God Has Done."*

When upon life's billows you are tempest tossed,
When you are discouraged thinking all is lost,
Count your many blessings name them one by one,
And it will surprise you what the Lord hath done.

So amid the conflict, whether great or small,
Do not be discouraged God is over all,
Count your many blessings angels will attend,
Help and comfort give you to your journey's end.
Johnson Oatman, Jr.

1 Chronicles 16:12
"Remember the wonders He has done,
His miracles, and the judgments He pronounced..."

Finally, I came to realize again in a real way that God is in control. Nothing happens by chance and He would bring to pass His purposes in my life as He had done so often in the past. Yes, I could count many blessings and remember all that the Lord had done. I came to the conclusion: *He is still in control; this will all work out!*

Slowly the darkness began to lift. The depression, stress, doubts, and fears began to fit into a greater scheme of me being just a small part of God's plans and purposes. I am just an ordinary human being who will have the same trials, burdens and blessings that will come to everyone in this life on earth. I have the added blessing of knowing that God has had His hand on my life. He has allowed good things and difficult things to happen. All of it has a purpose and perhaps the greatest purpose is to be drawn into a closer relationship with the Lord, knowing that He does love, care and provide. He is able to carry me through any dark or difficult situation. I can trust Him, He knows exactly the path set before me; He has never failed. I have failed often, but He never fails.

Thank you Lord! Now, what do you want me to do?

There were invitations to preach in many of our churches in the Sydney area and I even spoke at two camps during those first few months. Alan Tonkin was the camp director at one of those camps. I knew the Word and could teach from Scripture, but many times my teaching was coming from my head rather than from my heart. On other occasions, the message really helped me as the Lord used it to buoy me up.

I shared some of these thoughts with Sue who always came back with insightful verses, so appropriate for me at the time. Gradually I came out of that slump, and began to feel that the Lord still had plans for my life. I just needed to live by faith, not feelings, to trust Him and get on with whatever I had to do at that time. I wondered if Sue might be the one whom the Lord was going to bring to me. In our letters we had really enjoyed a closeness and freedom to express our deepest thoughts about the Lord, life in general, and sharing many of the difficult situations through which we had passed.

However, before long, some of the missionaries back in Colombia were suggesting I return to decide what to do with the printing and publishing work in Bucaramanga. A couple of them just wanted to shut it down as they didn't want the responsibility if it needed money to keep it going and someone to be in charge. I had set it up so that David Carreño was managing the publishing ministry with an excellent team working with him. The Editorial Luz, as it was called, was

266

self-sufficient, self-supporting and growing. It was a ministry on the cutting edge! We had a beautiful Heidelberg GTO press I had imported from Germany, and the only extra-large laminating machine in the city. We were publishing a bimonthly medical magazine as well as handling many orders for churches in the area, including the needs of the ECS Ministries work headed up at that time by Marcia Vanderlaan. The printing business was a self-supporting success and blessing to many in the city.

Another Wife?

In early August 1989, I decided to travel from Sydney to Bucaramanga to see what could be done to avoid the missionaries closing down the publishing ministry. I wrote to Sue telling her that my plane would make a stop in Philadelphia and I would like to see her on the way. Sue met me at the airport and we had a long talk on the way back to her apartment in New Hope, N.J. She had arranged for me to stay with the Dietz family who lived nearby, and over the next couple of days we had more long conversations.

The evening before I was due to leave for Colombia we had supper and were again discussing the possibility of marriage. Sue was still rather hesitant, not wanting to run ahead of God's plan for her, and having recently ended the other relationship. Finally I said to her, "What do I have to do to convince you that this is something we should do? Do I have to stand on my head and propose?"

Having said that I promptly stood on my head and said, "Sue, will you marry me?"

Sue, trying hard to get control of her laughter, finally said, "Of course I will, you clown!"

The next day I cancelled my flight to Colombia and called the missionaries telling them to allow the print shop to continue as it was running well and insisting that the business should continue. Then we went off to a jeweler where Sue chose an engagement ring and we were officially engaged.

"I want you to meet my family!" Sue declared.

"Okay, I'll be over in the morning," I said, as I left to go back to the Dietzs' for the night. The next morning I dressed in what I thought was something suitable on that summer day. I hadn't really prepared for a picnic in the USA so I arrived in a button down shirt, shorts with black socks and tennis shoes. Sue was laughing so hard I wondered what was wrong.

"We're going shopping," she said, and off we went to buy some suitable short white socks, and a nice Polo shirt. Being a missionary in Colombia for so long, I had no idea what the fashions were!

I had a great time meeting her parents, sister and a whole bunch of cousins, aunts and uncles, nieces and nephews. Then we began to make plans for the wedding. "No point in going back to Australia and coming back for a wedding. I suggest we just run to the registrar office and get on with it!"

"You're not getting off that easily!" she replied. And so, we began the process of planning a wedding, dates, chapel, reception and then travel plans back to Australia.

Meanwhile, the annual large Grove City conference I had attended in the past was coming up. It was about five hours away in Pennsylvania and Sue wanted to attend. There were about a 1,000 people attending that year. We enjoyed receiving all the congratulations and best wishes, as well as seeing Sue's friends and the many people I had met over the years.

Unknown to me at the time, as Sue and I walked hand-in-hand along the sidewalk at the conference, a single lady by the name of Barb was walking behind us. As she told me later, seeing Sue and me together she was thinking and sort of talking to God, "Now Sue is the same age as I am! How come she gets one and I don't?" God's ways are mysterious to say the least!

August 19, 1989, Sue and I were married at the Colonia Chapel in Clark, New Jersey. My daughter Diane was one of the bride's maids and one of Ann's brothers from New Zealand, Eric Sides, made the journey to show Ann's family's acceptance and support. Because of distance, the expense of travel, as well as the quick decision to marry while I was in the USA, my other children could not be there. I called the family in Australia to tell them the great news. I knew they were praying for me and now for Sue; and waiting for us to come back so they could meet her. Since the children had met her at the camp they knew of the lady who now would become their new mother.

Larry Ondrejack officiated at the wedding and spoke about Abraham sending his servant to get a wife for Isaac. On arrival at

Nahor, the servant asked God to show him the right person. He suggested that when he would ask a girl for a drink from the well, she would not only give him a drink, but offer to water his camels also. Larry said that when Sue agreed to marry me, she was also agreeing to care for my three children also. I wasn't sure if he was saying that my kids looked like camels, but anyway it made a good analogy!

We left for a short honeymoon and drove to Florida in Sue's car.

Sue and Ian's wedding - 8/19/89

We left it with Bill Van Ryn until we returned the following year, thinking we would settle there to live.

On the flight back to Australia someone on the 14-hour flight from Los Angeles to Sydney was chain-smoking all the way which resulted in Sue having a very serious asthma attack the first day in

269

Sydney. The following night she could hardly breathe and I thought she was dying. I called an ambulance at 2:00 AM and she was taken off to hospital. I was thinking, "Lord, don't let her die. I couldn't take having a wife of two weeks dying on me!"

Sue spent three days in hospital until she was back to normal again. I was very thankful I could bring her home to our apartment and the three kids she had inherited. She already knew Adri and Phil well, having been their teacher at the Bible camp just two years before. David was staying with mum in her apartment as she had a spare bedroom. But we all had meals together and began to put the family back on track.

Some years later Sue handed me a list she had written many years before meeting me, describing the husband she would like to marry. I thought it was interesting and funny as she showed me the list and said, "I did get most of what I had wanted!" I still don't know which one was not fulfilled.

Sue's description of the husband she would like. 7/29/1970
1. *Good looking*
2. *Ambitious*
3. *Intelligent*
4. *Responsible yet impulsive*
5. *Exciting*
6. *Likes to travel*
7. *Classy, but not a snob*
8. *Fun*
9. *Friendly and Outgoing*
10. *Kind and generous*
11. *Loves kids, 'cause I want 4*
12. *Demands respect, is respected, & respects others*
13. *Considerate*
14. *Enjoys music and sport.*

Wow! Not a bad list!

By the end of 1989 I was in the process of obtaining resident visas at the US Embassy for the children and myself. There were no problems getting the visas as being married to a US citizen made the application merely routine. However, there was the need to get birth certificates from two countries, for Adri and Phil. They had birth certificates from Colombia, which had to be officially translated, as well as having Australian citizenship-by-descent documents. Finally the paperwork was in order and we made plans to return to Florida in January 1990.

Because of her declining health, my mother, along with my sisters, thought it best that we sell my townhouse in which she was living. She moved in with my sister, Anne, and I was able to give some assistance to getting her settled before I moved away again.

Reorganizing our lives in Florida, USA

Through all the years of serving in Colombia it was my belief that God had brought me there and that I would live out my life in Colombia. I had no intention of ever leaving. However, with Ann's sudden passing and other circumstances that following year God seemed to be showing me that my ministry was taking a different turn. During the year in Australia I prayed earnestly seeking the Lord's mind; and just where He would have me to serve and what He would have me to do. I was willing to go back to Colombia if that is what He directed. When I married Sue and we discussed ministry possibilities I believed that God was directing me to move to the USA, to live in Florida, and therefore be able to visit Colombia regularly as well as other Latin American countries.

Having worked with Bill Van Ryn for the Intensive Bible Study classes in Colombia and other mission activities I thought it would be good to live in the same area as he and his wife Fayette. This would allow us to both serve the Spanish communities and for me to make trips to Colombia or elsewhere in Latin America as God directed.

We were able to rent an apartment in Palm Beach Gardens, Florida not far from the Van Ryns and then went about enrolling the children into schools. David, then 17, went to Jupiter Christian School but being mid-school year in the USA he repeated the second half of his junior year, graduating the following year. Philip was 9 and also attended the same school, as it provided K-12 instruction and was near our house. Adriana was enrolled in the local public school where she could receive the special help needed to be successful. Sue was a great help in working with school officials for the right placement because she knew the USA system with her Special Education experience.

Once again I could look back and see God's hand as He controlled our lives. The arrow had been re-sharpened, and I was ready to be used in whatever way God directed me. It was good to have the family settled again.

Ian, Sue, Adriana, Phil and David - in Florida

19

NEW BEGINNING AND MINISTRIES

A Visit to Colombia

During the summer of 1990 we were advised that the missionaries had invited several overseas men to come to Colombia. This was done to give backing to their desire of closing down the printing and publishing ministry. I also needed to close our home and sell off the furniture, as well as pack up personal effects that should be brought to the USA.

Sue and I traveled to Bogotá, staying a day with my cousin Bill Corson and his family, then going on to Bucaramanga. Without relating all the pain and my arguments for not closing the Literature Ministry, it was finally and wrongfully thought that the Colombians managing the ministry could not do so effectively. Also the printing equipment would be sold and the money redirected into Grace and Truth Publishing in the USA. This action was eventually accomplished and Grace and Truth was able to purchase a four-tower web press, which proved to be a tremendous help for the printing of the millions of tracts and the continued Spanish literature under the auspices of Good Tidings Publishers, which I had been handling since 1986.

Knowing that some of the missionaries wanted to also take over the bookshop, I was able to state, as part of the agreement, that Marina, who at that time had been working for me for 17 years and had really managed the running of the bookshop well for those last six years, should be given the stock as her severance payment. She would rent-to-own as payment for the purchase of the book-shop property, which was in the name of the Corporación Maranata,

273

and eventually complete payment for the property and continue that side of the Literature Ministry. A couple of years later Marina and her husband Miguel sold their home and gave the funds as full payment for the bookshop property to Andrew Rothlisberger, who at the time was president of the Corporation. Since then, as owners, they have continued to administer the bookshop. Marina (and her husband Miguel), has been able to continue this important ministry in the State of Santander, having worked there for 41 years as of 2015.

Having settled the literature work situation and closed out my house we prepared to return to the USA. I was happy to have some of my books and other household items with us and it was time to get on with serving the Lord as He directed.

Are We Too Old?

Finally life had begun to settle to some routine in the USA when Sue and I discussed the possibility of having our own children, taking into account that I was already in my 50s, she was 40, and that we would be "older" parents for any that came along. "Do you think you can handle being a father in your 60's and 70's?" Sue asked.

Well, I was feeling pretty strong at the time and said, "I don't see why not!"

By the end of July 1991 Sue announced that she thought she was pregnant and the doctor confirmed it a couple of weeks later. Those were days of excitement for us both and as time went along and Sue began to show, she was a very proud mother-to-be, just loving the fact that she would have the joy of bringing a child into the world.

April 9, 1992 Jillian Suzanne was born and our lives changed again with this little life. However, that excitement lasted only a few days after she arrived home. Jill would cry whenever we put her down. I don't know if it was because my mother had come from Australia for the event and she was always holding Jillian and spoiling her, or if it was just Jill's nature or some other issue. After mum returned to Australia we had to decide what we would do. Finally, we left Jill in her crib in our bedroom and we slept on the pullout couch in the living room for several days, until Jill learned that it was easier to go to sleep than cry and wait for someone to pick her up.

274

Our family grew in other ways also. June 5, 1993 I was privileged to officiate the wedding ceremony of son David to his high school sweetheart, Hannah. We had a great time celebrating with them and the anticipation of more grandchildren in years to come. I was thankful to be settled and serving the Lord as He opened up opportunities.

Ministry – Visits To Cuba

Conference in Cuba during the '90s

In 1991, I began receiving letters from people in Cuba asking for the bimonthly Tri- fold tract "Buenas Nuevas," (Good News.) It seemed that some governmental ties were loosening politically in Cuba. In one of those letters there was a request from someone, giving us a post office box number and speaking about needing the tracts and quantities of Buenas Nuevas for their work in their "Sala de Reunión," (Meeting Room – or Hall.) This was a very common description of Plymouth Brethren Chapels and I immediately thought, "There must be Brethren assemblies in Cuba. I should go there and try to find them."

I made bookings to fly to the Bahamas and then on to Cuba. Since I was traveling on an Australian passport I felt the restrictions for Americans to travel to Cuba did not apply to me. I did not know whom I could trust in communist Cuba and I knew there would be security people watching tourists. However, my daughter Diane was still working at Trans World Radio in Bonaire at the time, and she gave me the contact information for a pastor in Havana whose son was also working at TWR.

I had a load of my tracts in Spanish along with my VHS video camera in my travel bag and arranged for some tours since I was there as a "tourist." I had a tour of Havana, seeing the old city and the Spanish-built fortifications, then another tour to the Bay of Pigs. The folk on the bus knew I was an Australian and they said they really loved the Australians, as some of the men from the Australia Communist Party were there when the US invaded Cuba at The Bay of Pigs. I didn't say much, just said, "All us Australians try to be helpful." Of course I meant, without stating this, that getting the gospel to the people was the best help anyone could give.

I made contact with the pastor who invited me to visit a youth camp the following Saturday and Sunday. I agreed and we made plans for how I could meet him without drawing attention to our contact. Saturday morning after breakfast and after the maid had made up the bed I packed my small bag with tracts, my camera and some changes of clothes. I messed up the bed so that the maid would think I had slept in it Saturday night. It was always my habit to keep the hotel key in my pocket and not hand it in to the front desk so that no one would know if I was in or out.

The youth camp went really well with over 100 attending for the weekend. I got to preach during the camp session and finally arrived back to the hotel Monday morning. By that time the maid would have seen that I hadn't slept in the bed Sunday night. I didn't know what to expect so went right up to my room since I had the key, and therefore the hotel people at the desk could not give warning. When I opened the door, three men were in the room. One was going though my suitcase and with a screwdriver opening up the lining. The other two were doing something with their screwdrivers to the wall.

I asked them, "What are you doing?"

"We are fumigating!"

"What? Looking for bugs?"

They all hurriedly packed up and left. I guess my absence had aroused some suspicions and they were checking me out.

When I was leaving the country, fortunately, I decided at the last moment to keep the VHS recordings in my carry-on, as my checked bag never arrived at my stop-over in the Bahamas. I guess they wanted to do some more "fumigating!"

While in Havana the pastor I met told me about a small group of people who were meeting in a home that he thought might be those for whom I was searching. We visited them the following Sunday afternoon and discovered that they had just finished breaking bread as they celebrated the Lord's Supper. There were just six believers together that day.

I assured him I would be back in a few months, and early the following year when I visited that same home there were 40 baptized believers, 80 people coming to a weeknight Bible study and over 100, including children, coming to the Sunday School. Also I was able to visit a couple of other Brethren churches during that visit. The brother who was the leader of that first group said, "Things seem to be opening up and we have many home Bible studies going on. We even have one brother here who rides his bicycle as much as two hours each way to conduct several Bible studies during the week. Do you think you could come and give teaching on how to turn these Bible studies into churches?"

I excitedly said that I would love to do that and we set up a date. There were 12 different Brethren churches functioning at that time. This fellow was to coordinate getting believers to attend a conference for studies in helping home Bible study groups to also become functioning churches. I spoke to my long-time friend Bill Van Ryn and, together with his son Todd, we prepared the studies as well as printed notes of our studies for each person to keep and use in their home areas.

There were about 35 who attended those studies, all very enthusiastic, so the time we spent there was really worthwhile. Today there are many more local churches and the work continues to grow. During the 90's I visited Cuba some ten times.

Wise As Serpents And Harmless As Doves

On one occasion when I arrived in Havana, I had not put the name of a hotel where I would be staying, as I planned to stay with some of the believers. I was in line to see the immigration agent and finally handed him my passport and entry paper.

"You don't have a hotel here," he stated.

"No, I will be staying with some friends."

"You are in trouble, go and stand over there until I finish the rest of the passengers," he ordered.

I went over to the corner of the immigration area, like a naughty boy in school!

When everyone had gone he called me over and said, "You can't do that, tourists can't stay with Cubans; you have to be in a hotel. You are in trouble," he said again.

"When I travel in different parts of the world I usually stay with the people I know. I thought I should be able to do the same here."

"You are in deep trouble, really big trouble," he went on. "Where are you going?"

"Well, I was going to Pinar del Rio, and if you like, you can book me in to the hotel Pinar del Rio." I didn't even know if there was a hotel by that name, and I was sure he didn't either.

"You can't do that. You are in real trouble!"

"Why don't you go to the travel section over there and book a hotel for me?" I asked.

"I'll see what I can do." And with that he walked over to the tourist desk and spoke to the people there for a couple of minutes. I knew that most of the telephone lines were not at all reliable and was curious about what he was doing.

"I couldn't get through to Pinar del Rio, so you are really in trouble."

By this time I was getting sick of hearing that I was in trouble and was sure he was just looking for a bribe.

He finally asked, "What is it worth to you to get out of all this trouble?"

"Are you looking for a bribe?" I asked, purposely not using the Spanish word for a tip. "How much? Ten dollars?"

"Make it twenty," he replied.

278

I started to pull out my wallet taking out a US $20 bill. "No. No! Put it in your passport and I will meet you at the luggage carousel."

There were security cameras all around that area, so I just stepped back a few steps, took out my wallet and put a $20 bill in my passport with about half sticking out the top of the book. I held it up so that the cameras would get a good look at it then walked over to the carousel, picked up my bag, still with the passport in my hand and the money sticking out. I waited for a few minutes. The guy didn't come over, so I just picked up my bag and walked out of the terminal and met the believer who was giving me a ride. He loaded my bag and off we went.

The strange thing was that this friend was driving a 1949 Ford Mercury and it sounded like a tank. I asked him about the motor and he said, "The motor died in this car many years ago. But there were some old Russian buses left in a field nearby so I was able to get one of the diesel engines and built it into this car." It sounded more like a large tractor going down the main street of Havana, but no one seemed to notice as there were many more very old vehicles chugging along on the Cuban streets.

After another visit to Cuba I was back in the Havana José Marti International Airport waiting to board my plane for the Bahamas. In the waiting room there was a lady with a baby about 10 months old also waiting. She looked like an American and I wondered what she was doing in Cuba.

The call came to board and as I walked out to the plane I could see that it was an old Russian model. There were two jet engines at the rear end and behind the jets the plane was black with exhaust fumes. That didn't give me a lot of confidence! I boarded, found my seat and as I sat there I began to get a very strange feeling that something was not right.

The lady with the baby came on board and sat in her seat about three rows in front of mine. I felt a real urge to pray for the safety of that lady and her baby. That was strange enough, but then I found myself thinking about how I could tie my jeans in such a way that they would become floats if we crashed in the Caribbean. We went through the usual take- off procedures and were soon up to 33,000 ft. I was sitting in the aisle seat so could look forward. The cockpit door was open and I could see the pilots and out of the plane wind-screens.

I still felt strange and continued to pray for a safe trip, when suddenly the plane made what felt like a 90° turn to the right. I had never experienced a turn like that in a plane after many years flying commercial flights. In a couple of seconds the plane went into a steep dive. As I looked forward through the cabin, I could see the ocean through the plane's front windows. We seemed to be diving directly down to the ocean.

The man beside me was reading and hadn't seemed to notice anything. I said to him, "Looks like we are going down!" He looked up from his book, then looked out the window and started to hold on to the armrests. We dove down for what seemed like a very long time and I expected to hit the water soon. I suppose we were at about 4,000 ft. although at the time is seemed a lot closer to the water, when the pilot pulled the plane level again. It had seemed like we had been diving for 10 minutes, but it had to have been less than half that. I know I did have time to thank the Lord for having given me a fantastic life and prayed for Sue and Jill and the coming baby.

After a few minutes the pilot spoke on the P.A. system, "Sorry about that folks. We have an engine problem and we are going to attempt to get back to Cuba. We will try to get to Varadero, which is the nearest airport. We will keep you informed!"

Well, that was exciting news. They were attempting to get back to Cuba and trying to reach Varadero airport on the North Coast of Cuba! Great!

We were flying at just a few thousand feet and could see the ships and boats on the waves below us. About 20 minutes later we came over the coast, and no doubt Varadero wasn't too far away.

The pilot came on again and said, "Well, we have made it here and so we are going to try to make it all the way back to Havana as they have better facilities for maintenance."

We did make it to Havana and landed safely with fire trucks running along beside us. As I deplaned I saw that the jet engine on the right side was blackened and was no doubt the cause of our problem.

The passengers all returned to the transit waiting room and as we sat, the lady with the baby came and sat at my table. Waiters brought "free" coffee to us all, and we sat and chatted while we waited. I wanted to ask what she was doing in Cuba. But Cuba, being a police state with security people always close by, one has to be cautious about those with whom you speak. So it was a very general conversation until someone came and stood across the room from us and took out a camera.

I was in Cuba as a tourist, but had spent many days visiting churches and preaching in different places, which was not officially allowed. I didn't want to find out that, "You are in deep trouble, really big trouble," again. I didn't want my photo on any security camera and so ducked down and re-tied my shoelaces that were perfectly all right. As I glanced across from me under the table, I noticed that the lady had also ducked and was picking up something off the floor that wasn't there! We smiled at each other, waited a couple of minutes more, then sat up again with our backs away from the area where the photographer was doing his deed. Now my curiosity was running wild with all sorts of ideas about what that lady was doing, but neither of us asked any of those sorts of questions. Obviously we were both being careful not to get into discussion about any topics that were off limits. I have no idea about her activity and I was wise enough to just mind my own business.

The replacement plane eventually arrived and I had an uneventful flight back to the Bahamas, then on to Fort Lauderdale and home.

We never know what trials God will lead us through in our service for Him. If we knew ahead of time we might just say, "No, thank you; I'll stay home." But learning to put our full trust in Him for all circumstances brings the greatest blessing both to God and to us. I am thankful that God gave me the strength to rest in His care through each event. I truly wanted to be an arrow in the Archer's Hands.

20

DARK CLOUDS

Another Baby And Another Life-Changing Challenge

By March 15, 1994 Sue was again six months pregnant and really excited about having another child. One evening as we lay in bed Susan suddenly asked, "Please feel this."

I felt her right breast and there was a lump the size of a gumball.

"If this lump is cancer, I'm dead!" she exclaimed. Sue had told me that her birth father had died of colon cancer at the age of 31, an uncle about the same age had also died of cancer and Sue had feared that she might have a family gene that could cause cancer. (At that time Sue did not know that her mother would later have the same diagnosis.)

We visited the OB-GYN the next day. He said we needed to see a specialist and arranged an appointment for two days later. The specialist was also concerned and decided that a needle biopsy was needed. He performed that procedure right away, and we left for home feeling scared and wondering what the result might be. There was so much to pray about.

"I can't believe this is happening to us," Sue stated, "How is this possible? We have been so happy and the Lord has blessed us wonderfully."

We hardly slept that night hoping against hope that the biopsy would show a benign tumor. At 10:00 AM the following day the phone rang and we both picked up an extension. It was the specialist.

"I'm sorry to have to tell you that the biopsy showed a very aggressive form of cancer and the best solution will be immediate surgery." He went on to explain that he had arranged for us to see an oncologist and had set the date for the surgery just a few days later.

We visited the oncologist who walked us through the steps of chemotherapy and strongly suggested that Sue abort the baby so that the chemo could begin as soon as possible. Of course, this was not an option for Sue or me, so the oncologist then stated that Sue would need to wait for the chemo treatment until the baby was born. She suggested that we should consider inducing labor a few weeks early in order to start the treatments as soon as possible.

Also, during one of these visits the doctor asked me if I planned to stay around. With a curious look I asked what he meant by that. He went on to explain that many husbands can't live with the idea that their wife had a mastectomy and therefore file for divorce or just leave the family. Again, this was a preposterous idea to me and I informed him that I would be alongside Sue no matter what developed.

Sue and I did a lot of praying over the next few days pleading with the Lord that the surgery would get all the cancer and that the cancer would not metastasize to the other breast or anywhere else in her body.

Sue always kept a journal of her thoughts and had started one for this little baby:

4/19/94

My darling little one,

What a sad time we are going through. Mommy has just been diagnosed as having breast cancer. It is too hard to contemplate what the future may hold. At the moment we are dealing with some pretty scary things - I feel so sorry for you, my sweet as you will have to go through some of these things with Mommy, I'm afraid.

Later this week I will have a mastectomy - surgery to remove my breast. (If the cancer is found to have spread, then I may lose both breasts.) For a woman this is a terrible trial, but what frightens me more is the prospect that the cancer may have already spread elsewhere. If it has, I may not have much time with you. If God allows, however, for me to recover we will praise Him together for such mercy.

284

Meanwhile, my darling, I'm afraid you must endure the surgery with me. You are too little to be taken yet, so you will have to go through it under anesthetic, just like Mommy. All the doctors assure me that you will be safe. There is some risk but most are optimistic. Our God has you in His hands, I am trusting He will shield you from all harm.

In about 2 months we will have to deliver you a bit early. The doctors would like to wait until we get to within 2 weeks of your due date (July 4.) Then as soon as you are born, Mommy will get chemotherapy. I will not be able to breastfeed you - even if I have a single breast, because of the chemicals. This saddens me, but I am willing to sacrifice my breasts, my breastfeeding, anything, if I can just have a chance to live to see you grow up.

Darling, my heart is so heavy. I feel as if it is breaking into little pieces day by day. Yet God is our refuge - don't ever forget that, when in your own life you face trials.

This afternoon Daddy and I will go to the doctor's to check on you. We hope that we will be able to tell clearly if you are a girl or a boy - then we will name you and pray for you by your name! How lovely to think we might know you that well. It will be a joy for Mommy to contemplate before surgery.

All will be well, my sweet. God is in control.

Love, Mommy

4/21/94

Dear Little One,

In just a few hours you and Mommy will go through surgery. Please be strong, my darling. Please take care and stay alive! Stay in mommy for a while - be strong, my sweet! I love you so - all the more for what you do - all the more for what you are going through. We are in God's hands. Praise God - He is good!

5/1/74

Dear Little One,

You did so well! We got through the surgery just fine. You were monitored the whole time and the surgeon said they could hear you kicking and bouncing around even during the surgery! In the recovery room everyone was puzzled by the sound of an amplified heartbeat - <u>yours</u> on the monitor! (Not many pregnant women go through surgery!)

I have been healing well, but feeling so tired and sluggish. The weight of you plus the pain of surgery has made it hard for me to sleep comfortably.

We have many decisions to make re your delivery - when? How, where? All is in God's timing - We need His wisdom.

5/15/94

Dear Baby,

It's been difficult these days handling the responsibilities of house and children while feeling so tired. At times I get really discouraged - I look at the calendar and think of what could/should have been - you are due July 4th! Independence Day! What fun it might have been to have you then. But now we have to rush you into the world - perhaps before you're ready, poor thing. Thankfully the doctors say we can wait until later June. That will be good for you, my love, but I still worry if you'll be o.k.

Our lives have changed so dramatically, so suddenly. Sometimes it overwhelms me to think of having to go through chemotherapy during the first months of your life when you will need and demand so much attention; perhaps I'll be too sick to give it to you! It breaks my heart to think of the joy of your birth being overshadowed by the pain of cancer and the trauma of treatments. I cling to the thought that a cure will make it all worthwhile! May our prayers be answered.

6/3/94

My darling little one -

We saw you today on the ultrasound and we now know you are a little <u>BOY!</u> How lovely to think of my little son and how we rejoiced to know that Daddy will have a "bit" of his little Alan back. (You will learn all about Daddy's other little boy, Alan, who died at age 2). We know you are a different child - you are a very <u>special person</u> all by yourself, but having a little boy will, I think, help Daddy get over losing Alan. It will keep Alan's memory alive, while yet bringing new joy to Daddy. He's so excited about you! We are naming
286

you SEAN ALAN (Sean = a form of <u>Ian</u> and <u>Alan</u> in memory of your brother.)

Jill has learned to say your name and waits patiently for you to "come out". She kisses my tummy and talks about when she can give you a bottle and rock you (not too hard, I hope) and give you a "little tiny binky" when you cry, etc. She loves you, too, as we all do.

You are being planned for delivery around June 20. We'll see how things go. As you are no longer breech, we hope to deliver naturally. That will be better for both of us. The Lord knows.

Mommy will have to start chemo a week later. We will try to enjoy a week of <u>bliss</u> before that! Your crib is ready and so are we to receive you into our arms.

I love you, darling, Mommy

June 20, 1994

Happy Birthday, Sean Alan!

Born 8:33 p m   BEAUTIFUL!

You have slate blue eyes and very pink skin. You have a nice soft covering of black hair - not too thick.

6/27/94

Darling Sean,

I need to take a break from record keeping to tell you how much I love you! I am, in fact, <u>in love with you!</u> You touch my heart with a tenderness I cannot describe. I look at you and well up with love. I wonder at your beautiful, peaceful little face. You look like an angel to me! You bring a calm to my spirit and joy to my heart beyond words. I am so thankful to God for you. May you feel this love I have for you, darling. Be assured of it!

Mummy

PS Mommy began chemo yesterday (first of 12 treatments over the next 9 months)

287

Jillian and Sean with Sue during her Chemo treatment

A Father Doing Midnight Feeds

With all of the challenges of missionary life, learning a new language and culture, dealing with diverse situations, the idea of a wife with cancer, and all that is required for a new baby was a new challenge. Once again, I knew that God was in control. I had the pleasure of bottle-feeding Sean, evenings, 2:00 AM, 6:00 AM etc. Sue was able to feed him a few times during the day, but with the chemo treatments she was always extremely tired and had little energy for many of the household chores. Those first few months were really difficult for us both as I still had the literature work, as well as preaching and teaching, on top of caring for Sean, two-year-old Jill, and the others. Fortunately David, Adri and Phil were older and could help with many of the household needs.

I really enjoyed looking after Sean and we bonded quickly. That bond has continued to this day.

God Opens Doors Of Ministry

Sue's treatments brought about remission and when she was well enough I continued to make trips to Cuba. There was real revival in Cuba and just about every time I preached, souls were saved. On one occasion the believers had a conference with about 150 attending. Twenty-one people made decisions to receive the Lord after I spoke that afternoon, one of whom was a communist party member.

I also continued visiting churches in the USA as well as participating in the Winter Youth Retreats being held in Toledo, Ohio at that time. They were held between Christmas and New Year's Day, with as many as 400 high school and college age young adults attending. On one occasion we took some young people from the Bahamas with us. They flew in to Fort Lauderdale and we hired two 15-seat vans and drove all night to the Retreat. As we were leaving Ft. Lauderdale, one of the Bahamians asked, "When does the blacktop finish?" That was his first time in the US. He had no idea of the distance and didn't realize the roads were paved all the way to Toledo.

On several occasions I was asked to speak at Family Camp at Hickory Cove Bible Camp in North Carolina. In July 1993 with Sue, one-year-old Jill, Phil and Adri we drove to the camp. I spoke for the main sessions and that same trip my son Phil was baptized at the camp. We met some old acquaintances, including Barb Martin, who had been the dorm mother at the Grove City Conference when Diane was there back in 1982. Barb was usually at the registration desk at the Winter Youth Retreats and also helped at the camp each summer.

Bill Van Ryn and I often took turns visiting a church in Miami where we were asked to speak at the ministry service after the worship meeting. On one of those occasions one of the elders mentioned to Bill that there was a group of Guatemalans in our area who had asked the believers in Miami to visit them in order to help establish a church in the Lake Worth area. Because we lived closer, Bill and I followed up and made contact with some of those believers whose background was with the churches with whom we were associated in Guatemala. We were able to have some conversations and finally rented a large second floor room at the back of an English speaking church in the area.

Bill and I began with Bible studies and after a couple of months felt we had a good core group of believers who understood how a New

Testament-type church should function and we finally decided to establish the group as a local church of believers. We spoke to the believers in the English church we had been attending who were generally happy for us to move forward with an Hispanic church in the Lake Worth area.

There were many seasonal workers in Florida and the fact that there was an established Plymouth Brethren Hispanic church functioning, caused many more Guatemalan workers to find their way to the meetings. Others from other Latin American countries began to attend and it wasn't long before there were people getting saved and baptisms to perform.

The baptisms were held in the inlet near Jupiter, FL and with permission from the authorities. Generally, a fairly large crowd of Hispanics gathered to sing and pray at the baptism. Bill and I mostly did the baptizing, but we were rather surprised when on one occasion we invited a mature brother to baptize a couple and he very readily did so but with his suit and tie on. Apparently that was how it was done in Guatemala!

Bill and I were working closely together with the Spanish Literature Ministry. He had a paper he had been publishing called, "El Joven Viajero," (The Young Traveler,) and we also produced another teaching paper called "Escudriñad" (Search the Scriptures). I continued to write and prepare the *Buenas Nuevas,* and Bill was generally updating and rewriting the line of tracts we were publishing under the name of Good Tidings Publishers, *(Editorial Buenas Nuevas.)* There was always so much work to be done.

21

CANCER TAKES OVER

Sue had been in remission for about six months after her initial nine months of chemo treatment and the oncologist was keeping a close eye on her platelet count and cancer markers. She had been having some hip pain and the cancer indicators had increased, so the oncologist ordered X-rays of Sue's pelvic area and hips. Cancer had returned in the bones in the hip area.

Another round of chemo began along with the lack of energy, tiredness and continuing pain.

Move to Wisconsin

In 1996 Sue and I began to think about the future, the possibility of Sue's passing, and the fact that there would probably be very little support for the children and me from the little church at Lake Worth. The church was made up mostly of retirees and very few children. As I was invited to speak at different churches and camps, we used those opportunities to look for possible places where we might be able to fit in to a well-established church with families and children.

Later, when further x-ray's were taken that showed four cancer spots on Sue's liver we both realized that a cure was not really a possibility. Sue was heartbroken and the thought that hurt her most was that she would not be around to see her children grow up.

November 25, Sue asked, "Why is the Lord allowing this? I really believed He was going to cure me." She came to me later that day and said, "I really would like to have a day of fasting and prayer to just seek the Lord and try to come to grips with what's happening in my body. Would you mind looking after the children and let me lock myself in the bedroom for a day to read, pray and seek the Lord?"

"Of course. When would you like to do it?" She chose the next day.

The following day I prepared the children to go to the park gathered some snacks and worked out a plan to keep the house quiet while Sue had her time alone with the Lord.

(The following are notes Sue made during the day of fasting and prayer which reflect what we were both experiencing in facing this trial. All Scripture quotes are from the New King James Version as that is what Sue was reading at the time.)

A day for Fasting and Prayer - Tuesday, November 26, 1996
Some notes from my personal studies during this recurrence of the cancer.

Last Friday at 9:30 I had more X-rays and now I have learned that the cancer, after returning in the bone of my hips some months ago, has now returned as several small spots on my liver. Lord I'm scared!

I asked Ian if he could just take care of the children for the day so that I could shut myself into David's old bedroom and fast for the day, to be able to pray without any interruptions and just find out what the Lord is doing. I'm so afraid that I will not see my darling children grow up, I don't want to leave them and my heart just aches at the thought of dying and leaving them all.

I. Confession, sin, acceptance of God's judgment.
    Psalm 109:21-27   It is God's doing.

Our Ministry 2 Cor. 6:1-10
"¹As God's fellow workers we urge you not to receive God's grace in vain."
Lamentations 3:21- 5:21
 3:21 Wait on the Lord!
 3:31-33 God's compassion
 3:39-44 Is there some sin?
 3:49 "My tears are now constant, no joy! My eyes will flow unceasingly, without relief."
 3:55-57 "I called on your name, O LORD, from the depths of the pit."

5:15-21 "Joy is gone from our hearts; our dancing has turned to mourning."

II. Confession as to my own selfishness
Loss of focus on God;
Loss of that beautiful vision of helping Ian, and seeing him and bringing him joy;
Him not me; Focus/order; God, Ian, me.
Is it too late?

Reading in Job, he passed through deep waters!

III. Blessings in my affliction - Job
Blessings if in my affliction, I can accept that God has given me a path to walk that is hard.
My calling is to walk that path faithfully; I have been given an opportunity to show forth Christ that would otherwise not have happened, my pain has returned me to the Lord - caused me to be "better" for Him and my family.

My body is not my own - it was fashioned by God for a purpose – with cancer!
To glorify Him! Job - afflicted yet worshiped.
   1. Lord gives - heals, blessed by God
   2. Uttered not a word against God
   3. Held fast to his integrity
   4. Shall I receive good at the hand of God and not evil?
   5. His friends - happy to be corrected
   6. Seek God and commit cause to Him.

Job 5:8-9   "But as for me, I would seek God."
Marvelous things without number. God wounds and makes whole. (He was wounded but His hands also healed)
5:18 "For he wounds, but he also binds up; he injures, but his hands also heal."
5:26-27 "You shall come to the grave at a full age," (hope!)

IV. Hope for Healing

For every hope of healing, there comes a thought of despair; for every Scripture of encouragement, there is one, which rings of truth and deceit and distrust. I don't have hope, yet I want to.

Job 7:11 "Therefore I will not restrain my mouth; I will speak in the anguish of my spirit; I will complain in the bitterness of my soul."

7:13-21 When morning comes!

That You should set Your heart on him, That You should visit him every morning."

Job 9 tells of God's power; who is justified before Him

God's right to do as He pleases.

Job 12:10 "In whose hand is the life of every living thing,

And the breath of all mankind?" All life is in God!

13:15 "Though He slay me, yet will I trust Him.

Even so, I will defend my own ways before Him."

Job 16 -17 Job senses the grave

16:22 "For when a few years are finished,

I shall go the way of no return." I will go the way from which I will not return!

17:1 The grave is ready for me...! My fear!

"My spirit is broken, my days are cut short, the grave awaits me."

17:7 "My eye has also grown dim because of sorrow,

And all my members are like shadows."

Job 22

1. I need to have eyes for the Lord. Good will come from this.

22:22 "Now acquaint [submit] yourself with Him, and be at peace;

Thereby good will come to you."

2. Return to the Lord.

22:23 "If you return to the Almighty, you will be built up;"

3. Delight in the Almighty, He will hear your prayer.

22:26-27 "For then you will have your delight in the Almighty,... He will hear you"

Job 23 The Test

I cannot see/feel God, yet I know he knows my ways.

23:10-11 "But He knows the way that I take;

When He has tested me, I shall come forth as gold."

God is always right!

Job 34:12 "Surely God will never do wickedly, Nor will the Almighty pervert justice."

294

Job's choice
24:14 "If he set his heart upon man, if he gather unto himself his spirit and his breath; All flesh shall perish together, and man shall turn again unto dust."
Need for confidence in God
Job 34:28-29 "For He hears the cry of the afflicted.
When He gives quietness, who then can make trouble?"

God's power and purpose
Job 37:13 "He causes it [rain] to come, whether for correction, or for His land, or for mercy.
37:14 "Stand still and consider the wondrous works of God."

The entire discourse between God and Job is amazing.
That God would reason with man!
Who am I?

Job 40:1 "Moreover the LORD answered Job, and said, Shall he that contends with the Almighty instruct him? "
Rom. 9:20 "But indeed, O man, who are you to reply against God? Will the thing formed say to him who formed it, "Why have you made me like this?"
Job 40:8 "Would you indeed annul My judgment?"
Job 42:6 "But now my eye sees You. Therefore I abhor myself, And repent in dust and ashes."
After the trial Job lived another 140 years and the Lord blessed the latter end of Job! He died, old and full of days.

Sue finally came out of her room at 8:00 PM that night and stated, "I have been fighting with the Lord about getting cured, and He hasn't given me any direction that it will happen. I finally had to come to the place where I could say to the Lord, "I am ready to accept whatever is Your will for me. I am still heartbroken, but can now accept whatever His plan is for me. I will not continue to ask for healing, although I really want it so badly, but I can now say Lord, Your will be done."

Preparing For The End

January 1997 Sue had been having headaches and the oncologist arranged for a CT Scan that showed the cancer had metastasized to the fluid in the spinal column. This was obviously serious and we didn't know how much time Susan would have. Previously I had read an email, which came through our church email group from Brian Glaeser. He mentioned that several families had moved away from Kenosha in Wisconsin, and he had some questions about what might be needed to help the local church there to revive and grow. I answered with some ideas and was surprised when he answered my email asking if I knew of any full time workers who might be able to go to Kenosha to help. "I know you can't come because your wife is so ill, but if you could let us know of a worker who might be free to come, it would be a great help."

After speaking with Sue, I wrote telling Brian that we had been praying about moving from Florida and that Kenosha might be what the Lord had in mind. We decided to drive to Kenosha to visit and check out the possibilities of living there.

In March we arrived and were very happy with what we saw. The church family was very accepting and friendly and we believed this was what the Lord had for us. While in town we looked at several possible homes suitable for us and got an idea of location and prices. We made plans to return to Kenosha in June that same year to look for a suitable house.

On that second visit we found a home that we thought would be ideal and began the paperwork to purchase it with a contingency loan from a local bank on the basis of the sale of our home in Florida. While in Kenosha Sean celebrated his third birthday in mid-June and we hurried back to sign the contract as we had a buyer with a bank loan that would be transferred directly to our Wisconsin bank. The sale went through on a Friday in early July and the closing date for our new home in Kenosha was for the following Monday afternoon.

In early July, while the two trucks were being packed, I visited the oncologist and asked her to be frank and honest with me, and tell me how much time she thought Sue really had left to live. She said, "Sue has at the most two months, and I'm so sorry I have to tell you that."

We had been packing and boxing our household goods for several weeks and one Friday we had some professionals pack our goods into two U-Haul trucks. Bill Van Ryn drove one of the trucks with David for company while I drove the other truck with Phil and Sean along. We pulled the cars on trailers. Since Adriana had completed high school she chose not to move to Wisconsin with us.

By that time Sue was weak and really sick so I arranged for her and Jill to fly to Chicago. Abby John, a good friend who just happened to be traveling to Chicago at that time also accompanied them. One of the couples in the Kenosha Church, Don and Karen Ditthardt, whom we had met while house-hunting, had promised to collect Sue and take her to their home until we had our household goods unpacked from the trucks.

We arrived on Sunday afternoon and Monday morning there were about 15 men from the chapel there to help unload the trucks, carry the beds, dressers, tables and appliances, etc., setting them up in the correct rooms as I directed. This was a tremendous help and I was so thankful for a local church so ready to be there for us as a support.

Sue couldn't do more than sit and watch, as her strength was gone. Knowing that the cancer had moved up the spinal fluid to the brain I took her to the local oncologist who suggested she have radiation to the brain to try to alleviate the pain and perhaps slow down the process. That process went on for a couple of weeks every two days, but really had no positive affect.

In late August, Diane and Bob with their two boys, who are the same ages as Jill and Sean, came to the house. They were in the USA awaiting visas, etc. after leaving Bonaire before going to Bucaramanga for another mission work. When they realized the serious condition of Sue they decided to stay at the house. This way, Diane was able to take care of the domestic chores and the children while I looked after Sue.

Also, Sue's parents and her sister flew out to see her. I had kept them informed of the situation and they wanted to say "good-bye." While there the ladies also unpacked more boxes and made some sense of the kitchen.

Shortly after Diane arrived I drove Phil to Florida State University in Tallahassee FL, where he had already enrolled for his freshman year. Then before leaving I called home to check on Sue, but there was no answer of the phone. We did not have a cell phone in those days so I set off at 6:00 PM for the long drive and was in a real hurry, not knowing what may have happened. I arrived back in Kenosha at 9:00 AM to an empty house and quickly called Gisela Habel, who was one of the ladies from the chapel who lived nearby. Gisela told me that the children were with her because Sue had been admitted into the hospital. I showered, changed and drove to the hospital to find that Sue had experienced a tremendous amount of pain and was receiving some strong painkillers. A number of people visited her and I stayed with her during the day.

Not having had any sleep the night before, I went home to nap and didn't wake till the next morning. I hurried off to the hospital only to find that Sue had been moved somewhere else. Urgently asking the nurse where she was, I was told that Sue had been screaming in pain most of the night and disturbing other patients.

With that I asked why the doctors had not given her morphine or some other painkiller and was told, "The doctor on call couldn't be contacted and we don't have the authority to dispense those sorts of drugs." I was really upset and began to tear into the nurses for not having enough brains or initiative to call some other doctor or give Sue something to stop the pain.

After that episode I decided to take Sue home, and the hospital arranged for a hospice nurse to come to the house each day. The oncologist prescribed morphine that I was to administer to Sue each day. I had the prescribed dosage and kept a record of how much and the times of the dose being given.

Sue asked the hospice nurse, "I want to talk with my five-year-old daughter before I die. When do you think it would be a good time to do that?"

"You should do it today," she replied.

That afternoon I told Jill to come and see her mother. Jill wasn't sure what that was about and stood quietly by Sue's bed.

"My darling little Jillian," Sue began. "Very soon I am going to go and be with the Lord Jesus in heaven. I want you to know and always remember how much I really love you. I'm sorry I won't be here to see you grow up, but I want you to always love the Lord and follow Him with all your heart. One day we will all be together in heaven and there will be no more tears or sorrow. Always put the Lord first in your life and He will care for you and give you the help you will need in every circumstance.

"One of these days the Lord will bring along another mother for you and Sean, and I want you to love her just the same as you love me. I really love you and I am sorry it has be like this."

Sue was tired after all the effort of that talk. She closed her eyes and slept. A little later she woke and was groaning so I gave her the prescribed dose of morphine. After a short time she could relax and we talked some more, but then her eyes closed and she slept. I had rented a special hospital bed and the next two nights I slept in the regular bed beside her. I could hold her hand and from time to time she would give a gentle squeeze.

That second night, around 2:00 AM she stirred and I began to sing some of her favorite hymns. I sang first, It Is Well With My Soul; then followed with, Great Is Thy Faithfulness, and another she loved was, How Great Thou Art.

We sat on a chair with Jill on my lap and cried together. I drifted off to sleep holding her hand and suddenly awoke at 4:00 AM. I don't remember what woke me, perhaps it was Sue's last sigh as her spirit went to be with the Lord. I switched on the light and as I looked at Sue I could see, indeed, she was with the Lord. I checked her heart to make sure, then called the nurse as instructed who told me she would come at 6:00 AM. The date was Tuesday, September 2, 1997.

I went upstairs to let Diane and Bob know that Sue was with the Lord and they both came down to see Sue and then pray with me. We cried on each other's shoulders for a little while then made decisions about the children. When the nurse arrived she confirmed what we already knew and went about taking out the tubes and cleaning the body. The nurse also called the funeral home to tell them to come for the body, telling them not to come until 7:00 AM as I wanted the children to see Sue and say their good-byes.

At 6:30 AM I woke both Jill and Sean and told them that their mother had gone to be with the Lord and to come down to see her before the funeral people came. They were both in shock and just stood there for a few moments. Jill remembers that she didn't believe me. She reached out to touch Sue's hand and said, "No, she's not dead." Then Sean asked, "Why is her mouth still open?" Sue's mouth was slightly open and I had to explain that when the person's spirit leaves the body to go and be with the Lord Jesus, the body just relaxes and I even had to close her eyes. We sat on a chair with Jill on my lap and cried together. By this time Diane's boys were awake and all four children went in to see Sue before the funeral men came. Right on 7:00 AM the funeral people came and that left the rest of us to tidy the downstairs room, fold up the medical bed I had rented and then get breakfast for the family.

One Day At A Time

Using e-mail I was able to let many of our friends and family know that Sue had passed away, and I asked one of the believers at our chapel to get the news out on the phone prayer chain. It wasn't long before several of the church friends called to offer to bring lunch and supper and some sort of roster was made up so that different families brought us meals for the following two weeks. This was really appreciated, as Diane, Bob and I, had to arrange the funeral, the speakers and songs for the funeral at the chapel and the burial at the Sunnyside Cemetery Gardens.

Sue's parents, Jane and Elmer Bozza had returned, as well as her sister Pat with her husband Tom Raab. My good friend Bill Van Ryn spoke at the funeral and began by saying, "Three great women passed away this week, Princess Diana, Mother Teresa, and Susan Taylor." He went on to speak about Sue and her love for the Lord and presented a good gospel message.

Another good friend of mine, Brian, was living in Canada at the time. He and I had served the Lord back in Australia in the late 50s, starting a youth ministry and preaching in the streets during our lunch hours with the Open Air Campaigners. I appreciated that he was able to say a few words and have the closing prayer.

I had been to the cemetery, chosen and paid for the plot, and they knew the time for the funeral. When we arrived the grave had not been dug and one of the workers told me they had made a mistake and dug a grave somewhere else. They humbly apologized and told me they would get it done as soon as possible. Meanwhile, all the visitors were at that area so I suggested we go ahead with the service with the casket still on the funeral home's stand. We all stood in a circle around the coffin and after a prayer, Sue's brother-in-law, Tom, brought a good message with a challenge that all the people there should be ready when their time came to meet the Lord.

When Tom finished I spoke, "It's hard for us at times to understand why the Lord takes to Himself a life so young, (Sue was just 47.) Sue was an answer to my prayers at a time of terribly difficult circumstances and challenges in my life, and I am thankful for the eight years we were able to spend together.

"I believe that just as Sue was there for me during those difficult times in my life, the Lord allowed me to be there for Sue during the terrible struggle she had when the cancer came, with the pain and suffering that eventually took her life. Sue loved the Lord and is now in His presence, free from pain and sorrow."

Sean, and a couple of other little boys were playing nearby and thankfully didn't really understand all that was involved in our lives at that time. Jill was quietly observing.

The workers at the cemetery came to me as we closed the "graveside" service, to tell me that the proper grave would be opened by 2:00 PM. We went back to the chapel where the ladies had prepared a meal for all who were there. Many came from distances and had travel plans for later that day.

At 2:00 PM Diane and Bob with their two boys Alister and Malcolm, and me with Jillian and Sean went to the cemetery for the actual burial. Because Diane had been traumatized when her little brother Alan was so tragically killed in Costa Rica and there had been no closure for her because she did not attend the burial; we decided to have the children at the actual burial so that they could know that Sue was with the Lord and her body was in the grave to await the resurrection.

There was a canopy over the grave with 10 seats to one side. We sat there for a few minutes and then I spoke about the resurrection and prayed. Each of us threw a rose onto the coffin and I then asked the men to fill the grave.

We returned to our seats and three-year-old Sean, who was sitting there watching as a front-end loader came and began to push earth into the grave asked, "Why are they putting dirt on Mummy?" I explained to him why this was done, and when the grave was full, we all threw another rose onto the mound and left. The adults were all heavy-hearted as we left the cemetery for home. The absence of Sue in the home began a heavy painful loneliness, for me.

Susan Vorberg Taylor
December 28, 1949 – September 2, 1997

Susan Gail Vorberg was born December 28,1949, to Elmer and Jane Vorberg and joined her two-year-old sister Patricia. She grew up in Irvington and Fanwood, New Jersey. At the age of two years old her 31-year-old father died of colon cancer. For the next nine and one-half years her mother worked diligently to provide for the girls. They lived in the upstairs flat over their grandparents who would babysit when needed. By the time Susan was 11 years old, Jane had found a loving, caring man also named Elmer and they married. Elmer #2 loved both girls and he became a wonderful Daddy to them.

Growing up in the 60s was a challenge for everyone at that time. Susan did very well at school, graduating high school with honors in 1967 and then going on to attend Trenton State College, graduating in 1971. She was enjoying life, and being a determined young lady was living life to the full.

By 1969 Pat married Tom Raab and before long Susan was an Aunt to three sweet children. While Susan had several boyfriends she had not found "Mr. Right" and pursued her career in teaching Special Education students, specializing in those with hearing impairment. Also, during this time Pat was introduced to knowing the Lord Jesus as her Savior. She and Tom attended a Bible-teaching church and she shared her faith with Susan. While the sisters had been raised to attend church they had never come to a full understanding of committing their life to the Lord. Susan did not appreciate her sister and brother-in-law's efforts to lead her to Christ.

Sue's best friend through junior and senior high school, Betty Ann, had married a man who was not the best example of a fine man as he had been into drugs and so forth. However, at some point he became saved and in a long distance conversation from California to Pennsylvania, he witnessed to Susan for a very long time (when phone calls cost by the minute). Sue was saved that very evening over the phone at the age of 30 and then began to read the Scriptures and to serve the Lord. This couple had no money, they had married very young and with a baby on the way; they really couldn't afford that phone call. On the day the phone bill arrived, a check from the IRS for some vague unexpected refund in the exact amount of the phone call (not the bill, just the one call) was in the same mail. God had provided for Sue's need of salvation even in that phone call.

Having given her life to the Lord, Sue became involved in a church in Hightstown, New Jersey, while continuing her profession of teaching the hearing impaired. Her first Bible camp experience was at Mountain View Bible Camp in Sunbury, Pennsylvania. She attended Family Camp in 1980 with Tom, Pat, and their family. Because she was a teacher, with time off during the summers, she decided to use her time to serve the Lord. She was a counselor and children's teacher at the camp for many years, for many camp sessions. This led her to explore what God wanted from her life and she took a year's sabbatical from her teaching of the deaf in Bucks County, Pennsylvania to spend a year teaching at North Pole Christian Academy in North Pole, Alaska from 1983-1984.

Coming back to teach at her old school she again found herself at Mountain View Bible Camp during school holidays. It was while she was there in 1986 that she met the Ian Taylor family and became close friends with his wife Ann. They carried on a written correspondence regularly until Ann passed away. Sue was very helpful in giving Ann suggestions for helping daughter Adriana, who had some learning challenges. Therefore it was understandable that Sue would write to the children after their mother suddenly passed away.

As noted in Chapter 19, Susan became the new mother for Ann's children. She was so thrilled to have married a godly man and also to be blessed with children. After the move to Florida and life settled she was even more thrilled to be pregnant with Jillian. The following year she had a miscarriage, but recovering well, soon she was pregnant with Sean. Knowing that she was past the "magic" age of 30, the doctors were monitoring her but all was going well, and then the cancer showed up. As related in Chapter 21, this was a most difficult time for everyone, especially Sue.

Throughout her battle with cancer she worked with all her strength to provide a normal family life for the children. All of the treatment and medications caused her much grief when it sapped her time and energy for them; but she persevered.

Sue kept copious journals. She also began writing her thoughts and love to Jill and Sean. She expressed her greatest fear – that she would not see them grow up to be godly, loving adults. They have those journals today to remember her thoughts and love for them.

Susan loved her Lord, her husband, and her children. Now I had to not only comfort two small children but also try to understand why God had chosen to take yet another companion and helper from me, having been through this once before.

22

BEGINNING THE CLIMB
BACK UP

Lord, What Now?

Once again I found myself with two small children needing a mother, and myself needing a wife, a companion to serve the Lord with me. What to do? Thankfully, Diane and her family were living with us for a few months to help keep the household running. But I knew that they were only waiting for their visas to be finalized, because they were preparing to go to Bucaramanga and continue their mission work. Saying that life was difficult does not adequately describe my thoughts, feelings and emotions. I prayed; oh yes I prayed. From past experience I knew that God was in control, but it surely seemed strange to me that He would, yet again, take my wife and helpmate leaving me with two small children.

Of course being September this was the beginning of the school year in the USA. Diane and I had enrolled our two oldest, Alister and Jill, in kindergarten at the local Christian School. Sean and Malcolm were enrolled in a pre-school two days a week. This gave us some peace and quiet to try to make sense of the house and also gave them something positive to do. Sean was not very excited about leaving me those days. He needed much reassurance, which I surely gave him. Jill seemed to get back into school easily after missing the week of the funeral. Her teacher was very understanding and encouraging.

Soon after Sue passed away Jill began to pray, "Lord, I don't know why you had to take our mother. You know we need a mother. We need someone who loves You, who loves Daddy and who will love us." How do you respond to a child's prayer like that? We were all praying for the same person, we just didn't know who it might be. I was careful not to raise any hopes for the children or myself, knowing that God was in control, and His timing is always perfect.

Life reached some sort of order and I continued to pray for direction. As the months wore on I was beginning to preach at the chapel again and also received an invitation to participate in the Winter Youth Retreat. I had often been invited to speak at this event held during the Christmas break and focused lessons for university-age students. With Sue's illness I had not been able to participate for a few years. I accepted the invitation, knowing that it would be good to get back to disciplined study of the Word preparing messages and also that Diane and Bob were there to take care of Jill and Sean.

Helper And Companion #3

Phil came home for his Christmas break and we had some kind of family celebration for the sake of the children. Then, on December 26, 1997, I prepared to drive with Phil to Toledo, Ohio where the retreat was held at a Hilton Hotel. Since all roads south out of Kenosha lead through Chicago I agreed to meet a young lady from New Zealand who was flying in for the retreat and other visits in North America. We arrived after the initial registration but in time for the opening session.

As I entered the hotel lobby I saw the registration table ahead and the ladies who were there to register everyone for the retreat. First I greeted Betty (Montgomery) Cattrell who had been widowed, due to cancer, the previous year and had two small children. I had met her husband Willie who had corresponded with Sue during her cancer journey. Obviously Betty and I had a common understanding of my life situation. Further along the table was her sister, Barbara Martin, who, as noted previously, was often at these events serving the Lord during her teaching holidays. She greeted me with the usual Christian handshake and then suggested that we go directly to the first session, which had already begun, and then check-in later.

However, the moment she stood up from behind the table I got a sense, a thought ran through my mind, "This is the one." Barb says that she got no particular "vibe" or thought, but I sure did. We continued down the hall to the meeting and returned later to collect

306

our booklets, name tags, and room assignment from Barb. Later that evening we "older" folks were all visiting and enjoying catching up with each other, including Barb.

Now, here, I'll not give the full account of our daily conversations. But with each day God was impressing on me that Barb could be the person to fill the void which now existed in our family. I knew that she was a busy person serving the Lord. She was involved in a camp in North Carolina every summer, and the large conference in Pennsylvania, all the places where I had met her through the years. I also knew that she loved children because she had been teaching kindergarten for many years. At first she was unaware of what I was sensing from God but she soon got the idea the second evening when I asked her to go out to lunch for the following day. After her initial shock she said, "yes."

As the retreat ended I was certain, in my mind, that God had already prepared someone to meet my unique needs. However, I did not want to pressure Barb to make any sort of decision right there at the retreat. I told her that I had already purchased tickets to take the children to Australia to visit my family since we had not been able to go during Sue's illness. I explained that I would come to visit her in St Louis when I returned in February. However, I did make sure that she knew that I was serious in my interest in her. After a quick good-bye kiss at the car, we all left Toledo on the morning of Wednesday December 31, to go home.

When I got back to Kenosha from the Retreat I told Diane my thoughts and she was very positive in her reply. She knew Barb from the several times they had met at conferences. Of course, Phil had been at the retreat so he knew what was going on. I also wanted to make sure that Barb did not forget me or that I had said, with great realization, "If you decide to do this, your life will make a major change." However, I also told her I would not pressure her for any decision. Of course, I didn't actually voice what decision I was asking her to make. I called her daily, even after having to call Lee Baseler (her uncle) to get the phone number of her brother Dan's house where I knew she was spending New Year's Eve and Day. Naturally, having been on this road before, I also sent flowers to her house along with my calls.

By this time Barb was getting the idea that I was very serious.

307

When she got home from the retreat and with her three siblings, nieces and nephews gathered for their family holiday festivities she read *Our Daily Bread.* Once again, that publication had a most timely piece. This particular account was about walking by faith and that to move forward a person must take a step and keep walking. Based on Hebrews 13:5 *"...God has said, Never will I leave you; never will I forsake you."* The lesson said, "Go ahead, prayerfully step into the unknown future. God has promised to be there for you. You can be sure there'll be something to stand on, or you will be taught how to fly." This was a confirmation to her.

Since Barb's father had passed away many years before and her mother was in a nursing facility with dementia, she sought counsel from her aunt and uncle, Lee and Louise Baseler, as she knew that they knew me and had corresponded with letters of encouragement all during Sue's illness. They were in agreement that this was God's leading and gave their blessing, which was very important to her. Also, her brother Dan stopped by a few days later to chat with her and ask some hard questions particularly about loving and nurturing someone else's children. Her reply to this was, "I've always had to love someone else's children, from my nieces and nephews, to my school children." By Monday, when she returned to teaching her kindergarten class, she began to determine if she would still be able turn in her request to retire at the end of her 27th year of teaching. She was assured that this was possible although school personnel thought it strange for her to retire early since she was so near the 30-year mark and the bonus, which came at that time.

Tuesday, January 6, I told Barb that I could come to visit her at the end of the week as I had to travel to Danville, Illinois for a Good Tidings Publishers' annual meeting. Barb knew very well that St Louis was not on the way to Danville but she also felt a sense that the Lord was providing a way for us to be together. By this time she, also, felt that the Lord was directing us to marry and she wanted to tell me in person, rather than by phone, before I left for Australia. I was waiting for her when she arrived home from school on Thursday. She had prepared a lovely dinner, in her own home. We sat and chatted. Again, I assured her that I did not want to pressure her. She asked questions about the children, what they liked to do and

Barb Martin - engagement

other family questions Thankfully, she knew the older children from camp and conferences so that was good.

Then, she handed a piece of paper to me. It was an enlarged copy of the *Our Daily Bread* reading, which she had read on December 31. I thought it a nice article. Then she indicated to turn the paper over. On the back she had written, "Yes, I will take the step of faith, because God has sent YOU to teach me how to fly." I read it several times and then the light bulb went off in my head as to what she was referring. With that I scooped her in my arms. WOW!!! This was amazing! We talked about possible dates, and another wedding to plan. (I should be a pro by now.) I made the same suggestion of just going to the registrar's office, but also had learned that the ladies enjoy a special day, so I gave her permission to plan whatever kind of celebration she would like. With that settled, we called family members.

Knowing that this might possibly be the result of my visit, Barb had arranged to take off school on Friday. Her favorite substitute was available and promised not to tell anyone the reason, as Barb did not take off from teaching very often. I stayed at her brother Dan's house. First thing the next day we headed to the jewelry store. Barb tells me that she always had a ring design in her mind. When we walked into the store, I asked what she liked. "There, that is it. The one I've always wanted." And so, I bought it. We went to a coffee shop near-by and I slipped it on her finger, making all things official!

From the jewelers we went to the church she always wanted to use to get our name on the calendar for June 6. We visited a few more family members and then had dinner before I had to leave town. By the time I got to my meeting in Danville, Illinois the Retreat gossip was beginning to leak out. Some of the folks at this meeting had seen us talking at the Retreat, so I was able to give the official announcement. Since they also knew Barb, there was much happiness and rejoicing on my behalf.

Returning home from that trip late Saturday evening the children were already in bed. I went directly to Jill's room to kiss her goodnight but first I showed her the picture of Barb and said, "Here Jill, your prayers have been answered. God has sent you a new mother." She immediately jumped out of bed and ran into Sean's room exclaiming, "Look, Sean, we've got a new mother!" At only three years old Sean didn't quite understand the significance but he looked at the picture. We all hugged and I tucked them back into bed.

Another Trip to Sydney Without A Wife

Diane and Bob, with their boys, stayed with us until mid-January. Right after I left for Australia they went on to Colombia to continue their missionary work there. After Sue died September 2, I had made plane bookings to go to Australia January 15, taking Jill and Sean to meet, for the first time, my mother, their Granny; aunts, uncles and cousins.

I don't know if you have ever made a long international trip with a three and five-year-old, but it is really a challenge! The kids were awake and enjoying the plane ride from Chicago to Los Angeles, but by the time we arrived at 7:00 PM, Sean was so tired as we walked from the national terminal to the international terminal that he eventually went to sleep as I carried him on my back. Not only did I have Sean on my back, but also I had two suitcases to pull along, and Jill had her pull-along and Sean's small pull-along.

We rode the escalator up to the QANTAS check-in area and got in line. When I finally got to the counter, the lady there said, "I'm sorry but you are not booked on this flight."

I really wasn't in the mood for that. "What do you mean, I'm not booked on this flight? I made the booking back in September. It was confirmed and here are my tickets."

"I'm sorry but the flight is full and you are not on the list."

"Listen, as you can see, I'm traveling with two small children. I made the bookings months ago, paid for the flight and have the tickets dated September. I'm going on that flight, and if you really think I'm not booked, you can just call my cousin Mr. Jim Lucas who is a manager in the head office of QANTAS in Sydney. He will tell you that I am booked, and to stop giving me the run-around."

With that she went off to talk to someone and after about five minutes, came back and said, "I'm sorry for the confusion, a mistake was made and here are your boarding passes."

"Well, thank you," and with Sean still asleep on my back, but now with only the carry-on- bags, I headed for the transit lounge, which of course was full and no seats anywhere. Finally a couple of young people saw my dilemma and offered me their seats.

"Thank you so much. I'm running a little ragged and appreciate your kindness." Soaking wet from perspiration, it took me about a half hour to cool down. I still had about two hours to wait until the flight was to leave at 11:00 PM and gratefully sat down with Sean on my lap.

Finally we boarded and as soon as we took off, since we had three seats on the window side, I lay Sean on the floor; Jill had two of the seats with the armrests up to lay down and I reclined, (as much as is possible on a plane) and dozed during the 14-hour flight to Sydney.

My family and many friends were at the airport to meet us, and after the usual hugs and kisses, we were driven to my sister Anne's home in Marsfield, a northern suburb in Sydney where my Mother also was living. Anne was a great help with the children and they had fun going to the zoo, the lake where I had lived on my previous time in Australia in 1988, and other fun places. Of course, all the family and church friends wanted to see me and to meet the children. I was thankful that I could tell them that God had already provided another companion and helper for me and introduced them to Barb through her photograph. Everyone was so thankful of this blessing for the children and me.

The church, which had been my home church and supported me through all of my life, asked me to speak several times. One message was from Psalm 84, noting many blessings from God in which He gives us strength to go forward. Verse seven refers to people going through trials, "They go from strength to strength" which I took to mean that God provides for each problem as it comes along. I could surely attest to this fact.

After a short but very sweet visit to my homeland, and with great excitement for what the future would bring, the children and I made the long arduous flight back to the USA. Arriving in Chicago Monday February 23, the one-hour drive to Kenosha was filled with anticipation.

Now our house was truly empty of everyone but Jill, Sean and me. Diane and Bob had returned to South America and all responsibility fell to me to keep the household running. My first chore was the laundry. Thankfully there was not any snow needing to be cleared from our large corner block sidewalks and large driveway. I turned all my attention to organizing the house, getting Jill to kindergarten every day and Sean to the pre-school two days a week.

The Children Meet Their New Mother

Of course, I had already been in touch by phone with Barb, who was happy to be able to talk rather than send emails for communication. I told her that I wanted to bring the children as soon as possible to meet her and start to get to know their new mother. She informed me that her school was holding their annual Project Fair Night on Thursday February 26. I told her we would be there.

So, after being home for two days, still recuperating from jet lag, I packed our bags and we drove the six hours to St Louis. Again, we were waiting for Barb when she arrived home from her day of teaching. The children ran out the front door, in the drizzling rain, shouting, "Mommy, Mommy, Mommy." That did my heart good. After a quick supper, we returned to her school for the open house event. Barb was blessed to teach in a school where all the parents supported the activities. She expected a large crowd, but she did not expect as many as came specifically to her room. As she greeted the parents and children of her current class she noticed former parents and students appearing in the room. They would say to her, "I didn't come to see you; I came to meet him!" while pointing to me standing in the center of the room. Of course having an Aussie accent was some sort of a curiosity, but they also wanted to see this fellow who was taking away their beloved Miss Martin. I happily visited with them and was able to share the gospel when they enquired of my occupation. It was a very long night.

The following day Barb had arranged to take a personal day off so we enjoyed time together as a family, almost. We visited a local children's museum and she got to know Jill and Sean. They called her "Mommy" from the start. We had brought a few gifts for her and she was overwhelmed with the whole scene. Of course we discussed wedding plans and future arrangements for Barb moving to Kenosha. Thankfully, the three of us could stay with her brother's family, therefore not giving the neighbors any cause for gossip. We returned to Kenosha the following Sunday afternoon so that Jill could get back to school.

Just Another Glitch Along The Way

A few weeks later, in mid-March, our church arranged for the weekly children's club group to visit a nearby gymnastics club for open gym night. Having been in gymnastics in my youth I was quite happy to join the fun and brought the children too. Our good friend, Don Ditthardt said, "Hey, you were in gymnastics. Why don't you try the rings over there?" "What a splendid idea," I thought. It had been at least 40 years since I'd done that. So I mounted the Roman Rings, extended my arms and tried to do a "dislocation" turn – hearing a "pop" sound in my left elbow. I let go of the rings and landed face down on the mat. OUCH!!!! Upon further examination I saw that my upper arm muscle was not looking right and all bunched up near the shoulder. "This is not good," was my first comment. The tendon had torn off at the elbow, which then pulled the muscle up and I had no muscle in my upper arm.

I thought I could just ice it but that did not help. A lady in our church was the nurse for an orthopedist and said I should see him right away. I called Barb to inform her that I would need surgery to correct the "Popeye" arm, which I now had. After she digested that information we discussed what to do. Again, God provides a way. Barb had "planned" to take a few days off that week to sew dresses for the wedding; however she flew to Chicago instead. I met her on Tuesday, we drove the one-hour to our house to which I said, "Here's your new house." Then we promptly took the children to Gisela's house and we drove to the next town for my outpatient surgery.

This was an interesting experience for Barb as the nurses and doctor all assumed that we were married. It was too difficult to explain the exact situation. So she saw me as they prepared me for surgery; and throughout the procedure they came to her often to report, "Mrs. Taylor, your husband is doing just fine."

"Oh, thank you," she thought as she continued praying, asking God just what she had gotten herself into and waiting for me to be able to go home.

When the doctor finished he came to explain, "Mrs. Taylor, your husband has very good muscles for his age and he will be just as strong as before when he heals. I will give him some exercises to do so physical therapy won't be necessary." He went on to explain exactly what he had done to repair the damage. "Thank you, doctor. I'm glad all went well."

This was to have been an outpatient procedure. However, due to a delay in the schedule, it was well into the evening hours before I was out of recovery and still not finished with pain medication. Barb was getting a bit concerned about the late hour and taking me home. While she was standing next to my bed the doctor asked if she would prefer I spend the night and come for me in the morning. "Oh, yes, thank you; that would be good," she said. This was a relief as she was wondering how she would take care of her not-yet husband with his casted arm, limited mobility, and still needing pain medication. She kissed me good-bye and went home to pick up the children and get them into bed. Her first real "mom" duty and I wasn't even there.

The next morning, Sean was up with the sunrise looking for breakfast. He indicated that he wanted "Vegie toast". Barb was quite perplexed, as she had not yet been introduced to Vegemite, the staple Australian spread for toast. She had only heard of "Veggie Tails." Three-year-old Sean gladly showed her where it was in the cupboard and then explained how to make vegie toast. He was a sharp little fellow already. Jill had her preferred cereal; they got ready, and Barb brought them to pick me up from the hospital. Thankfully, Barb stayed the remainder of that week to help around the house. It sure was great having someone to wash, clean, cook, transport children and share family life, sort of. She stayed each night at our friends' Gisela and Bert's house not far from my house. Again, we were conscience of the testimony to neighbors and she did not want to spend the night at the house, so there was no cause for gossip.

One neighbor, Jeff Love had approached me the day after we had unloaded the trucks, to tell me that he had heard I had been a missionary and that he had just become a believer at a Promise Keepers meeting a year before. I had asked him if he would like to have a Bible study to which he agreed, and every Monday night we had a Bible study in his home. I already had some sort of testimony in the new suburb as a Christian worker and didn't want to damage that.

Once again God provided for a need. How was Barb going to get home? She had flown to Chicago, but in talking with her brother, she knew that he would be driving back to St Louis from northern WI after a business trip. On Friday March 20, we met him at the highway and he took her home. Sean was a bit disappointed when she told him she was going back and he said, "But I don't want you to leave. I like having a Mommy." Out of the mouths of babes.

Very Busy Months Preparing For The Future

Now I found myself being chief cook and bottle washer, mom and dad, while doing everything with my left arm in a sling. Ever try to tie your shoes with one hand? But God gave me strength, especially knowing that help was on the way. I even was able to build two sets of sturdy shelves in the basement for Barb's teaching supplies and other items. Sean was my "helper" and those shelves have been very useful to this day.

As had been originally planned, Barb was coming back during her Spring Break week, April 6-11, and then we were driving her back to St Louis to be there during Jill's Spring Break the following week. That meant two weeks together. Barb again flew to Chicago and went right to work at the house since she now knew where everything was in the kitchen. Also, she was in town for birthday week, mine on the 11th but Jill's sixth birthday on the 9th so she organized a sweet party with lots of pink and Barbie Doll decorations, etc. I had offered to hold it at McDonalds but she assured me that having a party for a six-year-old was nothing new for her after all those years in kindergarten.

We did spend the next week in St Louis. The children visited Barb's school and Jill spent a day in kindergarten there. This was a special bonding time for all of us. Barb had been sewing the dress Jill would wear for the wedding and she used the time to be sure the size was appropriate. Sean and I visited the tuxedo shop for our fittings. The next time we would be together with Barb would be for the wedding.

The Biggest Wedding And Another Companion And Helper

As I've said before, I would have been happy to go the registrar's office for a quick ceremony. However, realizing that this was Barb's first time to be married, and also having met so many people who knew and cared for her, I was happy to go along with her plans for our wedding. I can honestly say that with each of my marriages the weddings got larger each time.

June 6, 1998 all the details came together. Hundreds of Barb's family and extended family, former students and their parents, school personnel, friends of various music activities and church people from all over the country arrived to celebrate with us. We were blessed by so many who cared to celebrate that wonderful day with us. Of course, I was the one who was blessed more than any other because I was, once again, receiving a gift from God to be my companion and helper in ministry and raising my two small children.

316

Diane came from Colombia to help and to take care of Jill and Sean while Barb and I took a honeymoon. My sons David and Philip were groomsmen along with Barb's brother Bob, who escorted her down the aisle, and our friend from Kenosha, Don Ditthardt. Barb had her sister Betty as her maid of honor and her best friend, Jean Bassett, along with her two sisters-in-law as bridesmaids. Her twin nieces were junior bride's maids and Betty's young

Barb and I are married 6/6/98 - Jill and Sean with us

children as flower girl and ring bearer. Jill and Sean escorted me up the aisle as we awaited Barb's arrival. Her brother Dan officiated after my friend Bill Van Ryn gave a clear gospel message. We knew there would be unsaved folks in the audience and some who may not have seen a Christian wedding so everything said and done was to be a testimony to God's plan for marriage.

As a surprise to me, just after the vows and rings were exchanged and the official kiss, Barb broke into song. She sang "Love Will Be Our Home." I decided this deserved a second kiss as Jill and Sean came up to join us and then she kissed each of the children. It was a tender moment. After a closing prayer Dan introduced us to the audience.

Because of the large number of people we had a very simple reception at the church. Following that we had the usual photos taken. Then we prepared to go to the dinner reception with closest friends and family.

The dinner was fun for all with several family groups singing songs of greeting to Barb and me, and general fun. We cut the cake and shared a piece with Jill and Sean rather than feeding each other. As is the Australian custom, all the guests stood around the perimeter of the large banquet room as we went around in opposite directions greeting them one more time, and then out the door.

Thanks to the generosity of Barb's cousins Dave and Phyllis Baseler, we had use of their vacation house in the Smoky Mountains of Tennessee. We took two days to drive there and spent the time enjoying each other's company, discussing the future and seeing the area. I felt we needed more than one week to get to know each other as I had predicted to Barb, "Your life will be much different." Then, our last night in Gatlinburg, actually at 2 in the morning, the phone rang, which we thought was rather odd. It was Barb's brother Bob calling to say that her mother had been called Home to Heaven after suffering over 25 years with dementia. God had overruled and lifted this responsibility from Barb, as she was her mother's guardian.

We were leaving for home the next day, stopping at Betty's house in Michigan one night and arriving in Kenosha June 19. The next day was Sean's fourth birthday and Barb made special pancakes for him. Later that day we took Diane to the airport to return to Colombia and we headed to St Louis. On Monday June 22, I was asked to speak at the grave-side service for my mother-in-law whom I had never been able to meet when she was well.

After a few days at Barb's house, and loading some items to bring back to Kenosha, we went home to start our new family life. Because Barb would be so busy organizing the house, as well as preparing for the large Pennsylvania conference, we brought her twin nieces Heather and Sarah, then age 13, with us. They were a

318

great help with childcare and happy to be with Aunt Barb as they were not so happy that some strange man had come along and taken her away from their daily lives.

My Three Wives

As I look back over my life I have to marvel at the way the Lord has so perfectly organized the direction of my life and the many different ways he has protected me, prepared me for the different ministries, and above all how He brought three wonderful women into my life as a "help meet for me," or as the NIV translates it, "suitable helper." I sometimes wondered why He had to take the first two of my wives home to glory, seemingly ahead of what would have been my schedule. However, I have come to realize that His ways are perfect and those occasions have been major turning points in the Lord's arranging and preparing me for the ministries into which He has called me.

Ann (Married 1/20/62 to 12/20/87) had a Master's degree in linguistics and we married before I had any thought of becoming a missionary. She was proficient in several languages and as a teacher taught at least three of them. Ann was fluent in English, French and taught Latin, and when we eventually decided to follow the call and leading of the Lord to Colombia, we spent a year in Costa Rica studying Spanish, that came easily to Ann. I did not know that eventually I would be preparing message handouts and notes and eventually writing six books in Spanish as well as editing and preparing a monthly magazine. When I started a publishing work in Colombia, Ann, whose Spanish was grammatically correct, became a perfect proof reader for all our publications and also wrote and prepared a women's and children's section of the monthly magazine. She was just who I needed as a helper.

Susan (Married 8/19/89 to 9/2/97) had a Master's degree in Special Education, teaching and working with the hearing impaired. She taught signing along with all of the general subjects and also worked with students having speech disorders. Sue had been able to help Ann understand some of the problems Adriana faced in not being able to process what she heard or read. Then as Adriana's mother, Sue helped Adri when she began classes in the American schools. Knowing the American system, Sue was able to not only register Adri into the right classes, but also could help her at home with her studies and make sure she had the right sort of help at school. This meant that Adri, who had struggled so much in Colombia, was able to get a high school diploma. That was what Adriana needed to eventually be able to get suitable work. Sue was a great help to me in organizing the children in the USA.

Barbara (Married 6/6/98 to present) has a Master's degree in Early Childhood Education and was a kindergarten teacher. When we married I had a six-year-old daughter and a four-year-old son. Barb was able to easily understand the two children at those ages. Over the next few years she homeschooled both Jill and Sean who were then well prepared for traditional school when they each enrolled for seventh grade. Barb has also not only been the one who encouraged me to write this book, but has been my chief proofreader and a major help in getting this book ready for publication.

As I look back and see how the Lord sent just the right wives into my life, I thank Him for each one of them and can only say that His planning and choices were way beyond anything that I could have planned myself. All this is just another confirmation that:

"We know that in all things God works for the good of those who love Him, who have been called according to His purpose." Romans 8:28

23

MINISTRY FOR TWO

New Opportunities

Now, finally, I could get back to serious Bible study, writing and message preparation. I could go to my office in our basement and not have to worry about the children upstairs or what to fix for dinner. God had truly blessed us.

Barb also had ministry activities. She took on the household chores with ease and tried to get things running smoothly. As was mentioned in previous chapters she was heavily involved in the registration process of the large conference held at Grove City, Pennsylvania. All the registration cards were being sent to our home just after we returned from our honeymoon. Then it was her responsibility to organize the housing for over 800 people. We attended the conference the last week in July 1998. This was the same conference where Barb had been walking behind Susan and me wondering why Sue got a husband and she didn't. When she told this to me, I said, "God said, 'Just get in line!'"

After the conference, her nieces went back to St Louis with their family and we went on to New Jersey for the children to visit Sue's family. All of them were very welcoming to Barb and enjoyed hearing about the wedding, even watching the video. It was painful for them to think that Sue was not there with her children, but they were happy to see that Barb loved them as her own and would take good care of them. Every year, until the grandparents passed away, we visited them as Barb thought it important that the children should know their grandparents and aunt. They welcomed Barb as a member of the family. After that initial visit we made our way home to Kenosha and settled to some sort of "normal" life.

With the school year starting in September Barb discussed

home schooling as she was very familiar with the ages and stages of development at ages six and four. While I didn't want to add burden to her I knew that this would free us to travel together to places when I was invited to speak. By joining the local homeschool organization we both were able to be of help in various ways with that group.

By the year 2000 we had settled into a good routine of answering calls for ministry, which included traveling to various places in the USA and also to visit some of my family from time to time. I thought it would be good for Barb to meet the family in Australia so from January to April we packed up schooling materials and went "down under." It was a wonderful time of family, reconnecting, and Barb seeing my roots. This would be the first of three such visits. When we returned home it was soon time for summer activities in the USA.

Also in 2000 we had another addition to the family when Phil married Ann in a small ceremony before he was shipped out for his first deployment. We did not get to California for this event. However, in June 2001 we made the trip out there and I was able to officiate their re-commitment ceremony and participate in all the usual wedding festivities. Jill and Sean each were part of the wedding party and Barb was honored to represent the several mothers Phil had loved in his life.

Since we were already on the west coast of the USA we drove our motor home north to Seattle, Washington to visit Diane's family who by that time were back from Colombia. Routing back through Wisconsin, we went on to Florida to see David's family, and Adriana, and then to New Jersey to see Sue's family. Of course, Barb always in teaching mode, made certain that we stopped at historical places and noted various features of the large United States. The children even helped to plan our routes by reading maps and discussing what they would like to see. That was quite a traveling summer and one we will never forget.

Again, in 2003 we began the year with a trip to Australia and New Zealand. Because it is cold, snowy winter in Wisconsin in January but summer sun and fun "down under," that is a great time to visit. The visit to NZ also allowed Barb to meet some of Ann's family and gain a better understanding of my first wife. By the end of that year we were able to help at the Adventure Learning Center in Nassau, Bahamas. So, it was a year of sandy beaches, service and schooling.

I was very much enjoying our family being together and having time to study, write and speak as the Lord directed. Looking back I can see that the arrow was being re-sharpened for service. Before long an email, phone call, or letter would come with requests for something that I could do. I never seemed to have to wait long before God organized a request.

One such invitation was quite unexpected when a man from a nearby church asked if I would like to attend a conference for church elders at Emmaus Bible College in Dubuque, Iowa. "Yes, that would be great," I said. I did attend and was so impressed with the strong Bible teaching and encouragement that I made it a point to plan to attend each year, which I have been able to do.

Emmaus Bible College and Emmaus Correspondence School

In June of 2004, I received a call from the president of Emmaus Bible College requesting to stop by to see me, along with Barb, since he would be in Kenosha on other business. Barb rearranged her schedule so that she was available to fix dinner and we could meet in our home rather than a restaurant. The reason he wanted to visit with us was to ask if I would be willing to serve on the Board of Trustees for the college. I was very humbled and reticent to think that they thought I could be of help in the world of academia. However, the president explained that they were looking for someone with international experience, publication experience and a strong background in our church New Testament principles. Now, that did seem to fit what God had called me to do. I prayerfully accepted the invitation to become part of that Board and have found great blessing from serving in that capacity, even on the executive committee. How could I possibly know that God would shoot this arrow in that direction?

Because of my connection with Emmaus, I also became more aware of the Emmaus Correspondence School Ministries, which distributes millions of Bible study materials all over the world. For many years I had made use of these study materials in Colombia and knew them to be very helpful in Bible study with people I had discipled. I had offered a study book I had written, *"The Gates of Jerusalem"* for them to publish, which they did. After getting to know the director for that ministry, I was also invited to become part of their Board of Directors and have been so honored to serve in this capacity.

Having a connection with all of the Emmaus family has opened other doors of opportunity to serve as God leads.

Serving Together

Besides these areas of service God has continued to open doors. For two years during the spring we joined several others from our Kenosha church going to El Paso, Texas. While we stayed with the church folks there our purpose was to help with their work in Juarez, Mexico. Jill and Sean were impressed with the different culture and noted the blessings they have in the USA. Of course my speaking Spanish was helpful since no one else in our group was fluent.

There have been numerous camps and conferences where I was asked to speak or Barb would help with events. We both served on the Board for the Winter Youth Retreat for several years, until it no longer was being held. For several years it was not possible to travel often as the children became more involved in youth activities. I certainly did not want to be an absent dad, so it was important to schedule travel around their school schedule as we found it necessary to place them in Christian School rather than continue to home school.

In 2010 Jill graduated high school and in 2011 married her sweetheart, Josh. This was, yet again, another daughter's wedding I was privileged to officiate. They live in our area so her children are the only grandchildren living in the same city with me. We enjoy seeing them and watching them grow. We have 12 grandchildren altogether. Sean graduated high school in 2012 and was soon off to university to pursue his passion, playing soccer. He is seeking a career path in Sport Management, as God would lead him.

Now that we are "empty nesters," Barb and I are able to travel together and share in the ministries God gives us. Barb and I often counsel young people who are seeking advice for serving the Lord, "If you tell the Lord you are available, you had better mean it. He will take you up on your offer and your life will be busy."

One of our most gratifying trips was my return to Colombia in August of 2015 to visit all of the churches mentioned in this book, as well as many of the people whom I was privileged to disciple, teach and encourage and the different ministries in which I had been involved. Barb was able to join me and, while she does not speak Spanish, she was warmly welcomed by those who had known me for over 40 years and were happy to see that God had, once again, provided for my needs.

I am so thankful for the many opportunities to visit and speak at churches, camps and conferences across the United States, as well as invitations to speak at conferences, Bible schools and seminars in Latin America, Australia and occasionally in Europe. I am thankful for good health and strength to be able to travel, and for the Lord's provision to make those trips. We continually watch for what God has next for us to do.

Ian and Barb serving together - 2015

24

CONTINUOUS POLISHING

Psalm 92:12-14 *"The righteous will flourish like a palm tree, they will grow like a cedar of Lebanon; planted in the house of the Lord, they will flourish in the courts of our God."*

You may remember my first trip to sea with the opportunity to steer the ship, and when I looked back I could see the zig-zagging of the wake where we had been. (Ch.1) In a similar way I can now look back over my life and see all the ways the Lord has been directing and using me. I can see where I took control and the Lord had to return me back onto the path and plan that He had for my life. The smooth sailing was when He was in control and I was nothing more than a vessel to be used for His glory.

I am so thankful for the many blessings that completely overshadow the difficult days, the trials, the heartaches and the many problems that I have had to face. God's guiding hand is obvious in all the life-changing events, and He has used the tragedies, sometimes to redirect my life in order to extend and open new ministries, or to increase the opportunities and activities. Because of the many different experiences and trials, I have been able to reach and influence people dealing with difficult circumstances, giving instruction and practical teaching to encourage them in their spiritual and personal struggles.

Some of the areas where the polishing was roughest have been used to help and encourage people going through similar circumstances. Did someone lose a child? Did someone have a wife or close family member suddenly pass away because of sickness or accident? Was someone a caregiver through a time of prolonged illness like cancer for a wife or family member? Has anyone been left with children as a single parent facing tremendously new challenges? I have been able to "look back" and truly empathize and give encouragement to suffering people rather than a perfunctory statement, "I will pray for you," knowing that they would soon be forgotten. Has someone had to deal with persecution and the threat of death on a daily basis? I can say from experience in all these things; **God is in control. It will all work out.**

It is wonderful to be able say, *"For to me, to live is Christ and to die is gain."* Philippians 1:21

I know the Lord will continue to polish and care for this arrow until the day I am with Him. As Isaiah could say, *"He made my mouth like a sharpened sword, in the shadow of his hand he hid me; he made me into a polished arrow and concealed me in his quiver. He said to me, "You are my servant."* Isaiah 49:2-3 My desire is to finish my course well and to one day hear His voice saying, *"Well done, good and faithful servant! You have been faithful with a few things; ... Come and share your master's happiness!"'* Matthew 25:21   Until that day, the polishing process will continue and I pray that the Lord will be able to use this ordinary man, who is continuously being shaped and polished to serve at His pleasure, ready and willing to the end.

Psalm 90:10-12 *"The length of our days is seventy years—or eighty, if we have the strength; yet their span is but trouble and sorrow, for they quickly pass, and we fly away... Teach us to number our days aright, that we may gain a heart of wisdom."*

Psalm 91:1-10 *"He who dwells in the shelter of the Most High will rest in the shadow of the Almighty. I will say of the LORD, "He is my refuge and my fortress, my God, in whom I trust. Surely he will save you from the fowler's snare and from the deadly pestilence. He will cover you with his feathers, and under his wings you will find refuge; his faithfulness will be your shield and rampart. You will not fear the terror of night, nor the arrow that flies by day, nor the pestilence that stalks in the darkness, nor the plague that destroys at midday... If you make the Most High your dwelling—even the LORD, who is my refuge—then no harm will befall you, no disaster will come near your tent."*

To contact the author for discussion or speaking engagement,
write to:
asharpenedarrow@gmail.com

Book copies and e-books may be ordered from Amazon.com